C000137019

CHAMPIONS
20|13

CHAMPIONS
20|13

How We Got The Title Back –
The Players' Own Story

With Steve Bartram

**SIMON &
SCHUSTER**

London · New York · Sydney · Toronto · New Delhi

A CBS COMPANY

First published in Great Britain by Simon & Schuster UK Ltd, 2013
A CBS COMPANY

Copyright © 2013 by Manchester United Football Club Ltd

This book is copyright under the Berne Convention.
No reproduction without permission.
All rights reserved.

The right of Steve Bartram to be identified as the author of this work
has been asserted by him in accordance with sections 77 and 78 of the
Copyright, Designs and Patents Act, 1988.

1 3 5 7 9 10 8 6 4 2

Simon & Schuster UK Ltd
1st Floor
222 Gray's Inn Road
London WC1X 8HB

www.simonandschuster.co.uk

Simon & Schuster Australia, Sydney
Simon & Schuster India, New Delhi

Every reasonable effort has been made to contact copyright holders
of material reproduced in this book. If any have inadvertently been overlooked,
the publishers would be glad to hear from them and make good in future
editions any errors or omissions brought to their attention.

All photographs © Manchester United/Getty Images

A CIP catalogue record for this book is available
from the British Library

ISBN: 978-1-47112-820-2

Typeset in the UK by M Rules
Printed and bound by CPI Group (UK) Ltd, Croydon, CR0 4YY

Contents

Introduction

Typical. Just when it looks like normality has been restored, along comes something extraordinary. The 2012-13 season began as a quest to wrest the Barclays Premier League title back to Old Trafford, but wound up being a landmark season in Manchester United's history.

The Reds strode into the campaign determined to overcome the heartbreaking finale to the previous campaign in which two injury-time goals had given Manchester City the league title in the dying seconds of the season. Fuelled by that haunting experience and embossed by the stunning capture of Dutch striker Robin van Persie and the exciting enlistment of Japanese schemer Shinji Kagawa, United enjoyed a thrilling start to the campaign in which haphazard defending and incessant attacking served up a host of nerve-shredding comeback victories.

December's dramatic derby win at City fell amid a staggering four-month period in which only four points were dropped over 18 games, setting a pace which sent records tumbling and left the Reds' title rivals chasing a distant speck on the horizon. On an unforgettable April evening, when van Persie moved irreversibly to the top of the division's goalscoring charts with a superb hat-trick, a swaggering victory over Aston Villa wrapped up United's 20th league title with four games to spare and ensured another night of Old Trafford folklore.

Reaching the historic landmark and extending United's record as England's leading team more than offset the disappointment of cup exits at the hands of Real Madrid and, in both domestic competitions, Chelsea. Then, just when it appeared that the campaign would drift smoothly towards the Reds' May coronation, the season suddenly became a watershed in football history.

Sir Alex Ferguson, the man responsible for 38 of the 61 trophies gathered throughout the club's entire history, celebrated clinching United's 13th Premier League title by ending his managerial reign after 26½ years in charge. But, rather than bidding farewell to Old Trafford, the 71-year-old accepted positions as a United ambassador and a member of the club's board, while also recommending his successor: Everton manager David Moyes. Sir Alex's suggestion that his fellow Glaswegian should be tempted across the north-west from Goodison Park and offered the position was unanimously backed by the board of directors, and Moyes was announced as United's 18th manager just a day after Ferguson had stunned football.

For everyone associated with the Reds, the future is a thing of wonder and intrigue but, before looking forward to a new episode in the club's history, it's time to look back on the final chapter of United's tale under Sir Alex Ferguson: a mercifully happy ending reached, in true United fashion, with a few twists and turns along the way.

Steve Bartram, 19 May 2013

1

Pre-season

'It was a long summer, actually,' Michael Carrick smiles ruefully, eyes fixed on nothing in particular, mind replaying the gut-wrenching denouement to the 2011-12 season. Having a title seemingly sewn up, then surrendered, before a final day in which the unlikeliest late reprieve was suddenly snatched away, can make its mark on a man. And a team, for that matter.

'Initially, it was just getting over the impact that the final day had,' continues the midfielder. 'Obviously it was hard to take, but we got away on holiday pretty much straight away and tried to forget about it; there was no point in beating ourselves up about what happened. I just tried to get away, have a good holiday and it ended up being the longest holiday I'd had pretty much all through my career. So I came back really refreshed and looking forward to the season, having gotten the end of last season out of my system.

'I think the great thing about this club is that, regardless of what's happened in the last season, we always come back and look to achieve again. That's what I've found ever since I've been here, and it was the same situation this year.'

But the pain, and the manner of the events of 13 May 2012, was a feeling unlike any other. So often the purveyors of dramatic doom on opponents, the Reds had been on the wrong end of a most United-like dose of theatre. Amid the funereal atmosphere of the Stadium of Light's away dressing room, a pact was reached which assured that the day would provide a reference point to outlast the hurt.

'In the past few years the team had won at least one trophy, but last season we didn't win anything, so it was a bad season,' explains Chicharito. 'We didn't win anything and this is Manchester United. The feeling we had in the Sunderland dressing room after the game . . . straight away after that game we decided we never wanted to feel that way again. So we prepared well in pre-season and every week throughout the season we worked hard because we didn't want to feel that way again.'

Whether preparing for a season on the back of success or sorrow, Sir Alex Ferguson invariably freshens up his playing roster in advance of the new campaign, and it didn't take long for the manager to start the process for 2012-13.

The first day of June heralded the release of Michael Owen and Tomasz Kuszczak, news to which the former Tweeted: 'I have loved every minute of the three years I have spent at such a fantastic club.' Within three days, the Reds' first summer recruit had already been lined up: Borussia Dortmund and Japan playmaker Shinji Kagawa. A week on, he was followed through the doors of a mid-renovation Trafford Training Centre by Nick Powell, an England youth mid-fielder who had shone in Crewe's promotion to League One.

And still the squad shuffling continued. Paul Pogba had run down his contract in order to join Juventus and Zeki Fryers did likewise and moved to Standard Liege, while Ji-sung Park's seven-year Old Trafford career ended with a transfer to Queens Park

Rangers. The Korean livewire was followed to Loftus Road by Brazilian full-back Fabio on a season-long loan, and to complete a hectic news day for the Da Silva household, Fabio's twin brother Rafael signed a new four-year contract. Having always played and lived together, the twins were aware that the next year would test their mettle both personally and professionally.

'We're close and I have always been together with him, but it's good for us, just to become more mature,' said Rafael. 'I used to ask him all the time if I needed something, but now I need more of my own mind so I've grown more mature. It's bad, because I will miss him, but it's good to learn more.'

Rafael was among a clutch of players whose summer was heavily punctuated by international football. The Brazilian had joined Ryan Giggs, Tom Cleverley and David De Gea at the London 2012 Olympics, while Wayne Rooney, Ashley Young, Phil Jones, Danny Welbeck, Nani, Patrice Evra and Anders Lindegaard were all selected by their nations to attend Euro 2012.

That left a gaping hole in the Reds' squad for a rigorous pre-season calendar of fixtures in South Africa, China, Norway, Sweden and Germany, prompting the promotion of several burgeoning members of the club's youth ranks, as well as a quick-fire assimilation for new signings Kagawa and Powell. Only half of the 22-man squad had sampled first team football before with United, but for one of the comparative old heads, the trip would be a first.

'It was very special for me because it was the first time I went on pre-season,' says Chicharito. 'The last two, I met the team once they were on tour, both times in the USA. I missed the team bonding in America, so it was great to get a proper pre-season this time. I had the two weeks at Carrington before we went over to South Africa and China, so it was very good to prepare myself with a very good pre-season and be focused for the new campaign.

'Of course, out on tour we saw little bits of each country. In

South Africa, we went on safari. In China, every player did commercial appearances for the club, so you go out and see a little bit. South Africa for me was very special because I played the World Cup over there, so it's a very special place to me. I'd also never been to Shanghai, so it was very good to go and see. We enjoyed being out there because the fans are unbelievable – always waiting for us at the airports and the training grounds.'

The squad's collective encampment brought with it all the usual ingredients which comprise tours – matches, fitness work aplenty, commercial visits and a smattering of general hi-jinks. All of this was captured on camera by squad veteran Rio Ferdinand, who once again filmed a behind-the-scenes documentary for MUTV, the club's television station. 'We're used to it now,' says Michael Carrick. 'It's quite good viewing at times, because it gives everyone a chance to see what it's really like on tour. There are a lot of tired bodies and we go to the nice places, but we don't generally get to do an awful lot of sight-seeing. It's training, games and commercial activities, really, but it's nice to see the behind-the-scenes stuff, because you can see some funny things going on.'

For all the insight afforded to the downtime on tour, the over-riding focus was – as it has always been – readying the squad for the season proper. A daunting Monday night trip to Everton's Goodison Park provided United's Barclays Premier League opener, and the remit for Tony Strudwick, the Reds' head of fitness, was to have the roster fighting fit for a Goodison Park battle.

'In and around the tour matches, there are opportunities to top the players up with training but the target in these two weeks is to get the players exposed to match minutes, with the main focus being on getting the senior players who are on tour ready for that first match against Everton on the twentieth of August,' said Strudwick, speaking after Kiko Macheda's goal had ensured a winning start to the preparations with a hard-fought 1-0 triumph over AmaZulu in Durban.

'There's good energy within the group we have with us. Obviously some are away at the Olympics, while the European Championship players aren't back yet, but this tour has given the youngsters an opportunity to come in and do well and they've certainly done that so far.

'Another important part of the tour is to expose the young players, and the new lads, to what it is to be a Manchester United player and the experience that comes with travelling with the club around the world. You can tell all the lads are enjoying the tour and they're embracing all the extra bits that come along on the trip, such as the commercial activities. It's a good learning curve, full stop.'

A late equaliser from Bebe salvaged a draw from another stern examination against Ajax Cape Town, before a draining trip to Shanghai pitted the Reds against Shanghai Shenhua. There, as they had in South Africa, United's players spent their days on a timezone just two hours ahead of British Summer Time, in order to stave off jetlag. There were certainly no ill effects on Shinji Kagawa who, on his return to the Far East, turned home the only goal of the game against Shenhua to fan the flames of anticipation surrounding him.

'The thing that's impressed me is that every exercise we do on the training ground, he's never needed it to be explained,' Sir Alex said of the Japanese playmaker. 'After one demonstration he joins in, as if he's known the language forever. We know he doesn't speak the language, but it isn't a problem. It just goes to show that a good footballer can pick up exactly what's needed. He's been fantastic in that respect.'

With United still widely tipped for further transfer activity, a trio of names had regularly been tipped to follow Kagawa to Old Trafford. The first, Eden Hazard, claimed to have been close to joining the Reds until Chelsea's unlikely Champions League triumph persuaded him to move to West London instead. Lesser known was Sao Paulo trickster Lucas Moura, who ultimately plumped for a switch to Paris St Germain despite Sir Alex's confirmation that United were interested in him.

Most regularly linked of all, however, was Robin van Persie. The Dutchman, fresh from a staggering season's work at the Emirates Stadium, had confirmed that he would not be renewing his Arsenal contract; a stance which looked set to prompt the Gunners to sell their prize asset. United, Manchester City and Juventus were linked with the 29-year-old on a daily basis, but soon momentum was building behind rumours that van Persie was interested only in a move to Old Trafford, and news eventually broke that United had reciprocated with an offer to Arsenal.

'Obviously Arsenal have given out the fact that we've made a bid for him,' said Sir Alex. 'We try to keep business as close as possible to us until the moment we conclude a deal. There's no point talking about something that might not happen. There are other clubs interested in the player. We've shown an interest and that's where we're at.'

Negotiations with the Gunners would not prove straightforward – understandably, given the various factors to consider in appraising the Dutchman's value – while the Reds' pre-season concerns were primarily concentrated on the defensive side of the squad, with Chris Smalling ruled out for ten weeks after undergoing an operation on a broken metatarsal. The England international limped onto the sidelines to join Jonny Evans, himself recovering from ankle surgery undertaken at the start of the summer.

More positively for Sir Alex, however, the news of Smalling's setback was tempered by the twin return of Nemanja Vidic and Phil Jones. The pair had returned to full training in Shanghai, the latter having been out of action since suffering an anterior cruciate ligament injury in December 2011. With the season-opening trip to Everton looming ever closer on the horizon, there were still just three senior central defenders vying for inclusion. Michael Carrick was on standby to reprise his role as a moonlighting defender if required – indeed, the midfielder had performed the role in Shanghai, admitting: 'I don't mind it. From time to time, it happens, and you have to do a job!'

For Carrick and company, home comforts briefly beckoned, as the travelling party returned to Carrington to draw breath before the second half of a six-game pre-season calendar, featuring clashes with Valerenga, Barcelona and Hannover 96. Though the opening three games had yielded just three goals for his squad, Sir Alex was unperturbed by their preparations.

'That is not the most important thing,' said the boss. 'We want to keep our heads held high in terms of our performance level and making sure we get a result. But at the end of the day, when we get to that last pre-season game in Hanover we want to be confident the team is ready for the first game of the season.'

2

August

A new season brought a new start, but a familiar aim for Sir Alex Ferguson and his players. Deposed as Premier League champions by Manchester City some three months earlier, what mattered most to everyone at Carrington was reclaiming domestic rule.

'It would be special to win it back,' said the manager. 'If you look back over different periods, you see we recover. When Arsenal won the title from us in 1998, we went and won the Treble the next year. We accepted that challenge and did something about it. Then [under Jose Mourinho] Chelsea came along and got off to a flyer in the league for the first two years. We changed our pre-season a little to make sure we got off to quick starts. That allowed us to get the title back.

'That's happened three times in the last fourteen or fifteen years. Recovery is so important and the same applies this season. There's not any difference. We want to recover the title. That's our priority number one: to win the title back.'

The first test of that aim would come at Goodison Park against

Everton, and Sir Alex was still posed with personnel issues in defence as the trip to Merseyside loomed larger, with Chris Smalling and Jonny Evans both recovering from surgery, Fabio on loan and Rafael at the Olympics with Brazil. With three more pre-season games to negotiate first, a back four of Phil Jones, Nemanja Vidic, Rio Ferdinand and Patrice Evra would be precious commodities as the season proper hoved into view.

It was the form of Vidic, back in action for the first time since December 2011, which provided the greatest cause for positivity after a goalless draw with Valerenga. 'I felt well,' said the Serbian. 'After eight months without a game, it's obvious that you have to get used to your positioning, and still fitness-wise it's not as it will be hopefully in a few weeks, but I'm pleased.

'It was frustrating, but I knew I would be out for the rest of last season. I tried to make the best of it, to work hard and to be the same as I was before the injury. This was my target and we'll see how good a job I did in that six months. It's hard, but it's part of the football career. Any sportsman has the risk of injuries and hopefully this is the past and better days are coming for me.'

While Vidic showed no adverse effects to his return and continued his comeback in the Reds' next warm-up match – a goalless draw and subsequent defeat on penalties to Barcelona in Gothenburg – Lady Luck once again turned her back on United, as Phil Jones was forced to return to Manchester after suffering with back spasms.

Yet still, with just under a month remaining until the closure of the transfer window, incomings and outgoings were the only post-match topics awaiting Sir Alex in his Gothenburg post mortem. As Paris St Germain proclaimed victory in the race for highly rated Brazilian winger Lucas Moura – 'I find it quite amazing that a club can pay €45 million for a nineteen-year-old boy; you have to say the game's gone mad,' commented the boss – there was still no clear outcome looming in Robin van Persie's mooted move to Old Trafford.

'We have made a bid and they [Arsenal] have been trying to negotiate with other clubs,' said Sir Alex. 'We just have to persevere. Hopefully it will come our way. We're trying our best, but there's no progress at this moment in time. I don't have a gut feeling on it at the moment, I must admit. We're not getting any breakthrough with Arsenal. It's difficult to say why they're operating this way. I don't know what their thoughts are because they're not giving anything away.'

Neither were United's pre-season opponents. Having failed to score for a second successive game, and having netted just three goals in five pre-season outings, the Reds' shot-shy start to their preparations was becoming noteworthy but as yet was not an issue, according to the manager.

'I'm not concerned at the moment,' he insisted. 'I would be if we'd started the league. This is preparation for us and some players need game time after being involved in the Euros. They need that twenty-eight-day rest and, after that, there's make-up time. I'm trying to give them all enough game time to get them to the proper pitch before the season starts. That's what pre-season is for. We're just trying to get all the squad as much football as we can.'

Sure enough, Sir Alex's calm preceded a storm of goals, as the DHL Tour ended in scintillating fashion in Germany, where the Reds overcame Hannover 4-3, having trailed by two goals midway through the second half. A Wayne Rooney brace and Shinji Kagawa's slick winner secured a thrilling win to inject overdue excitement to United's preparations, though assistant manager Mike Phelan confessed to both enjoying and enduring an unpredictable display.

'It was exciting, all right,' said Phelan. 'We made a game of it because we gave a couple of sloppy goals away, which we shouldn't be doing. But credit to the players. They came back, they showed a little bit of spirit at the end and it was a good victory. It's important we score goals. We can't go into a championship and be struggling finding the net. We have progressed in that department, but we have to look at it from the point of view of how disappointing it was to give the goals away in the first place. We switched off. We look like a team that can go forward and score goals, but we also look as though we can concede as well, and that's not good.

'It's been a long tour; it took us all over the place, but that's part of being a Manchester United footballer. We've taken the team to numerous continents and we've come away relatively unscathed so we're happy with that. We now have to settle down a little bit and get focused on the Premier League. That will be a big challenge.'

Hopes of meeting that challenge were boosted in a vital final week of pre-season, in which a lengthy discussion between Sir Alex and Arsène Wenger, his Arsenal counterpart, finally prompted the Gunners to slacken their grip on Robin van Persie. After the Dutchman confirmed to Wenger that he wanted to move to Old Trafford and nowhere else, the two clubs struck a deal five days before United's opening night trip to Goodison Park.

The impact reverberated throughout English football, with the deposed champions strengthened by the league's finest striker, and the good vibrations shook Carrington more than anywhere. 'News like that galvanises you, definitely,' says Ryan Giggs, looking back at the deal's announcement. 'We heard rumours about him coming, but you never know, especially with a player like that where his team don't want to let him go. Ultimately, as soon as you hear the rumour that he wants to come, then it's just a matter of time, really. A player – especially with a year left on his contract – usually gets his way.

'Over the last few years we've probably bought players with potential. With some players you never can quite tell what will happen – we didn't know Cristiano Ronaldo was going to go on and become a world-beater – but with Robin, I think we had a ready-made star. A ready-made great player, a proven goalscorer, and he was a perfect signing for us.'

At the time, Sir Alex admitted it had required all his powers of persuasion to complete a deal he had been hankering after for months. 'It wasn't an easy one,' he said. 'Understandably, Arsène Wenger didn't want to sell to Manchester United. The boy wanted to come to us and that's important. He turned down various clubs to join us, because he wants the challenge of coming to the biggest club in the world. I think that's fantastic.

'That's what swung it and what made it possible. If he hadn't come out forcibly to Arsenal to tell them he wanted to go to Manchester United, it meant the negotiations were really over – the only negotiation left was agreeing a fee with Arsenal, as there was no one else in the picture because the boy wanted it and was desperate to come to Manchester United.

'You can't turn that down. I didn't think it was possible we could get van Persie when we talked about it last year but, when I heard he'd refused to sign a new contract and made it publicly known that he wanted to leave Arsenal, then we had to be interested – there's no question about that. I spoke to David Gill and David spoke to the Glazer family and we got the ball rolling, but that was some months ago. It's been a long haul and it's not been an easy one but, thankfully, we've got him here.'

The Dutchman wasn't the only player to pen a contract in the office of chief executive David Gill ahead of the new season. Danish goalkeeper Anders Lindegaard, like van Persie, signed for four years, extending his deal until June 2016, while 23-year-old Vitesse Arnhem left-back Alexander Büttner and 18-year-old Chilean striker Angelo Henriquez also jetted in to tie up transfers.

Another boon was provided by the shock appearance of Darren Fletcher at Neil Simpson's testimonial in Aberdeen. A youthful Reds side was beaten 2-1 by the Dons at Pittodrie, with Anderson scoring a sublime consolation goal for the visitors, but the return of Scotland captain Fletcher after ulcerative colitis was the game's major talking point.

'Darren's fantastic,' marvelled Sir Alex. 'Obviously we are in the laps of the gods in terms of Darren because he has a certain condition that he has to handle very well. At the moment he is doing very well at that, he has put the weight back on which was a big concern for the kid. But he came on for twenty-five minutes in Aberdeen and did very well.'

Fletcher's return to training meant he was on hand to meet the summer's major capture, and one of Robin van Persie's first deeds as a Manchester United player was to face the world's media and explain his reasoning behind leaving Arsenal for their fierce rivals.

'I'm proud to be here and looking forward to achieving big things with Manchester United,' the Dutchman told a packed Carrington press conference. 'Arsenal are a big club, but for me it's a big challenge to get to know players here. I had a good training session this morning – I noticed every single person was really helpful. It's a friendly club like I'm used to, so it's not a big difference. The language is the same.

'Everyone knows by now that I'm a lover of football. I'm quite principled in that respect. It's always difficult to find a perfect match, but I do feel this is the perfect match for me. Manchester United breathes football. If you look at all players at the club, the stadium and the manager, my choice was made based on those things. When I have to make hard decisions, I always listen to the little boy inside me and what he wants. That little boy was screaming for United. I'm looking forward to a big challenge – the biggest so far in my football life.'

That challenge would begin at Goodison Park three days later. Whether or not van Persie would start was the main topic of discussion among the assembled media, but for Sir Alex and his coaches, the focal point had to be a defence further weakened by the loss of Rio Ferdinand. With Phil Jones, Chris Smalling and Jonny Evans still absent, Michael Carrick would have to deputise in central defence – no small task against a notoriously physical Everton side.

Barclays Premier League

Monday 20 August | Goodison Park | Attendance: 38,415

EVERTON 1 Fellaini (57)
MANCHESTER UNITED 0

United stumbled into the first hurdle of the 2012-13 season as Marouane Fellaini's header tipped a hard-fought encounter the way of Everton at Goodison Park.

The Belgian capped an impressive individual display by heading home the only goal of a tight game shortly before the hour-mark, as the Reds tasted an opening-game defeat for the first time in eight seasons.

United's under-strength defence was targeted by the hosts' route-one approach, and only an inspired display from David De Gea kept Everton's margin of victory down to a single goal. Despite the late introduction of substitute debutant Robin van Persie, the Reds came no closer than when Tom Cleverley's effort was cleared off the line by Phil Jagielka.

Makeshift defender Michael Carrick partnered Nemanja Vidic – without a competitive outing since December 2011 – while Antonio Valencia started at right-back and Patrice Evra at left-back in an unfamiliar backline, and Everton were swiftly out of the traps.

Fellaini rattled the woodwork from close range on 14 minutes, before Nikica Jelavic and Steven Pienaar both prompted smart saves from De Gea. United briefly threatened when Tim Howard smuggled Wayne Rooney's free-kick around the post, but De Gea made three more eye-catching stops before the break, saving brilliantly from Pienaar, Leon Osman and Leighton Baines.

Restricted to half-chances narrowly missed by Rooney and Danny Welbeck, United arrived at the interval with parity intact, but a string of dangerous deliveries from Baines and Darron Gibson was proving a regular cause for concern – worries which were validated just before the hour. Shortly after Osman had battered a shot against the crossbar, Fellaini rose above Carrick to reach Gibson's corner and powered an unstoppable header past De Gea, sending Goodison Park into rapture.

Stung into life, United almost levelled after a goalmouth mêlée culminated in the ball dropping to Cleverley, but the diligent Jagielka alertly flicked out a heel to fend away the midfielder's effort and preserve his side's lead. Yet such clear-cut openings were at a premium, with Jagielka in particular conducting an impressive rearguard action for David Moyes' side, who rarely looked to be troubled by United's forward probing.

The introduction of van Persie for the final 22 minutes yielded just one real opening for the Reds, as the Dutchman's pull-back found the impressive Shinji Kagawa stealing in at the near post. Howard was quickly off his line, however, to curtail the danger and ensure the hosts' victory.

The Teams

EVERTON: Howard, Baines, Distin, Hibbert, Jagielka, Neville, Gibson, Osman (Coleman 81), Fellaini (Heitinga 90), Pienaar, Jelavic (Naismith 90)
SUBS NOT USED: Mucha, Gueye, Barkley, Anichebe

MANCHESTER UNITED: De Gea, Valencia, Vidic, Carrick, Evra, Nani (Young 78), Scholes, Cleverley (Anderson 85), Kagawa, Rooney, Welbeck (van Persie 68)
SUBS NOT USED: Lindegaard, Rafael, Berbatov, Wootton
BOOKED: Nani, Scholes

'I think it was a pretty good game, actually,' said Sir Alex. 'We had plenty of possession and made some great openings without actually finishing them. But I have no criticism of my team; they applied themselves well. We had a couple of moments. I thought maybe Danny Welbeck was pushed as he went into the box [before his first-half chance]. That was a big moment and Tom Cleverley had his shot blocked by Phil Jagielka on the line in the second half. We played really good football at times. We had some good combination play.

'Fellaini is a handful. He's a big, tall, gangly lad and they just lumped the ball towards him all the time. That's all they did and they worked it from that base. But he got the goal for them so it's justified.'

Bearing the bruises to back up the challenge of facing the Belgian, moonlighting central defender Michael Carrick admits the trip to Goodison Park was tough, but the opening-night defeat was never going to prompt panic in the Reds' ranks.

'It was a difficult game,' he says. 'Everton are tough to play at the best of times, but going there for the first game of the season, on a Monday night, was hard. I was playing with Vida and it was his first game in a long time, so it was a tough evening. I thought we started well for a period, had a couple of opportunities and then they scored in the second half. It wasn't an ideal start to the season, but we still took positives from that and didn't let it affect us too much. People were writing us off from day one and saying: "that's it, title over", but we knew that wasn't the case.'

Sir Alex's immediate reaction was to finalise deals for Alexander Büttner and Angelo Henriquez, as well as ending the long-running speculation over Danny Welbeck's future by having the England striker pen a new, four-year contract to run until June 2016.

'Playing for United is all I've ever wanted to do – it's the club I've supported all my life,' beamed Welbeck. 'I'm learning all the time from the best manager in the game and I'm keen for that to continue alongside the world-class players in the squad.'

The 21-year-old was joined by another pair of burgeoning talents in Büttner and Henriquez. 'Alexander is one of the best young left-backs in Europe and we're delighted to sign him,' said Sir Alex, who also shed light on the decision to bring forward a move for Chilean youth international Henriquez.

'We've had an option on him since he was fourteen when he played against our youth team,' said the manager. 'He came over when he was fifteen and then sixteen. We kept in close contact with him in that respect and, when he got to eighteen, it was a matter of whether or not we left him for another year or brought him in. But he had such a good summer with Chile's Under-20s that we thought it wasn't worth waiting.

'We may as well do it now. That took away a lot of interest from other clubs. We had the option on him, but options only last so long and we decided to take him in. He's quick and a good finisher and he has a terrific physique for a boy of eighteen.'

Henriquez quickly jetted back to Chile in readiness for his permanent switch to England, but Büttner instead went straight into the squad for United's first home game of the season, against Martin Jol's Fulham. The newcomer's instant assimilation hinted at the ongoing injury concerns besetting the Reds' defensive ranks, though Sir Alex remained jovial amid his personnel plight.

'I need to call Bruce and Pallister,' joked the boss. 'Phil Jones has started training, but it's too soon for him. It's pretty much the same as Everton, injury-wise. Alex will be involved because he gives that back-up. Robin has had a few days' training, it's a home game and there's every chance he could get a start. I went to see Fulham [in their opening-day 5-0 win over Norwich] and they played very well, but we're at home and we need to make an impact quickly after Monday's game.'

Barclays Premier League

Saturday 25 August | Old Trafford | Attendance: 75,352

MANCHESTER UNITED 3 Van Persie (10), Kagawa (35), Rafael (41)
FULHAM 2 Duff (3), Vidic (64 og)

United's season belatedly got off and running after the Reds came from behind to beat Fulham through goals from Robin van Persie, Shinji Kagawa and Rafael.

Damien Duff had fired the Cottagers into a third-minute lead, only for van Persie to sweep home a magnificent leveller soon after in his first start for the Reds. Close-range finishes from Kagawa and Rafael had the hosts in command by the break, though an unfortunate second-half own-goal from Nemanja Vidic ensured a nervy end to the afternoon for the hosts.

Further gloss was stripped from United's afternoon by a painful late injury to substitute Wayne Rooney, who suffered a badly gashed thigh after being accidentally trodden on by Hugo Rodallega.

Though Jonny Evans was fit enough to take his place on the bench, Michael Carrick again continued in central defence alongside Vidic, who made his first Old Trafford outing since November 2011. The skipper's homecoming began in dreadful fashion as Fulham forged ahead after little more than two minutes. Bryan Ruiz craftily rolled a free-kick to Damien Duff deep inside the United area, and the veteran winger shrugged off Ashley Young's attentions to slot a simple finish past David De Gea.

United's response was positive, and parity was restored in sensational fashion through home debutant van Persie. The lively Patrice Evra whipped in a cross from the left which skipped up awkwardly off the rain-sodden turf, yet the summer's marquee signing peeled away from Brede Hangeland before sweeping a majestic finish high into Mark Schwarzer's goal.

Old Trafford, inevitably, erupted in recognition of the new figure on centre stage, and not long after it was another new arrival who put the Reds ahead for the first time. Van Persie's right-wing corner was cleared only as far as Tom Cleverley, whose thunderous low shot was parried out by Schwarzer to the lurking Kagawa, who turned in a simple finish. Though he had appeared to be lurking offside, the Japanese international was played onside by Sascha Riether.

Rafael had a close-range finish correctly disallowed for offside two minutes later, but the Brazilian was not to be denied and soon had United two goals clear. Another spell of pressure from the Reds culminated in Young stabbing a left-footed cross to the back post, where Rafael had peeled away from Mladen Petric to head the ball inside Schwarzer's near post.

Fulham still had time to fashion another opening before the break, as Evra bravely blocked Petric's acrobatic effort, De Gea padded away Duff's follow-up and then brilliantly deflected Petric's shot against the underside of the bar with his legs, before Ruiz blazed the ball high into the Stretford End.

The second half began brightly for United as Young brought a fine block from Aaron Hughes and Rafael headed over from a promising position, only for Fulham to reduce the arrears in bizarre circumstances. Matthew Briggs clipped in a high cross from the left which De Gea, Vidic and Petric all went for, with the Fulham striker seemingly nudging the United stopper as the ball hit Vidic's heel and trickled over the line.

As nerves began to grip the home support, Rooney and Danny Welbeck were sent on to replace Kagawa and Young, but Fulham almost pulled level immediately and only two fine saves from De Gea prevented Moussa Dembele from bringing the visitors level.

Rooney almost put the result beyond doubt with a late block-buster, but the England international's afternoon was curtailed when Rodallega accidentally raked his studs down Rooney's inner thigh, leading to a lengthy stoppage with the game already in injury time. A dismaying end to the game might have plunged even further for United, who required another De Gea save – this time to fend away Ruiz's header – to preserve a hard-fought, bewildering victory.

The Teams

MANCHESTER UNITED: De Gea, Rafael, Carrick, Vidic, Evra, Cleverley, Anderson (Giggs 81), Valencia, Kagawa (Rooney 68), Young (Welbeck 68), van Persie
SUBS NOT USED: Lindegaard, Evans, Hernandez, Scholes

FULHAM: Schwarzer, Riether, Hughes, Hangeland, Briggs, Duff, Diarra (Baird 81), Dembele, Kakaniclic (Sidwell 62), Ruiz, Petric (Rodallega 72)
SUBS NOT USED: Stockdale, Kelly, Kasami, Halliche
BOOKED: Hangeland

'I think I'll always look back on this game; that we won on my home debut and that I scored a good goal,' said Old Trafford's newest hero, Robin van Persie. 'I came here a couple of times before but I always liked this stadium, the size of it. The pitch is big, the pitch is always nice. Now I'm a United player, everyone knows that and I'm look-ing forward to this challenge. The fans have been brilliant today, supporting us and they gave me a very warm welcome, so I'm very pleased.

Of his breathtaking first goal for the club, the Dutchman remained modest, saying: 'I think I could only do one thing there, because it came with a little bit of a bounce, and so I had to time it well. Sometimes you're lucky and I was today, luckily enough. The game was a bit nervy, but we held on and the main thing was that we got the points, so that's out of the way and it was a good day in the end, a good three points.'

Van Persie's goal was the highlight of a solid all-round display, and he remained patient over his steady ascent towards top form. 'Training sessions have been very good and with all the guys it's a process,' he said. 'I have to get used to them, they have to get used to me, because I've still only been here a week. We have all the time in the world. I don't want to rush into things. I'm not one hundred per cent match fit. It's my first game of the whole pre-season in over a month, so I have to get fitter and fitter. I'll get fitter by playing games, basically, so I still need a couple of weeks before I'm fully match fit.'

For Wayne Rooney, even longer would be required after his stomach-churning injury. 'It's a very bad one,' Sir Alex solemnly admitted. 'He's gone to hospital. It looks as if he'll be out for maybe four weeks. I don't know what happened. I think the player must have followed through after he shot. He's got a bad one.'

Overall, the manager could see both positives and negatives in a display laced with attacking ingenuity and defensive fragility. 'I think we saw the two sides of Manchester United,' he confided. 'We made a terrible mistake for the second goal and it became a match. It should never have been a match, some of our football was fantastic.'

For Rafael, who capped a sparkling individual performance with what proved to be the afternoon's decisive goal, excitement was on the horizon for the coming months. 'Everyone knows everyone has these skills and everyone scores,' grinned the lively Brazilian. 'We will score a lot of goals this season, I hope.'

After a chastening 2011-12 assault on the UEFA Champions League, Rafael and his cohorts were aiming to reserve some of their finest play for the European stage in 2012-13. After being drawn against Galatasaray, SC Braga and CFR Cluj – another apparently navigable group, as in the previous season – Sir Alex was forthright in declaring: 'After the experience of last year, we don't want to make any stupid errors this time. We will play our strongest team to make sure we get through.'

The manager's selection process would not include Dimitar Berbatov, who ended a four-year stint at Old Trafford with a late transfer window move to Fulham. 'Dimitar was always going to be going,' admitted the boss. 'I said last year he'd be leaving at the end of the season. He's a very talented player and his contribution is good, particularly in home games. He's the only player to score a hat-trick against Liverpool for United [under Sir Alex]. When we changed our game, it didn't suit him. We wanted to play with more speed and teams were getting organised very quickly against us. Therefore, we had to change the way we wanted to play and it didn't suit Dimitar, but he's a very talented player. He'll do well.'

While the Old Trafford career of the club's record signing came to an end, however, United could focus only on the future. Off and running in the hunt for the title, things were only just getting started.

3

September

The start of any season is rarely a good time to face a freshly promoted club. Full of *joie de vivre* and eager to prove themselves equal to the step up, the newcomers often exceed the sum of their parts – as United memorably found at Burnley in 2009.

Thus, a hefty trip to Southampton carried with it no shortage of menace. Even though Nigel Adkins' Saints had lost their opening two games of the campaign, they had led champions Manchester City and threatened Premier League regulars Wigan Athletic, and Jonny Evans – in contention for involvement after featuring for Warren Joyce's Under-21s – anticipated a tricky afternoon on the south coast.

'Southampton have lost both of their games but they'll want to do well at home against us,' said the Northern Ireland international. 'I think everyone, especially the teams that come up, will be targeting their home games for points and they'll want to get their season up and running this weekend. So we'll be expecting a really tough game.

'I think you always get funny results at the start of the season.

Teams are still finding their feet and that means you sometimes see some strange results. Going away to Everton is tough at any point in the season, but we put that game behind us and had a good result against Fulham and we want to kick on against Southampton now. We've played a couple of FA Cup games there in the last few years and managed to win both, so hopefully we can continue our form there.'

Sir Alex Ferguson had conceded that his summer recruitment drive had created a welcome selection headache, and Evans concurred: 'The squad is so strong; just looking at the numbers we have in training is unbelievable. It's important to have that, though, because you get injuries through the season and we want to do well in every competition we play in, so we're going to need everyone. There is plenty of strength in depth in the squad.'

Barclays Premier League

Sunday 2 September | St Mary's | Attendance: 39,609

SOUTHAMPTON 2 Lambert (16), Schneiderlin (55)
MANCHESTER UNITED 3 Van Persie (23, 87, 90)

Just as United looked set to suffer a second defeat in three games, Robin van Persie struck twice in the dying stages to complete his first Reds hat-trick and pilfer the points from a battling Southampton side.

Twice the Saints had led, before eventually running out of steam and succumbing to a visiting side inspired for the final half-hour by substitute Paul Scholes. Van Persie, who had earlier cracked home a first-half leveller and also missed a penalty, turned in a close-range finish before powerfully heading home Nani's stoppage-time corner to send United's travelling supporters feral with joy.

Van Persie had looked United's likeliest saviour all afternoon, steering Michael Carrick's lofted pass wide of Kelvin Davis's post with the Reds' first opening. United's new number 20 would make no mistake from a similar position after 23 minutes, cracking home an angled left-footer after Antonio Valencia's flighted cross had coaxed Nathaniel Clyne into an untimely slip. By then, Southampton had been in front for seven minutes following Rickie Lambert's towering far-post header.

Despite the quick restoration of parity, the hosts seemed unperturbed. Bar a downward header from Patrice Evra, which Davis fended away in relative comfort, Southampton were rarely troubled. It was little surprise, then, when they retook the lead ten minutes into the second period. This time it was Evra who lost his footing, allowing Morgan Schneiderlin to power in a free header.

Anders Lindegaard – restored in goal in place of David De Gea – then showed sharp reflexes to repel Jason Puncheon's low, near-post shot before Sir Alex Ferguson, in his 1,000th league game at the Old Trafford helm, threw on Paul Scholes and Nani. The change had a dramatic impact, with the former dictating the Reds' attacking tempo and the latter teeing up van Persie to win a penalty, conceded by Joos Hooiveld's rash challenge.

The Dutchman's audacious clipped effort was comfortably batted away by Davis, but United shrugged off the setback and continued to turn the screw. A leveller belatedly arrived with three minutes remaining as Rafael's cross was headed against the post by Rio Ferdinand, with the rebound falling perfectly for van Persie to haul the visitors back on terms.

In injury time, van Persie completed the Reds' comeback and his own personal redemption by emphatically heading Nani's perfect corner past Davis, prompting wild scenes of celebration among the away supporters, who could embark on their lengthy homeward journey thoroughly entertained and relieved.

The Teams

SOUTHAMPTON: Davis, Clyne, Fonte, Hooiveld, Fox, Puncheon (Mayuka 74), Davis, Schneiderlin, Ward-Prowse, Lallana (Rodriguez 78), Lambert (Guly 75)
SUBS NOT USED: Lee, Gazzaniga, Richardson, Seaborne
BOOKED: Hooiveld

MANCHESTER UNITED: Lindegaard, Rafael, Ferdinand, Vidic, Evra, Valencia, Cleverley (Scholes 61), Carrick, Welbeck (Hernandez 71), van Persie, Kagawa (Nani 61)
SUBS NOT USED: De Gea, Evans, Giggs, Powell

A decisive hat-trick was not enough to save Robin van Persie from a post-match inquest over his missed penalty, with Reds legend and MUTV pundit Paddy Crerand giving the Dutchman a half-playful, half-serious dig on the arm for his fluffed spot-kick. Moments earlier, van Persie had admitted culpability in his post-match interview with the club channel.

'It's three points and a little headache for me,' he confessed. 'I don't know what I was thinking with the penalty. I wanted to hit it hard like I always do, but at the last second I changed my mind, somehow. That wasn't good enough so that was a bit of a down. I'm quite disappointed, to be fair. I ask a certain standard from my game and when something like that happens, when you're two-one down, you can't take a penalty like that. It is me who is to blame. I don't know what went wrong but something went wrong big time, so I have to work on that. After that, I was very relieved that we got the three points, trust me.'

While the Reds' match-winner was in critical mood regarding his own input, his manager could only marvel at yet another entry to a seemingly endless list of rousing comebacks. 'We never give up,' marvelled Sir Alex. 'We do that all the time at our club and I expect ten like that a season so that's one out of the way! It's unbelievable – it really is.'

They were to prove prophetic words from the manager. Having shipped five goals in their opening three games, United's porous start to the season was already a concern for skipper Nemanja Vidic, who demanded a quick improvement, despite the mitigation of the injury crisis claiming United's defensive ranks.

'It was a difficult game and we conceded two goals we're not happy with at all,' stated the Serbian. 'We've been told before the game what Southampton's strengths are, what their game is and what they're trying to achieve. In the end, they did it, so it's disappointing. I think it's only the second time in a year myself and Rio have played together, so it's a long time and obviously it's tough as everyone needs more games.

'I have to say, we are not really pleased with the goals we've conceded. There was a lack of concentration, I think, for all four goals we lost [in the previous two games], but we have to work on it. You have to say we've had a lot of turbulence in defence with so many changes and people going in and going out. We didn't have a constant back four and sometimes it causes a problem, but we look forward to the next games. We have over a week to improve our fitness and obviously our form, so we are going to be right for the next game in the Premier League.'

For Vidic, the chance to hone his game and fitness at Carrington was most welcome. For a host of his team-mates, however, a week-long international break thrust upon them the draining effects of travel and different surroundings at a time when settling into a rhythm with United was the primary aim. Yet, while Sir Alex and his staff held their breath awaiting a spate of walking wounded returning from Manchester Airport, it was Phil Jones – who had remained at Carrington – who provided the Reds' next injury scare. A torn knee meniscus muscle sustained in training prompted surgery for the 21-year-old, who was swiftly ruled out for up to ten weeks.

That crystallised Rio Ferdinand's importance to the cause, with only Vidic, Jonny Evans and the England veteran available and recognised as senior central defenders. Ferdinand, on the verge of his 400th Reds appearance, rued the timing of the international break and was itching to welcome Wigan to Old Trafford.

'You really feel it when you're not involved in international football,' said the defender. 'You're just sitting and waiting around thinking: "When is the next game coming?" When the games are coming week in and week out, with two or three matches a week, this is the time when you enjoy it the most.

'Against Southampton I thought that myself: "We can't lose this game because it's going to be a long two weeks' wait until the next game." A fortnight where you go out of the house at times and see people, and you don't want that laying in the back of your mind waiting to see if someone will mention it or talk about it. We needed to get a win to have a good break to prepare for Wigan.'

Ferdinand wasn't the only United player in line to reach a milestone against Roberto Martinez's Latics. Ryan Giggs would make his 600th Premier League outing, while Paul Scholes would reach 700 appearances in all competitions, almost 16 months after retiring. Inevitably, the trio of veterans invited pre-match praise from their manager.

'It's a landmark for the three players and it's a great example to the younger players about what can be achieved if they sacrifice in football,' said Sir Alex. 'These players have done that or they would never have got to this stage.'

Against a Wigan side who had dealt the Reds a damaging defeat five months earlier at the DW Stadium, the trio's know-how would be a valuable weapon.

Barclays Premier League

Saturday 15 September | Old Trafford |Attendance: 75,142

MANCHESTER UNITED 4 Scholes (51), Hernandez (63), Büttner (66), Powell (82)
WIGAN ATHLETIC 0

Paul Scholes marked his 700th United appearance with the opening goal against Wigan, before a trio of players from the opposite end of the age scale secured a comfortable victory.

Having had his early spot-kick saved by Ali Al-Habsi, Chicharito turned in Alex Büttner's shot, then the Dutchman marked his home debut with an impressive solo goal and fellow new boy Nick Powell rifled in the Reds' fourth from distance to cap a fine second-half display from the hosts.

With all bar Phil Jones, Wayne Rooney and Chris Smalling available, Sir Alex had several selection dilemmas to ponder, the end result being five changes from the side that won at Southampton. Scholes and Rio Ferdinand moved on to 700 and 400 United appearances respectively, while Ryan Giggs made his 600th Premier League outing. Büttner made his maiden appearance at left-back, while fellow summer signings Powell, Robin van Persie and Shinji Kagawa were on the bench.

Despite the raft of changes, United should have moved ahead inside the first five minutes. Danny Welbeck latched onto a searching through-ball from Giggs and reached the ball ahead of the onrushing Al-Habsi before tumbling to the ground. Though Welbeck made no appeal, referee Michael Oliver pointed to the spot, to the understandable outrage of the visitors. Their ire was soothed, however, when Al-Habsi plunged to his left to comfortably palm away Chicharito's effort from the spot.

Welbeck appeared to place himself in sole charge of enlivening the crowd again, turning in a lively attacking display and coming close four times in the opening period, while Nani fell foul of an untimely bobble and clipped well over the bar after being released by Giggs. Wigan threatened for the first time as Ivan Ramis headed wide from Shaun Maloney's out-swinging free-kick, before Emmerson Boyce scuffed a shot narrowly wide of Anders Lindegaard's near post.

Arouna Kone prodded wastefully wide of the target in a huge scare for the hosts, who responded by moving into the lead shortly after the break. Michael Carrick's incisive pass pierced the visitors' well-organised defence and released Nani, whose cross was palmed out by Al-Habsi and into the path of the merciless Scholes for a simple finish.

Shortly after the hour mark, United struck a quickfire one-two to end the contest, with Büttner heavily involved in both. With both teams encamped in the Wigan area, Welbeck nicked possession and fed Giggs, who teed up Büttner. The Dutchman's shot appeared to be clearing the far post, but it was instead diverted past Al-Habsi by Chicharito, lurking with intent and played onside by Boyce.

United's players rushed to salute Büttner's part in the goal, and the left-back was soon at the epicentre of celebrations again as he marked his debut with an unforgettable goal. Picking up the ball on the left flank, the 23-year-old shrugged off the attentions of Kone, motored past Boyce, nicked the ball away from James McCarthy and then beat Ramis before unleashing a shot which squirmed past Al-Habsi.

Sir Alex took the three-goal advantage as his cue to ring the changes, first replacing Scholes and Giggs with Nick Powell and van Persie. In the game's final act of note, Powell followed Büttner, van Persie and Kagawa in marking his home debut with a goal, cutting infield and arrowing in a 20-yard shot which sped past Al-Habsi to set the seal on a thoroughly enjoyable afternoon's work for the goal-hungry Reds.

The Teams

MANCHESTER UNITED: Lindegaard, Rafael, Ferdinand, Vidic (Evans 77), Büttner, Giggs (Powell 71), Carrick, Nani, Scholes (van Persie 71), Hernandez, Welbeck
SUBS NOT USED: De Gea, Valencia, Cleverley, Kagawa
BOOKED: Büttner, Welbeck

WIGAN ATHLETIC: Al-Habsi, Caldwell, Boyce, Ramis, Figueroa, McCarthy, Maloney (Gomez 59), McArthur, Beausejour (Jones 69), Kone, Di Santo
SUBS NOT USED: Crusat, Watson, Pollitt, Miyaichi, Boselli
BOOKED: Boyce, McArthur

'It's a dream for me,' grinned Alexander Büttner, one of the Reds' two scoring debutants. 'If I play I want to let the manager see that I can do a good job. I think I did that. I'm happy that I can play my first minutes in the first team. It's great that we won and I scored and gave a pass for Chicharito to score.

'I wasn't nervous until I was standing on the field, looking around. I think it's normal to be a little bit nervous if you play in front of so many people. In Holland, I played in front of twenty-three thousand, so it's beautiful to play for so many more people. I'm happy today. I've scored my first goal in my first game and I'll never forget it.'

'It's great to make my debut,' echoed Nick Powell, 'And to then cap it off with a goal is what I've been working for. But my dad will keep me in touch, I'll tell you that. I'm just going to go home, have this great feeling and I'll keep myself on the ground. When I first came on it scared me a little bit, to be fair, because I'm only used to five thousand people now and then, but it's a great atmosphere – the fans are great.

'It wasn't the hardest game because they made it easier for me, but I'm happy to be on the pitch getting minutes. I learn every day, especially from the midfielders – Scholes, Carrick, Giggsy – they're all great, they've all been through it and won trophies. That's what I want to do, so I hope to learn off them every day.'

Having watched the greenhorns and the old masters mingle with devastating results, Sir Alex was delighted with the input of every age bracket. 'Once we got the speed of the game right in the second half, it made a difference for us as we became more aggressive in terms of getting the ball back and making good tackles in midfield,' said the boss. 'That got the crowd up and we ran out good winners.

'It turned out to be a good day for us. It's fantastic Paul scored – that is what we always remember him for as a young player, ghosting into the penalty box. Obviously, as he's got older, he doesn't need to do that, as we prefer him to play in central midfield, but he scored on his hundredth appearance, two hundredth, three hundredth, four hundredth, five hundredth, not his six hundredth, but now on his seven hundredth appearance – and it's fantastic.

'We think Büttner can be a really good addition to the team, and Nick Powell is going to be a really good player who, we hope, will fill Paul Scholes's boots in terms of he's got terrific vision, good temperament, two great feet, is quick and is a great striker of the ball.'

Having continued a largely successful start towards the reclamation of the Barclays Premier League title, United's attentions could now switch to the European stage. The manner in which the Reds had exited the Champions League at the group stage a year earlier had remained a source of embarrassment, and with the visit of Galatasaray looming, there was a steely determination within the squad and staff to set the record straight.

'Galatasaray is a good game for us,' said Rio Ferdinand. 'The Turkish fans will come over and add a lot of noise to the stadium. They are very vocal. We're expecting a tough game, but it's one we're expecting to win as well. I don't take too much notice of who we have got. There are big teams we could have got that we have missed out on although, as we found out last season, people said it was a so-called good draw on paper but we didn't get through, so you've got to make sure you apply yourself correctly. If we do that this season, we'll get to the next stage of the tournament and that's definitely our aim.'

'The Champions League coming around again is always special,' added Ryan Giggs. 'You know it's a test and can't take any game for granted. That was shown last year when we didn't get through the group stage, so we need to be starting well to make sure we get our results at home, which we didn't do last year, and hopefully go a long way in the competition.'

In order to stave off the ghosts of 2011-12, only a win would do.

UEFA Champions League

Wednesday 19 September | Old Trafford | Attendance: 74,653

MANCHESTER UNITED 1 Carrick (7)
GALATASARAY SK 0

United took the first steps towards European redemption with a narrow, hard-fought victory over Turkish champions Galatasaray at Old Trafford.

The Reds survived an early penalty scare before taking the lead inside seven minutes through Michael Carrick, who latched onto Shinji Kagawa's incisive pass and calmly converted, despite being hooked to the ground by visiting goalkeeper Fernando Muslera. The

Uruguayan stopper repelled a second-half penalty from Nani – a third successive missed spot-kick for United – before David De Gea sprung to prominence with a fine display to preserve the hosts' invaluable clean sheet.

Sir Alex Ferguson made good on his promise to play his strongest team. Robin van Persie and Shinji Kagawa returned to the starting XI, while Patrice Evra was recalled at left-back, but the most noteworthy snippet of team news concerned Darren Fletcher's inclusion as a substitute after ten months on the sidelines with ulcerative colitis.

That pre-match boon for the home support was almost instantly forgotten as all attentions switched to referee Wolfgang Stark in the opening minute. Nemanja Vidic, attempting to reach a short Evra pass, caught Umut Bulut inside the penalty area, only for Stark to wave play on.

At the other end, Muslera did well to bravely block Nani's clipped effort after a smart interchange with Kagawa on the edge of the box. The Japanese schemer was soon involved again for United's goal, combining well with Carrick to send the midfielder clean through on Muslera. Carrick calmly circumnavigated the goalkeeper and, though he was tripped, still managed to hook the ball into the empty net.

The visitors responded admirably to the setback, however, striking the crossbar through Nordin Amrabat and the post through Hamit Altintop. In between, United might have been awarded a penalty for handball by Emmanuel Eboue, but that opportunity did arrive just eight minutes into the second period after Rafael was brought down by Burak Yilmaz. Nani's tame effort was easily saved by Muslera, however, adding further nerves to an already jittery atmosphere.

Selcuk Inan's glancing header sailed narrowly past the far post, before Vidic spurned a chance from close range and Evra flashed a shot across goal at the other end. A lightning Galatasaray counter-attack prompted two fine saves from De Gea – from Yilmaz and then Colak – in the visitors' clearest opening of the game.

Darren Fletcher's introduction in the 79th minute added gloss on a night when the result outweighed the performance, and United could reflect on a satisfactory start to life back at Europe's top table.

The Teams

MANCHESTER UNITED: De Gea, Rafael, Evans, Vidic, Evra, Valencia, Scholes (Fletcher 79), Kagawa (Welbeck 84), Carrick, Nani, van Persie (Hernandez 81)
SUBS NOT USED: Lindegaard, Ferdinand, Anderson, Cleverley
BOOKED: Vidic, Evra, van Persie

GALATASARAY SK: Muslera, Dany Nounkeu, Balta, Kaya, Eboue, Altintop, Inan, Melo (Aydin Yilmaz 79), Burak Yilmaz, Bulut (Elmander 15), Amrabat (Colak 63)
SUBS NOT USED: Ceylan, Cris, Riera, Baytar
BOOKED: Melo

'I think there was a lot more on that game than there had been in recent years, obviously with us not doing so well last year,' reflected Michael Carrick. 'It was a home game against the team we and most people regarded as our strongest rivals in the group, so it was our chance to get a real good start to the group. Especially after the way it finished last year, it was crucial we did that. To win the game was vital, really.

'It was nice to score, obviously. If I wasn't going to get the next ball then I would've stayed down when the keeper brought me down because it was a clear penalty – no arguments about that – but once there's a little carrot there of having a tap-in, I got up as quick as I could and made the most of it!'

That the midfielder did decisively open the scoring so early was an overwhelming relief to Sir Alex, who saw his side contrive to miss a penalty for the third successive game and gradually labour along the scenic route to a valuable victory.

'I don't want any more penalties,' he laughed. 'Maybe the confusion arose from the fact that Chicharito took it on Saturday, when Robin wasn't available, and today Nani grabbed the ball because he wanted to take it. Robin van Persie, to me, takes great penalty kicks. I don't see why he shouldn't take them.

'But Galatasaray have got more experience in their team and in the first half we gave the ball away and they counter-attacked well from that. I think there was a lack of concentration at times. It's unusual for us to be as frivolous with the ball. In the second half we did much better in that respect. I was pleased with the second half – it was more solid, we had better concentration and we saw it out really well.

'They never made any chances and all the chances fell to us – we could have scored four or five in the second half. They were very confident in their play and possession. You get that with these European teams. It's not a problem; you just have to be patient and make sure that when you're in possession you make it count, and with missing the chances we did in the second half, we keep ourselves on the edge.

'I think getting three points in the first game is a bonus,' he said. 'If you go back to last season we got a point in Benfica, then a point at home . . . so three points are really important. Cluj beating Braga away sets up a really interesting game for the next European match.'

More compelling still would be the Reds' next domestic outing: the short but perennially intriguing trip to face Liverpool at Anfield.

English football's grandest fixture is renowned as combustible, but United's looming trip to Merseyside fell in unusually sensitive circumstances, arriving less than a fortnight after the Hillsborough Independent Panel absolved Liverpool fans of blame in the 1989 stadium disaster.

'It shouldn't need what happened [the ruling] to change things,' declared Sir Alex. 'Two great clubs like ourselves and Liverpool should understand each other's problems. The fact we're playing them after the findings we've been reading about in the last few days does bring a focus to it. Both clubs have suffered such tremendous fatalities through football. Maybe this will be a line in the sand now, in terms of how supporters behave towards each other. The reputation of both clubs doesn't deserve trouble. You hope supporters of both teams support their club and that's the end of it.'

Despite the heightened importance of matters off the field, the manager still had several considerations in assessing his available personnel for the trip to Anfield. Nemanja Vidic complained of tightness in his knee and was omitted from the squad. Wayne Rooney – who had revealed that Hugo Rodallega's studs missed a major artery in his leg by a matter of millimetres – was edging towards contention but would not be risked, while the ongoing rotation of goalkeepers David De Gea and Anders Lindegaard kept everybody guessing as to who Sir Alex regarded as his first-choice stopper for what promised to be an emotionally charged afternoon on Merseyside.

'The most important thing I'm trying to do is give both of them experience in the English game,' explained the man with the answer. 'Neither is as experienced as Edwin van der Sar or Peter Schmeichel. Alternating isn't a problem for me. They're both equally very good goalkeepers. That's the policy we've adopted this season and last season, although De Gea played most of last season after Lindegaard was injured. I'm comfortable with this situation.'

Barclays Premier League

Sunday 23 September | Anfield | Attendance: 44,263

LIVERPOOL 1 Gerrard (46)
MANCHESTER UNITED 2 Rafael (51), van Persie (81 pen)

A first Anfield win since 2007 was procured in taxing circumstances as a sensational goal from Rafael and Robin van Persie's late penalty sealed a comeback win over ten-man Liverpool.

Steven Gerrard had fired the hosts into a deserved lead in the opening minute of the second half, only for Rafael to quickly curl home an unstoppable finish to level matters, and van Persie crashed home the decisive penalty after Antonio Valencia had been fouled by Glen Johnson.

The victory came despite a largely off-colour performance from the visitors, who toiled for long periods even in spite of the 39th-minute dismissal of Jonjo Shelvey for a two-footed lunge on Jonny Evans.

The game's events heightened the tension on a day already shrouded in pre-match fervour. Nevertheless, all fears of unruly fan behaviour from either end of the East Lancs Road proved unfounded. On the field too, there were handshakes throughout both sets of players and Sir Bobby Charlton presented Liverpool ambassador Ian Rush with flowers to commemorate the much-publicised Hillsborough ruling.

Amid all the issues surrounding the game, the major piece of team news was provided by Sir Alex Ferguson's omission of Nemanja Vidic as a precautionary measure, after the Serbian had already – for the first time since November 2011 – completed two full games in a week. Rio Ferdinand returned to partner Jonny Evans in his stead, while Ryan Giggs stood in as captain.

After a strong start from the visitors, it was Giggs who had the game's first opening. Nani made progress down the left flank and fed the ball inside for Shinji Kagawa, who in turn teed up his captain for a poked, 20-yard effort which narrowly skirted by Pepe Reina's top corner.

Liverpool's riposte was to quickly seize control of the game. Anders Lindegaard palmed out Luis Suarez's drilled cross before Steven Gerrard fired a low shot just past the Dane's post after a well-worked short corner. United were rattled, and just before the quarter-hour the visitors' defensive ranks were breached again, but a heavy first touch from Fabio Borini took him away from goal and allowed Evans to take the sting out of the Italian's subsequent shot.

The Reds' game was disjointed – too often giving away possession or too pedestrian to counter – and an injury to Ferdinand looked set to further hamper Sir Alex's gameplan. Instead, the veteran played on despite his discomfort and emerged as one of the Reds' most important players in the first period, constantly repelling the hosts' forward forays.

The game remained poised in that manner, with Liverpool's possession only undone by their own attacking bluntness and solidity in the United defence. Then, with six minutes of the half remaining, the complexion of the game was completely altered. Giggs was caught in possession by Shelvey, who sprinted into a 50-50 challenge with Evans. Both players left the ground, Evans reached the ball first and Shelvey crunched into him. Referee Mark Halsey took his time, assessed the situation and dismissed the Liverpool midfielder.

Nevertheless, it was Liverpool who continued to boss matters and soon after the re-start, after Glen Johnson's shot deflected to Gerrard, the hosts' skipper had time and space to bring the ball under control and direct a left-footed volley past the sprawling Lindegaard.

The circumstances demanded a response from United, and it was quickly forthcoming: less than five minutes had passed before the scoreline was levelled in sensational fashion. Valencia crossed from the right and Kagawa chested the ball neatly down to Rafael. The Brazilian cut inside on his left foot and, despite having little room for manoeuvre, curled an unstoppable shot high into Reina's goal, via the Spaniard's upright.

Having drawn level before building any real momentum, United's flurry of intent fizzled out. Suarez drew a fine stop from Lindegaard with an arrowed left-footed effort, before the Dane tipped over Suso's side-footed shot as Liverpool continued to threaten. Then, with 15 minutes remaining, the Reds were awarded what was only their second Anfield penalty of Sir Alex's Old Trafford reign.

Valencia showed mind-boggling speed to nip between Johnson and Daniel Agger and reach a loose ball, and as the Ecuadorian bore down on Reina and weighed up his options, Johnson's attempts to recover culminated in Valencia being bundled to the ground.

Van Persie was subjected to a four-minute wait to take the spot-kick as Agger received treatment, but the Dutchman showed nerves of steel to smash his kick high into Reina's goal. There was one late scare as Martin Kelly headed wide from a promising position but – despite eight minutes of added time – United were able to bask in the unfamiliar glory of winning at Anfield for the first time in half a decade.

The Teams

LIVERPOOL: Reina, Johnson, Agger (Carragher 80), Kelly, Skrtel, Gerrard, Allen, Sterling (Henderson 66), Shelvey, Suarez, Borini (Suso 46)
SUBS NOT USED: Assaidi, Jones, Enrique, Sahin
BOOKED: Reina
SENT OFF: Shelvey

MANCHESTER UNITED: Lindegaard, Rafael (Welbeck 89), Evra, Ferdinand, Evans, Valencia, Giggs, Carrick, Nani (Scholes 46), Kagawa (Hernandez 81), van Persie
SUBS NOT USED: De Gea, Anderson, Cleverley, Büttner
BOOKED: van Persie, Scholes

'It was a great day,' grins Jonny Evans, looking back on his first-ever victory at Anfield. 'I always remember Gary Neville talking to me about going to Anfield and the game being one hundred miles an hour, and you don't really understand that until you're out there. Watching the game from the sidelines doesn't give you the true feel of it. Until you're down on that touchline you don't see the true speed and intensity. It's in everyone's faces. You can see it in people's expressions. Sometimes you've just got to ride the storm there.

'They get the crowd right up and come at you, so I think in that game especially the first twenty minutes were tough. I think as well that maybe the sending off for them settled the game down a bit. I think just before that we were starting to get in the game anyway, but that probably swung it in our favour. They got the goal after half time, which we were disappointed about, but we got a great goal from Rafael and the penalty from Robin after Antonio's run.'

Evans played a major role in the incident which led to Shelvey's dismissal, and still insists that it highlights a disparity between football in the youth ranks and the highest level.

'By the letter of the law it's hard to judge,' he says. 'He caught me right up my shin and I got a big gash. I think the referee sent him off before he'd seen that, actually. It was just one of those collisions. People said I should have been sent off as well, but I think from both of us, it was two young players just going in for the ball as honestly as we could.

'That's the way we did it growing up playing Academy football. It's probably never been punished then, then you come into the

Premier League and suddenly these tackles are highlighted on TV and everyone's talking about them. That's a problem that should be sorted out at younger levels. Some of those tackles were daily things we used to do in training.'

By hook or by crook, United's barren run at Anfield was finally over, and the result left the Reds a point behind pace-setters Chelsea, while the winless Merseysiders occupied a berth in the bottom three. Points and positions could briefly be shelved, however, for the commencement of the Capital One Cup.

A home draw against Alan Pardew's Newcastle United ensured a stern examination for the Reds, who had surrendered four points to the Magpies in 2011-12, but assistant manager Mike Phelan confirmed that the game would provide a timely opportunity to field players in need of playing time.

'We've got options and we have to make sure this game helps us involve other players as well as the ones who have been playing in the last five or six games,' he said. 'It's important we give them the opportunity to perform.

'We've got a good mix of youth and experience, and we want to make sure we perform and the players involved show their abilities and what they can offer. The manager has always seen these games as an opportunity to look at individuals' progress, to see where some players are at and if they're capable of being part of a long season. The hardest part is giving them the competitiveness and the games in order to prove that. You don't just want one game, either – you want more than one. And hopefully this cup competition offers us that.'

The Reds' preparations were hit by the news that Nemanja Vidic had undergone an operation after further investigation had revealed underlying meniscus problems in the defender's right knee. The Serbian was initially expected to miss two months of action, giving a clutch of youthful defenders a chance to play themselves into prominence against Newcastle.

Capital One Cup

Wednesday 26 September | Old Trafford | Attendance: 46,358

MANCHESTER UNITED 2 Anderson (44), Cleverley (58)
NEWCASTLE UNITED 1 Cisse (62)

Despite a late fightback from Newcastle, United reached the fourth round of the Capital One Cup through Anderson's scorching long-ranger and Tom Cleverley's first senior goal for the Reds.

The Brazilian opened the scoring just before half time, while Cleverley atoned for an earlier miss with a neatly crafted finish in the second period. Papiss Cisse quickly reduced the arrears, however, and came close to forcing extra time when his overhead kick rebounded off David De Gea's crossbar.

United's diamond formation in midfield featured Wayne Rooney as its attacking tip, and the England striker shone in his first outing since suffering a gashed leg in August's victory over Fulham. A strong home side bore the hallmarks of a League Cup selection only in defence, where an inexperienced quartet of Marnick Vermijl, Michael Keane, Scott Wootton and Alexander Büttner protected De Gea.

Though Dan Gosling miscued a presentable early chance for the visitors, United's defence was seldom tested in the first period. Newcastle goalkeeper Rob Elliot produced a superb save to push away an Anderson drive, and was just as solid in repelling Danny Welbeck's powerful effort.

The visiting stopper was beaten shortly before the break as Javier Hernandez released Cleverley, only for the midfielder to slot his left-footed effort wide of the post. A lead did materialise before the interval, however, as Anderson wound infield and unleashed a 25-yard crackerjack which thudded against the inside of Elliot's post and into the net.

Both the Brazilian and Chicharito might have embellished United's lead in the early stages of the second half, but the deed was eventually done by Cleverley. A patient move involving Rooney and Welbeck worked the ball to the midfielder on the edge of the Newcastle area, and Cleverley impishly steered a shot wide of the unsighted Elliot and into the Stretford End goal.

Having negated his earlier miss and broken his goalscoring duck, the 23-year-old celebrated with understandable relief and delight. The air of jubilation inside Old Trafford was quickly dulled, however, when visiting substitutes Shane Ferguson and Cisse combined to halve the arrears, with the latter nodding in the former's cross.

United's response was swift: Hernandez lifted a shot against the bar, Anderson had a powerful effort deflected wide and Keane almost got on the end of a Rooney corner, but the closest either side came to providing the game's fourth goal was when Cisse acrobatically looped the ball against the top of De Gea's crossbar.

The Teams

MANCHESTER UNITED: De Gea, Büttner (Brady 86), Wootton, M.Keane, Vermijl (Tunnicliffe 77), Anderson, Cleverley, Fletcher, Rooney (Powell 76), Hernandez, Welbeck
SUBS NOT USED: Johnstone, Evans, Kind, Lingard

NEWCASTLE UNITED: Elliot, Coloccini (Ferguson 61), Williamson, Perch, Tavernier, Gosling, Marveaux, Tiote (Bigirimana 71), Obertan, Vuckic (Cisse 61), Shola Ameobi
SUBS NOT USED: Harper, Anita, Amalfitano, Sami Ameobi
BOOKED: Bigirimana

United's reward for progressing was another all-Premier League tie in the fourth round, with a taxing trip to Chelsea following hot on the heels of the Reds' league trip to Stamford Bridge. Nevertheless, Old Trafford's home dressing room was packed with delighted players after a game which provided a platform for individuals to achieve important personal goals.

'It's just over four weeks now since I last played and I'm delighted to have the time on the pitch,' sighed a relieved Wayne Rooney. 'It's always difficult, your first game back after a few weeks out, but it's great for me to get the minutes under my belt and hopefully that will benefit me. It was a good run-out for me and I'm obviously delighted. Hopefully there's a lot more games to come.'

Rooney's wait paled into insignificance compared to that of Darren Fletcher, who had completed 90 minutes in his first start in ten months, as well as skippering the Reds. 'It's my first time as captain of Manchester United,' said the Scot. 'It's a fantastic moment, something you dream about. Obviously, having done it for my country means a lot, but to do it for United as well is incredible. However, the most important thing, despite all these things like me coming back and being captain, was for us to win the game.'

The victory was assured by Tom Cleverley's fine finish, and the England midfielder admits bagging his first goal lifted a growing weight off his shoulders. 'That game was funny,' he recalls, 'because I missed a good chance on my left foot in the first half and I took a bit of stick for it at half time, so after the goal everything just came out in the celebration. I always thought that once the first one went in, more would come and fortunately that's what happened.'

Having shone against Newcastle, Cleverley, Fletcher and Rooney had thrust themselves into contention to face Old Trafford's next visitors: a Tottenham Hotspur side finding their feet under new manager Andre Villas-Boas. Though Antonio Valencia was doubtful after sustaining a knock at Anfield and Nemanja Vidic's operation had further weakened an already creaking defensive department, Sir Alex was still delighted with the attacking options at his disposal.

'We're having a terrible time with defenders at the moment,' he conceded. 'I think probably our strongest part of the club at the moment is the striking department. I think Welbeck and Chicharito have been doing really well and Shinji's been terrific, he's been settling in well.

'It's early doors, of course, but I don't know what my best partnership would be because I haven't seen Rooney and van Persie together. Wayne has to play games and get game time now. I think Robin has still got a bit to do as well in terms of game time, because he missed the whole of pre-season. In the Liverpool match he was playing against players who had ten or twelve matches under their belt. The combinations we have up front, I think are quite strong.'

Blessed with myriad attacking options, the Reds appeared equipped to handle a Spurs side still adjusting to their new management and nursing a dreadful record at Old Trafford. Yet, while the visitors hadn't mustered a victory in M16 during the Premier League era, records are made to be broken.

Barclays Premier League

Saturday 29 September | Old Trafford | Attendance: 75,566

MANCHESTER UNITED 2 Nani (51), Kagawa (54)
TOTTENHAM HOTSPUR 3 Evans (2 og), Bale (32), Dempsey (52)

Eleven years to the day that United came from three goals down to beat Tottenham, the Reds just fell short of another staggering comeback against Spurs, who registered their first win at Old Trafford in 26 visits.

From falling behind in the second minute, United were always chasing the game against Andre Villas-Boas' side. Jan Vertonghen's shot deflected in off Jonny Evans, before Gareth Bale's surging solo run doubled Spurs' lead. The Reds dominated the second period, however, and strikes from Nani and Shinji Kagawa flanked Clint Dempsey's tap-in in a madcap spell of three goals in as many minutes.

It seemed inevitable that United would level, but the hosts never came closer than when Wayne Rooney's free-kick thudded off the outside of Brad Friedel's post, and Tottenham were able to hold on to a famous victory.

Just two minutes had passed when Vertonghen was allowed to meander unchallenged into the penalty area and fire off a right-footed effort, which struck Evans and shot past the wrong-footed Anders Lindegaard.

Amid a growing theme of falling behind in Premier League games, United's plight was familiar, yet the zip and hustle about Spurs' play was not. Only a last-ditch challenge from Rio Ferdinand prevented Aaron Lennon from doubling the visitors' advantage and Vertonghen also headed over a decent opening, but soon Bale broke the Reds' creaking resistance.

Again a Spurs player was given too much room in which to oper-ate, and Bale's powerful run into space between Ferdinand and Patrice Evra ended with the Welshman shooting calmly across Lindegaard from 15 yards.

The hosts appeared more shocked than invigorated by events, and it took a half-time regroup – and the introduction of Rooney for Ryan Giggs – to breathe new life into United's approach. Rooney's impact was immediate, as he crossed for Nani to prod home a simple left-footed finish.

Spurs quickly hit back, and Bale was again involved as his fiercely struck effort was parried out by Lindegaard, giving Dempsey a simple tap-in. Within a minute, the arrears were again halved as Robin van Persie fed Kagawa for a wonderfully calm finish via the inside of Friedel's post.

As Old Trafford shook with joy and defiance, United pinned Spurs back in their own half thereafter. Rooney looked to have levelled with a magnificent free-kick, but the ball curled against Friedel's upright and away to safety. Van Persie then had a goal correctly disallowed for offside and dragged a presentable opening wide, while Rooney drilled a low effort just wide.

Friedel repelled Paul Scholes' blistering 25-yard effort and Michael Carrick's improvised header clipped the top of the Spurs bar, but there would be no completion of another unlikely comeback on this occasion.

The Teams

MANCHESTER UNITED: Lindegaard, Rafael, Evra, Ferdinand (Hernandez 90), Evans, Giggs (Rooney 46), Carrick, Nani, Scholes, Kagawa (Welbeck 78), van Persie
SUBS NOT USED: De Gea, Wootton, Anderson, Cleverley

TOTTENHAM HOTSPUR: Friedel, Vertonghen, Gallas, Walker, Caulker, Dempsey (Sigurdsson 69), Lennon, Bale, Sandro, Defoe (Dawson 90), Dembele (Huddlestone 83)
SUBS NOT USED: Lloris, Falque, Townsend, Mason

'It was quite a game,' puffed Sir Alex. 'We never started in the first half. It was a poor start to the game and they got a little break with a deflected goal. We really defended poorly. From there we were playing against the wind, really, until half time came along and we were able to change things a little bit. In the second half we were fantastic. We should have got something from the game. We were very unlucky. It was a bad break for us after getting one back. If we'd have kept it at two-one for a few minutes we would have won the match.'

Patrice Evra, meanwhile, conceded that the Reds deservedly paid the price for a poor opening half. 'This is what happens when you only play for forty-five minutes,' lamented the Frenchman. 'The game is ninety minutes long and we deserved to lose because we only played for forty-five. To concede three goals at Old Trafford is not good enough when you want to win the game.

'The problem is about our heads – it looked like we stayed in the hotel. The first forty-five minutes had no speed, no focus, we didn't win a lot of challenges and we conceded some silly goals. Maybe I am hard with myself and the team, but we only showed the United face in the second half.

'I remember, it was three years ago, when we were losing two-nil against Spurs and we won the game five-two. That is why I believed we could do it again, but their third goal killed us a little bit. We scored again to make it three-two, but missed a lot of chances afterwards.

'You could say we maybe deserved to win because we created a lot of chances, but we were punished in the first half and that is really painful. If we want to talk about positive things, we need to make sure we play like we did in the second half, so it's difficult for any team to beat us. We played with a different attitude and mentality in the second half, with speed and the anger. We had a winning mentality, but we have to play like this from the first minute. That is why I say our problem was inside the head.

'It wasn't tactics or because people were tired. We couldn't play a second half like that and make an excuse about being tired. It is just about our head. We didn't start well and we have been punished.'

Despite a second defeat of the season only six weeks into the campaign, Evra insisted a positive mental attitude was the only way forward, with a Champions League trip to CFR Cluj and a tricky visit to Newcastle looming large.

'We have to be positive. It's not a bad start to the season,' he said. 'We won at Anfield, which we didn't do last season, even if they played much better than us. We still have a lot to do, but we have to forget that first half against Spurs. I hope it was just an accident and we can get back the winning mentality in the Champions League and against Newcastle.'

A double-dose of European football, plus two tricky trips to Stamford Bridge and ever-awkward encounters with the Magpies and Stoke loomed large in October. If the Reds were to bounce back, it wouldn't be done the easy way.

4

October

The shock of slipping to a rare home defeat to Tottenham couldn't last long; United were quickly jetting across Europe to Romania for a first away tie of the Champions League campaign. Michael Carrick's early goal had secured a narrow but invaluable win in the Group H opener against Galatasaray, while Cluj had stunned SC Braga with a surprise victory in Portugal. Having fallen foul of what was widely admitted to be an underestimation of their rivals a year earlier, there would be no taking the Romanian champions lightly.

'We need it to be a no-nonsense campaign for us this time,' warned goalkeeper Anders Lindegaard. 'We cannot afford to make the same mistakes as we did last season. The Champions League is always a very special competition to be involved in. Hearing the music before the game and the whole atmosphere around the matches is something special every time.'

'The Champions League is completely different to the Premier League,' echoed Wayne Rooney, who missed the group opener with a gashed thigh. 'If you are not at your best you get punished, which is what happened to us last season. We have to make sure that won't happen again this year. It is a big game for us – hopefully we will get a win which will put us in a good position to go through so early on in the group. We are looking to get maximum points.'

Going for the jugular would carry costs, however. Cluj had picked off Braga in September despite being heavily pressured throughout, and the Romanians' swift, clinical approach mirrored a wider trend in European football, according to Sir Alex Ferguson.

'As part of our preparations we have to assess the opposition and we saw their performance in the last game against Braga,' he said. 'Before that they knocked out Basel, beating them twice. We know from our own experience last season that Basel knocked us out. That gives us every respect for Cluj because it tells you they're a good team.

'Cluj defend quickly and get plenty of bodies behind the ball. The main strength is counter-attack, as they showed against Braga. Counter-attacking has become a very important part of European football. Now it's done by four or five players, not one or two like twenty years ago, and the positive nature of the counter-attack has made the Champions League much better.'

With his side very much on their guard, the manager prepared to take another step down the road to European recovery.

UEFA Champions League

Tuesday 2 October | CFR Stadium | Attendance: 24,000

CFR CLUJ 1 Kapetanos (14)
MANCHESTER UNITED 2 Van Persie (29, 49)

United rung up a century of Champions League victories and maintained a perfect start to their European return as Robin van Persie's double secured a comeback victory over CFR Cluj.

Pantelis Kapetanos gave the home side a shock lead on 14 minutes with a close-range finish, but the Reds gradually established a foothold in the game and drew level when van Persie contrived to shoulder home Wayne Rooney's free-kick, before the pair combined again in more orthodox fashion soon after half time.

The Dutchman's winner, an impish flicked finish from Rooney's fine searching pass, was the highlight of a match which rarely hit the heights of gripping entertainment, but still represented an invaluable stepping-stone for a United side still looking to rebuild its name in the Champions League.

Sir Alex Ferguson made six changes from the side that lost out to Tottenham in September, most notably in a midfield diamond of Rooney, Tom Cleverley, Anderson and Darren Fletcher, while David De Gea replaced Anders Lindegaard and Javier Hernandez returned upfront.

While much of the pre-match debate had centred on plans to address an unwanted knack of starting games slowly, United fell behind inside quarter of an hour. After the ball had been spread wide to Modou Sougou, the winger raced down the right channel before firing a low cross into the path of Kapetanos, who swept the ball past De Gea. It was a frustratingly simple way to fall behind.

United's response was positive, though, as Rooney had a shot parried by Mario Felgueiras and both Anderson and van Persie flashed efforts just wide. The leveller arrived just before the half-hour, as Rooney's in-swinging free-kick bounced off van Persie's shoulder and looped up and over the stranded Felgueiras. The Cluj stopper emerged triumphant from his next duel with the Dutchman, after a fine through-ball from Chicharito, but van Persie would have the last laugh.

Four minutes after the restart, Rooney arced an inviting ball over the Cluj defence and into the path of the Reds' number 20, who expertly flicked a finish past the onrushing Felgueiras. Cluj were defiant in their response, while United toiled unconvincingly. After Gabriel Muresan had crossed for Kapetanos to fire over, De Gea reacted brilliantly to tip Cadu's header, from a Rafael Bastos corner, over the bar.

Hopes of catching the increasingly committed hosts on the counter-attack never materialised and, though van Persie almost reached Rooney's centre with 19 minutes remaining, the Reds spent the remainder of the game keeping Cluj at arm's length, rather than looking to kill off the game. The hosts rarely threatened, but the Reds required a superb fingertip save from De Gea to thwart Bastos's injury-time diving header and ensure another important step towards booking a spot in the knockout stages of the competition.

The Teams

CFR CLUJ: Felgueiras, Ivo Pinto, Muresan, Sepsi, Cadu, Rada, Bastos, Aguirregaray (Nicoara 80), Camora, Kapetanos (Bjelanovic 61), Sougou (Luis Alberto 23)
SUBS NOT USED: Stancioiu, Maftei, Piccolo, Valente

MANCHESTER UNITED: De Gea, Rafael, Evra, Ferdinand, Evans (Wootton 79), Anderson, Cleverley, Fletcher, Rooney, Hernandez (Welbeck 83), van Persie
SUBS NOT USED: Lindegaard, Nani, Büttner, Kagawa, Powell
BOOKED: Ferdinand

'I think I'm on the way,' said United's match-winner, with a degree of understatement. 'I'd like to make more assists. I have seven goals but for me, as I've said many times, it's not only about goals. Of course it's about winning, but I want to make more assists. Until now, I gave only one so I want that to improve a bit. I'm on a good run but I can always do better.'

The room for improvement theme was continued by Wayne Rooney, who bemoaned the passing of another game in which United had to overcome an early concession before securing victory. 'It's something we need to make sure we stop doing,' said the striker. 'We can't keep affording to let teams get a headstart on us, especially in the Champions League when it's very difficult to win the game anyway. We have to make sure we're more solid than we have been and hopefully we can be in future games.

'It was quite tough at times but, thankfully, we've got the three points and that's the main thing. It was a difficult pitch to play on, really bobbly and hard. So we had to make sure we were fully concentrated to get our touch and passing right. The main thing for us is just getting out of this group and progressing to the knockout stages. We're in a good position now and, if we win our next game against Braga, we'll be in a great position.'

Just as Braga had been shocked by Cluj, the Portuguese had stunned Galatasaray with victory in Istanbul, leaving United three points clear at the head of Group H with a fortnight until Braga's trip to Manchester. Beforehand, of course, was the small matter of bouncing back to winning ways closer to home.

Spurs' victory at Old Trafford had allowed league leaders Chelsea to open up a four-point lead over the Reds at the head of the Premier League table, and that lead was extended to seven points ahead of United's Sunday trip to Newcastle. The Reds' ongoing defensive woes flared up once again with the possibility that Jonny Evans would miss out with a dead leg sustained against Tottenham and aggravated in Cluj, but that was offset by the promise that Michael Carrick, Ryan Giggs and Paul Scholes would return after missing the trip to Romania.

Such experience looked an invaluable asset to have on board for an invariably taxing trip to the north-east. The Reds' previous visit to the Sports Direct Arena had yielded a damaging three-goal defeat, and the Magpies were unaccustomed to dropping points on their own patch.

'It's always a difficult place to go,' Sir Alex said. 'They'll be buoyed by their support. I think Alan Pardew has a really good team there. After the game against Tottenham we have to make sure we don't lose.'

For Patrice Evra, captaining the Reds in Nemanja Vidic's enforced absence, United first and foremost needed to address the worrying trend of starting games slowly. 'It's a bad habit,' said the Frenchman. 'The positive thing is we can say we have had a good reaction but, in football, it's better to act not react – that's what my old coach taught me. We have to make sure on Sunday against Newcastle that we don't go behind and ensure we score first and, afterwards, control the game.

'I think last year was a disaster at Newcastle. We played very badly and lost three-nil. This year it's going to be really important. We've already lost against Tottenham and have to react. We must have a big reaction against Newcastle but it's not an easy game. We just need to be focused on trying to score first and making sure we control the game.'

The stand-in skipper's demands would be heeded in spectacular fashion.

Barclays Premier League

Sunday 7 October | Sports Direct Arena | Attendance: 52,203

NEWCASTLE UNITED 0
MANCHESTER UNITED 3 Evans (8), Evra (15), Cleverley (71)

No poor start, no sloppy concessions, no mercy. At one of the least hospitable grounds in the Barclays Premier League, everything fell into place on a clinical afternoon for Sir Alex Ferguson's side.

A blistering start sent United into the international break on a high, as Jonny Evans and Patrice Evra both powerfully headed in corners inside the first 15 minutes, before Tom Cleverley's speculative,

Moments after being pipped to the 2011-12 title, Sir Alex Ferguson sets his sights on ruling the Premier League once again.

Pre-season preparations begin in South Africa, with Rio Ferdinand capturing the Reds' reception for MUTV.

The coup of the summer. Sir Alex Ferguson poses for the cameras with his new recruit: Robin van Persie.

Tim Howard denies new signing Shinji
Kagawa as the Reds' season begins with
a frustrating defeat at Goodison Park.

Robin van Persie becomes an
instant United hero with a dramatic,
match-winning hat-trick to take the
spoils at Southampton.

Nemanja Vidic rises to the
occasion as the Reds return to the
Champions League with a narrow
win over Galatasaray.

A first win at Anfield in five years is secured, as Antonio Valencia wins a penalty which is eventually converted by Robin van Persie.

Nani is aghast after being denied a penalty, as Tottenham shock United with a first Old Trafford win since 1989.

In a see-saw encounter with Stoke, Paul Scholes battles Robert Huth for possession.

David De Gea turns in another eye-catching display at Stamford Bridge, with the Reds edging a five-goal thriller.

Robin van Persie's inevitable goal against Arsenal provokes wild scenes of celebration, even if the Dutchman doesn't partake.

Anderson helps United wrap up qualification for the Champions League knockout stages with a fourth straight Group H victory in Braga.

Ignoring the Dubious Goals Panel, Chicharito claims a hat-trick as the Reds come from behind to overcome Aston Villa.

Darren Fletcher caps a remarkable return to action with a towering header in another comeback victory, this time against QPR.

Rafael – one of the stars of the season – leaps to head clear against West Ham.

Another ding-dong afternoon unfolds at the Madejski Stadium, with Wayne Rooney bagging a brace in a 4-3 win.

'One of our greatest wins,' declares Sir Alex after Robin van Persie's injury-time free-kick decides the Manchester derby in United's favour.

Michael Carrick and Tom Cleverley man the midfield at Swansea, but the Reds can muster only a draw at the Liberty Stadium.

A starring role for Jonny Evans against Newcastle, with a goal at each end for the Northern Irishman in a seven-goal thriller.

Old stagers Paul Scholes and Kevin Nolan get stuck in during an entertaining FA Cup draw at West Ham, who ultimately succumb to the Reds in a replay.

Patrice Evra revels against Liverpool at Old Trafford, although the Frenchman's header is later credited as a Nemanja Vidic goal for the hosts.

Trading places: ex-Fulham defender Chris Smalling wheels away from former Red Dimitar Berbatov in United's FA Cup stroll.

Wayne Rooney jabs home his second goal of the evening as the Reds fight back to beat Southampton at Old Trafford.

Milestone man Ryan Giggs curls home the opener against Everton, scoring for a record-extending 23rd top-flight season in succession.

spectacular second-half strike capped United's most eye-catching display of the season so far.

Alan Pardew's hosts rarely threatened a steadfast Reds defence, coming no closer to scoring than when David De Gea brilliantly clawed Papiss Cisse's 50th-minute effort off the line, despite vehement protests from the home support that a goal should have been awarded.

Sir Alex again opted for a diamond approach in midfield, with Wayne Rooney dropping deep to assist Cleverley, Shinji Kagawa and anchor Michael Carrick. Just as it had been in September's Capital One Cup victory over the Magpies, the decision was soon validated.

The opening quarter showcased some breathtaking football from the visitors, as Newcastle were blown away in front of their expectant home crowd. Cleverley's weighted pass was headed down by Robin van Persie for Evans to brilliantly flick into the path of Danny Welbeck on five minutes, but the striker's finish couldn't match the build-up.

After Steve Harper had turned van Persie's effort behind, the Dutchman's resultant corner was thunderously headed home by the soaring Evans, sending the travelling support wild – and nothing that followed would dampen their joyous mood. The one-way traffic continued with Rafael coming within inches of a scorching goal: collecting a De Gea kick-out, swapping passes with van Persie and sending a thumping drive inches wide of Harper's right-hand upright. Welbeck robbed Harper but could only drag off target from a tight angle, and the Newcastle stopper then tipped Rooney's curling free-kick around the post.

That reprieve was only temporary, however. Rooney swung in the subsequent corner and there, charging through the crowd of players, was Evra to power home his first Reds goal away from Old Trafford.

Newcastle's attempts to haul themselves back into an increasingly fractious game included Demba Ba and Yohan Cabaye blazing over, while Jonas Gutierrez's effort was deflected behind for a corner. It was United who menaced most from set-pieces, however, and Rooney was inches away from converting Carrick's flick from a van Persie corner as the half drew to a close.

Having been caught cold in the first period, Newcastle set about finding a route back into the game after the break. Ba headed against the bar with De Gea stranded, only for the Spaniard to recover and claw away Cisse's diving header from the rebound – with replays unclear over whether or not the whole ball had crossed the line.

The officials deemed that it had not, and the hosts' hopes of getting back into the contest were dashed. Van Persie had a goal chalked off for offside before Cleverley ended the scoring in spectacular fashion: picking up Rooney's pass on the left flank and arcing a magnificent effort over Harper and into the far top corner. Though the game again descended into ill-temperedness in its late stages, with van Persie and Cabaye clashing without censure, nothing could overshadow an eye-catching result for the Reds in a taxing fixture.

The Teams

NEWCASTLE UNITED: Harper, Santon, Williamson, Perch, Ferguson (Anita 63), Cabaye, Ben Arfa, Gutierrez, Tiote (Bigirimana 80), Cisse (Shola Ameobi 63), Ba
SUBS NOT USED: Alnwick, Obertan, Sammy Ameobi, Simpson
BOOKED: Perch, Tiote, Gutierrez, Bigirimana

MANCHESTER UNITED: De Gea, Rafael, Evra, Ferdinand, Evans, Carrick, Cleverley, Kagawa (Valencia 55), Rooney (Scholes 79), Welbeck, van Persie (Giggs 87)
SUBS NOT USED: Lindegaard, Wootton, Anderson, Hernandez
BOOKED: Ferdinand, Kagawa, van Persie, Scholes

For all the plaudits and attention showered on the Reds' obvious attacking talents, the victory on Tyneside provided a glimpse into a growing trend: United, suddenly, were a genuine threat from set-pieces.

'Every time I go up now, I feel like I've got an opportunity of scoring,' says Jonny Evans, scorer of the opener against Alan Pardew's side. 'Whereas before I was that desperate to get my first goal after so long, that I was probably trying a bit too hard. The pressure's off now and every time I go up into the box I do everything I can to get the ball in the net. That's the other side of it: it's made me hungry for more now. I think you have to be aggressive in those situations.

'Robin van Persie has come in and every set-piece he takes, he puts in the right area. It's made the others realise. We did get a few goals from that side – both sides sometimes, like at Newcastle Wazza was whipping them in from one side, Robin from the other and they were putting them in really good areas – people probably expect people like them to be in the box trying to score goals; that's their job, but when they put the ball in such good areas for us to come and attack, then it's going to provide us with opportunities for us to score more often.'

'A lot of people ask me if we are working on set-pieces more,' adds Patrice Evra. 'I'll be honest: we're not doing anything different that we've not been doing in the seven years I've been here, it's just the coaching staff have said: "Pat, if you go in for the corner kicks you can surprise a lot of people. With your size they will not expect you to jump so high and you can surprise them." I enjoy it because I'm coming really far before the corner is taken, I'm going everywhere and it's hard to catch me and I'm jumping very high. We just decided that I would go forward now for the corners and be another threat for the team. I don't know why, because I have small calves, but that's one of my strengths.

'I feel freer now because in seven years of playing for Manchester United I hadn't scored enough goals. People knew me as an attacking player for bombing forward, but I was giving more assists than scoring goals and to be fair it was frustrating on a personal level to end a season with one, two or even zero goals. It's different now, I'm looking forward to scoring more, but I haven't forgotten that I'm a defender and I have to defend well before I can think about going forward!'

For the Reds' other goalscorer, Tom Cleverley, there was a battle to be fought to convince all onlookers that his spectacular strike was wholly deliberate – 'I still say it's a shot,' laughed the midfielder. 'The more you look at it, the more it looks like a shot,' – but Sir Alex was more taken by the work done by Cleverley and his midfield cohorts in their diamond formation.

'I wanted to try the diamond again after some success against Cluj, which is not an easy place to go to, and against Newcastle in the Capital One Cup,' he said. 'It worked very well for us. Obviously there were moments in the second half when we felt we had to change.

'The diamond closes off the midfield. The only problem is when the ball goes out wide, how far your midfield gets separated. If you try to keep it tight in the centre of the field, then the opposition have to go wide. Okay, we took a gamble today because Newcastle are so big up front and they're good crossers of the ball. But the football we played from the central midfield positions through Cleverley, Kagawa, Rooney and Carrick was terrific. We've got to get consistency in the perform-ances and in the results. Once we get that, we'll get into a rhythm.'

A midweek international break threatened to knock the Reds back off-beat, but for once it came and went without incident. 'Everyone came back from the internationals fit,' Sir Alex marvelled ahead of the Old Trafford visit of Stoke City. 'It is always a time when you're a bit concerned about getting the players back but, fortunately, we've been lucky this time. Also Ashley Young is fit. Chris Smalling is not quite there but is making progress.

'Young gives us another option. As I've said many times over the last few weeks, the strength of our squad is the attacking options we have and we're getting better, with Darren Fletcher coming back which has been terrific for him and for us. There has been some progress with players like Nick Powell, who is doing well, as is Tom

Cleverley and Anderson is getting better all the time, so all the fears about the midfield positions are evaporating quite well.'

The boss's selection in central areas would be key against a Potters side renowned for their physical approach, but increasingly armed with guile to match their graft. Having faced Tony Pulis's side before, Paul Scholes was all too aware of the task awaiting the Reds – especially on the back of suffering a rare home defeat against Spurs.

'They probably will be inspired by Tottenham, by the first twenty minutes especially,' said Scholes. 'We can't let that happen again. Stoke have got some quality players now. They have had good players over the last couple of years, don't get me wrong, but I think they've stepped up even more now. We just don't expect them to be down struggling near the bottom these days. They're more likely to be at least a top ten side, maybe even top six or seven. That's how far they've come. It's a game we'll be hoping to win, but it's one we know won't be easy.'

Having taken the comfortable route to victory against Newcastle, all eyes were on whether or not United could once again despatch tricky opposition with minimal fuss. Instead, a return to madcap character beckoned.

Barclays Premier League

Saturday 12 October | Old Trafford | Attendance: 75,585

MANCHESTER UNITED 4 Rooney (27, 65), van Persie (44), Welbeck (46)
STOKE CITY 2 Rooney (11 og), Kightly (58)

United's deadly array of attacking talent combined to devastating effect as the Reds overcame Stoke City in another enthralling, goal-laden encounter at Old Trafford.

Once again, a comeback was required as Wayne Rooney's early own-goal put the Potters ahead, only for the scoreline to be flipped by the interval as Rooney nodded the Reds level and Robin van Persie steered home a clinical finish. Danny Welbeck's diving header put United in a position of comfort and, although Michael Kightly's solo effort hauled Stoke back into contention, Rooney quickly struck again to ensure the victory for Sir Alex Ferguson's side.

The United manager could reflect on another pulsating home game in which his side showed occasional frailties – particularly in the first period – but also demonstrated the mouth-watering potential afforded by his versatile attacking options.

In the 11th minute, however, Rooney's goalscoring instinct proved wayward as the visitors took a shock lead. Charlie Adam, a funnel for all the visitors' best play in the first period, curled in a fine, right-wing free-kick which Rooney was helpless to avoid as he jostled with Ryan Shawcross, and the United forward inadvertently diverted the ball past David De Gea.

The euphoric away support were still celebrating when Adam almost doubled Stoke's lead, firing in an audacious effort from the left touchline which De Gea alertly scrambled to safety. The Spaniard also fended away a Jonathan Walters effort after neat interplay from the Potters, as United toiled in vain.

Yet, shortly before the half-hour mark, Rooney atoned for his earlier opener. Van Persie, having pulled wide left in the Reds' revolving attack, received the ball from the Reds' number ten, then swung a magnificent cross into the six-yard box, where Rooney had superbly manoeuvred between Shawcross and Robert Huth to nod home.

United suddenly sprang into life. Welbeck fired over under heavy pressure from Shawcross, then clipped Asmir Begovic's bar with a stunning 25-yard curler, before van Persie ensured the Reds were ahead just before the interval as he stabbed home a clinical finish from Antonio Valencia's low, drilled cross.

Welbeck's endeavours brought a deserved goal just two minutes after the restart, as Rooney swung in a delightful right-wing cross which the Reds' homegrown forward nodded beyond Begovic on the stretch. A suddenly rampant home side threatened to pull away, as Jonny Evans brought a breath-taking point-blank stop from Begovic, while Welbeck was inches away from converting Rafael's cross, but Stoke unexpectedly halved the arrears when Kightly charged through the centre of the United defence, capitalised on a ricochet off Rio Ferdinand's heel and finished via the inside of De Gea's post.

Any nerves – which could be forgiven, such was the open nature of the game – were quickly settled when the Reds' two-goal lead was restored. A van Persie corner nicked Shawcross and hit Welbeck, falling perfectly for Rooney to squeeze a left-footed finish past Begovic from close range. Inevitably, a breathless game lulled in the dying stages and United ensured a serene denouement by comfortably snuffing out Stoke's attempts to coax late drama from a game which had thrilled for much of the afternoon.

The Teams

MANCHESTER UNITED: De Gea, Rafael, Evra, Ferdinand, Evans, Valencia (Nani 74), Carrick, Scholes (Anderson 70), Rooney, Welbeck (Hernandez 78), van Persie.
SUBS NOT USED: Lindegaard, Giggs, Powell, Wootton
BOOKED: Scholes

STOKE CITY: Begovic, Cameron, Huth, Wilson, Shawcross, Nzonzi, Adam, Whitehead (Palacios 86), Kightly (Owen 74), Walters (Etherington 70), Crouch
SUBS NOT USED: Sorensen, Jones, Upson, Wilkinson
BOOKED: Kightly

'We're giving ourselves uphill fights,' lamented Sir Alex. 'We keep starting badly in games, in the first twenty minutes. We conceded an early goal against Fulham, an early goal against Tottenham, an early goal today . . . but there's a goal threat about us, that has to be said, and some of the movement from the forwards was excellent.

'The forwards are digging us out of a hole at times. There's no doubt our attacking play has been the strongest part of our game. The more games Wayne gets, the better he's going to become and I am pleased he's off the mark with his two goals and Danny's off the mark, too. I think that's about fifteen [different] goalscorers already this season, so that's good. I'm glad they have started to gel quite well.'

Aside from the continuing trend of his side making life difficult for themselves, Sir Alex was also disappointed with Rio Ferdinand's decision not to wear an anti-racism 'Kick it Out' t-shirt in solidarity with his brother Anton, who had been the victim of racial abuse by Chelsea skipper John Terry. But, though he ominously warned 'we'll deal with it, don't worry,' in the aftermath of the Stoke game, the United manager subsequently met with his defender to discuss the incident. He later confirmed: 'I've spoken to Rio. I think there was a communication problem. He felt I should have spoken to him on Friday and I obviously didn't anticipate that he'd have a problem wearing the shirt. But we've resolved the situation, there's no lingering problem and we move on. That's the end of the matter.'

Ferdinand would, however, be missing from the Reds' next outing: the Champions League visit of SC Braga to Old Trafford. With a Premier League trip to Chelsea looming large, Sir Alex opted to rest his veteran central defender as well as Patrice Evra, but still United's sights were set on registering a third straight victory in Europe – albeit with an air of caution.

'We are not getting carried away,' said Michael Carrick. 'We cannot afford to think that just because we have had a good start it is going to be an easy ride. That is not the case. It could come back and bite us. We will go into this game like any other and just look to put ourselves in an even better position without looking too far ahead.

'It isn't necessarily the teams that catch your eye who are the ones that cause you problems. We know even in Cluj, it wasn't straight-forward. The lads had to play well to get a result. That is the nature of European football. Braga are a good team. You have to respect them for getting to this stage to start with. They are going to be of a certain standard and we have to match it.'

Much of the pre-match debate centred around how United would go about matching and bettering the visitors tactically, with a choice to be made between a traditional approach employing ortho-dox wingers – all of whom were back to match fitness – or utilising the narrower diamond formation which had worked well domesti-cally and in Cluj.

'The diamond is seen as a little revolutionary, because it goes against our history,' conceded the manager. 'But the level of the game in England and Europe is so high now that making yourself unpre-dictable is a strength. Teams will now have to think about whether we will play with two wide players or in the diamond because we have the players who are capable of doing both.'

And, it would transpire, they could switch between the two as required.

UEFA Champions League

Tuesday 23 October | Old Trafford | Attendance: 73,195

MANCHESTER UNITED 3 Hernandez (25, 75), Evans (62)
SC BRAGA 2 Alan (2, 20)

Another game, another nightmare start rescued in dramatic fash-ion. United's knack for doing things the hard way reared its head

**again, as the Reds battled back to overcome SC Braga and extend
a perfect start to the Champions League.**

Alan's double within 20 minutes stunned Old Trafford and put
the unfancied visitors in a position of power, only for Chicharito to
quickly commence his side's fightback. Then, after Jonny Evans had
scrambled United back on terms, the little Mexican powered home
a late header to decisively swing a thrilling game in the hosts' favour.

The Reds made a disastrous start to the evening, conceding in
just the second minute of the game. Hugo Viana's cross hardly
appeared threatening, but Braga skipper Alan forced his way in front
of Alexander Büttner to steer an unstoppable header wide of David
De Gea. As United struggled to cope with the slick passing of the visitors, and with little joy afforded by the lack of width inherent in the
diamond formation, the evening's plans continued to unravel. In the
20th minute, Eder tricked his way past stand-in centre-back Michael
Carrick to tee up Alan for a well-taken second goal. The small band
of travelling fans rejoiced, while the home support sat in stunned
silence.

They soon had something to shout about, however. Within five
minutes the deficit had been halved, as Shinji Kagawa pounced on
a loose ball and chipped a cross onto the head of Chicharito, who
stretched to power the ball past Beto, who was only able to help the
ball over the line.

United's dander was up, with Robin van Persie and Wayne
Rooney increasingly prominent and Chicharito soon denied a tap-
in after Kagawa was incorrectly ruled offside. Though Braga carried
their advantage to the interval, it seemed inevitable that the Reds
would haul themselves back into the game.

Nani's introduction at the expense of the injured Kagawa and the
redeployment of Rooney as a winger added much-needed width and,
before long, United were back on terms. Van Persie's low set-piece
was flicked on by Carrick for his defensive partner Evans, who missed

with his first swing at the ball but was alert enough to roll it in when the rebound fell kindly for him.

Suddenly Braga were rattled. Chicharito – enjoying his best performance of the season so far – did brilliantly to release Nani, only for Beto to fend away the Portuguese's blistering effort, but nobody could stop the Mexican having the game's decisive input with just 15 minutes remaining. As Braga dallied in closing down Tom Cleverley on the right flank, the midfielder arced a magnificent cross towards the far post, where Chicharito rose unmarked to thud a header beyond Beto and deservedly cap a scintillating personal display.

United were able to ride out the remainder of the game in near-total comfort, having spent the vast majority of the game – once again – putting all Reds through the wringer.

The Teams

MANCHESTER UNITED: De Gea, Rafael, Büttner, Evans, Carrick, Cleverley, Fletcher, Kagawa (Nani 46), Rooney, Hernandez (Giggs 79), van Persie
SUBS NOT USED: Johnstone, Ferdinand, Anderson, Young, Welbeck

SC BRAGA: Beto, Nuno Andre, Echiejile, Vinicius, Ruben Amorim (Barbosa 80), Ruben Micael (Ze Luis 88), Leandro Salino, Custodio, Viana, Eder, Alan (Mossoro 86)
SUBS NOT USED: Quim, Baiano, Anibal, da Solva
BOOKED: Echiejile

'In the early games of the season, I didn't play a lot,' recalls Chicharito, of a fixture which kick-started his own campaign. 'I played some, but you could see that match against Braga was special for me. It was a good game, we got the three points and we had to come back from two goals down, so it was a very good comeback and the most special thing was that we won. For me it was important because I scored the two goals and then after that the goals started coming for me.'

The Mexican certainly posed his manager issues with the level of his display against the Portuguese. With a trip to Stamford Bridge next up, plus Chicharito's strong goalscoring record in previous encounters with Chelsea, there was much to mull over after the dust had settled on a third straight Champions League victory.

'Chicharito has given me a good problem,' admitted the manager. 'He's got me thinking, I must say that. He and van Persie and Rooney and Welbeck ... I don't know what to do with them, to be honest with you. The boy is improving all the time. He has a great enthusiasm for the game, he trains magnificently, he practises all the time and his goal ratio is fantastic. It was a great ball from Tom Cleverley for the second goal, but Chicharito's movement in behind the defender for the second goal was terrific.'

Yet, despite the form of his strikers and an important result, the manager still couldn't consider himself delighted with the evening's work. Shinji Kagawa's knee injury would rule him out for a number of weeks, while yet again the Reds had fallen behind before bouncing back.

'It's been the story of our season really at home,' puffed Sir Alex. 'Starting badly, conceding goals and having to fight back to rescue games – and it's the front players who are doing that for us. It is a concern we're losing a lot of goals. We got a result most people would not have expected us to get after being two-nil down – being two-nil down in a European tie is very difficult – but credit to the players for the way we came back.'

For United, a similar comeback had been staged at Chelsea in 2011-12. Then, despite being three goals down early in the second half, the Reds had roared back to draw 3-3. The Blues' scintillating start to 2012-13 had not gone unnoticed at Old Trafford, and Ryan Giggs was in no doubt of the size of the task awaiting United at Stamford Bridge.

'What they've got is that experience and the know-how of how to win a league,' said the winger. 'Obviously, having added to the squad like they have, they're going to be right up there this season. Come the crunch, if they're there or thereabouts, they've got the experience, like ourselves and Manchester City now, to go all the way. I expect them to be up there at the end of the season.

'I think this is a different sort of Chelsea team. We've always thought of Chelsea as a big, strong, powerful team. They've still got that, but they've added the likes of Oscar and Eden Hazard, and Juan Mata is into his second season and coming along nicely. They've got clever players who can play in the pockets and make it difficult for teams. Sometimes new players settle in straight away and that seems to be the case at Chelsea. They've got off to a great start this season and we're going to have to play well if we're going to get a result.'

A positive result at Stamford Bridge would be a rarity. While the previous season's three-goal comeback was a progressive outcome and Wayne Rooney's solitary strike had swung 2011's Champions League quarter-final opener at the Bridge, United had not beaten Chelsea on their own patch in the Premier League for over a decade. For that to change, Lady Luck would have to pull on a Red shirt.

Barclays Premier League

Sunday 28 October | Stamford Bridge | Attendance: 41,644

CHELSEA 2 Mata (44), Ramires (53)
MANCHESTER UNITED 3 Luiz (4 og), van Persie (12), Hernandez (75)

United's thrilling season continued apace with a rollercoaster victory in a captivating, controversial top-of-the-table clash with Roberto Di Matteo's Chelsea.

Robin van Persie's shot thudded against a post and rebounded in off David Luiz to put United into a deserved early lead, which was duly doubled when the Dutchman cracked home Antonio Valencia's cross. The reigning European champions roared back to level through Juan Mata and Ramires, before they were hit by the double dismissal of Branislav Ivanovic and Fernando Torres.

The Reds piled forward in search of victory, and secured it when Chicharito turned home Rafael's drilled centre, though Chelsea's ire was further stoked when replays confirmed that the Mexican had been offside in converting the game's decisive opening.

The tone was set early on for 90 pulsating minutes, with United rapid and clinical on the counter-attack. Van Persie had already tested Petr Cech's handling by the time Wayne Rooney pulled the ball back invitingly for the onrushing Dutchman in the fourth minute. Though his effort thumped against Cech's left-hand post, it bounced against the helpless Luiz and into the untended goal.

Van Persie's previous visit to Stamford Bridge had yielded a hat-trick for Arsenal, and the Dutchman's purple patch on the Blues' turf continued with a superbly worked second in the 12th minute. Rafael's ball down the line fed Antonio Valencia and the Ecuadorian drilled in a centre that van Persie blasted beyond the exposed Cech with a superb right-footed finish.

Though stunned, Chelsea gradually clawed their way into the game and began to work David De Gea, who booted clear Luiz's dipping free-kick before brilliantly clawing away Torres' close-range header. Another Spaniard, however, found a route past De Gea just before the break as Mata curled an unstoppable free-kick past the United number one to inject belief into the home side and their support.

As the Reds wobbled, De Gea had to save from Mata almost straight from the restart, and only eight minutes of the second period had passed when Chelsea's leveller arrived. United might have cleared on numerous occasions during a spell of sustained Blues pressure, but failure to do so was punished when Ramires leapt highest to nod home Oscar's floated cross.

Though Chelsea's momentum had carried them to parity, United suddenly began to hit back, and landed a body blow from which the hosts would never recover. Van Persie brilliantly spun and released Ashley Young, whose run on goal was cynically halted by Ivanovic and prompted an inevitable red card.

Before long, Chelsea's plight worsened as Torres followed his Serbian colleague down the tunnel. Having already been booked for a shocking tackle on Tom Cleverley, the Spaniard was deemed to have taken a tumble under a challenge from Jonny Evans, prompting referee Mark Clattenburg to reduce the Blues to nine men with 22 minutes remaining. Time enough for United to capitalise.

Van Persie was again a central figure when the Reds moved back into the lead. The striker's powerful effort was half saved by Cech and spun agonisingly against the post. The Chelsea stopper managed to scoop the ball away, but only as far as Rafael, and the Brazilian's drilled cross was touched home by Chicharito, who had raced back into play from the Chelsea netting and, replays showed, an offside position.

Opportunities came and went for the Reds to rack up a more emphatic victory, as Chicharito volleyed over and Valencia dragged wide after rampaging through on goal, but an important result had already been secured and United were back within a point of the top of the table.

The Teams

CHELSEA: Cech, Ivanovic, Cole, David Luiz, Cahill, Ramires, Mata (Bertrand 72), Oscar (Azpilicueta 66), Mikel, Hazard (Sturridge 82), Torres
SUBS NOT USED: Turnbull, Romeu, Moses, Sturridge
BOOKED: Mikel, Torres
SENT OFF: Ivanovic, Torres

MANCHESTER UNITED: De Gea, Rafael, Evra, Ferdinand, Evans, Valencia, Carrick, Young, Cleverley (Hernandez 65), Rooney (Giggs 74), van Persie
SUBS NOT USED: Lindegaard, Anderson, Nani, Scholes, Welbeck
BOOKED: Valencia, Rooney

'I think that's probably the hardest game we've had this season, especially towards the end of the first half,' panted Jonny Evans. 'Chelsea really came at us and put the pressure on us. It was a tough game and we were probably lucky to see it out to two-one at half time. Going in two-one up was great, because it was a bit of an onslaught at that stage, but you've got to show character in games like this. We came out for the second half, and you've got to stand up coming to Stamford Bridge. It's a tough game; we knew we were going to be under pressure. They got the equaliser and obviously the sending offs are in between that, and we managed to finish the game off in the end.'

The manner of Chicharito's winner was unquestionably slightly fortuitous, even if the speed of the incident provided mitigation for the officials who allowed it – but while Sir Alex admitted United had enjoyed a slice of luck, he added that it was long overdue.

'It's ten years since we won here in the league,' he said. 'We've had some shocking decisions down here. It's very difficult to come here and get all the decisions as it's a very difficult place. They said the winning goal could have been offside, so that's a bit of luck we got, but we started the game so well. We were absolutely brilliant but then, ten minutes from half time, we lost our way a bit. I couldn't wait for half time, to be honest, then they got the second goal and, from that moment, we had to start performing properly and I think we did that.'

The dismissal of Fernando Torres attracted much post-match scrutiny, with Sir Alex insisting: 'He did go down, so it's his own fault.' Evans, a central figure in the Spaniard's second booking for diving, concluded that referee Mark Clattenburg had ultimately made the right call – despite admitting he had brushed Torres.

'I've seen it again and there was a bit of contact but I didn't feel like it was enough to bring him down,' said the Northern Irishman. 'I think he probably realised he wasn't getting the ball, he's gone down and I think the referee's made the right decision and sent him off.'

Inevitably, Chelsea failed to share Evans' view, and a post-match storm overshadowed the myriad positives in an enthralling game, with referee Clattenburg inaccurately accused of racially abusing Blues midfielder John Obi Mikel. Wild press speculation surrounded the alleged incident and subsequent post-match fallout, with Chelsea lodging an official complaint ahead of United's swift return to the Bridge in the Capital One Cup.

Sir Alex's focus was on the game rather than any juicy subplots, and he confirmed that he would again be rotating his squad for the competition, despite the taxing nature of the tie. 'We'll make changes for Wednesday,' he confirmed. 'The squad that played against Newcastle will be in place again. I think I will make some changes there, but not a lot as we don't want to lose down there anyway. We want to continue in the Cup, but there will still be some changes.

'Chris Smalling has been doing training with us back on the football side of it and we'll try to push him on quickly, but I don't think he'll make the game at Chelsea, although I'm sure he'll be ready for the following week. Phil Jones maybe needs another week on the physical part before he can train with us, but the good news is he's not far away.'

With the forthcoming Premier League visit of Arsenal to consider, that meant another evening on the sidelines for Rio Ferdinand and Patrice Evra, while the raft of central defensive injuries nudged youngsters Michael Keane and Scott Wootton into the limelight.

Capital One Cup

Wednesday 31 October | Stamford Bridge | Attendance: 41,126

CHELSEA 5 Luiz (31), Cahill (52), Hazard (90), Sturridge (97), Ramires (116)
MANCHESTER UNITED 4 Giggs (22, 120), Hernandez (43), Nani (59)

Sir Alex Ferguson's young side bowed out of the Capital One Cup at the second hurdle, but not without a gallant display against a strong Chelsea side.

Having led three times, the Reds were just seconds away from a sensational victory, only for a last-gasp penalty equaliser from Eden Hazard to force the game to extra time, where the Blues' experience and quality told in swinging a nine-goal thriller.

The Reds entered the game with ten changes from the side that had won at Stamford Bridge three days earlier, with only Rafael retained in the starting line-up. Much of United's youth was confined to the heart of defence, where Michael Keane and Scott Wootton had all the answers for early questions posed by Daniel Sturridge and Victor Moses. Conversely, lax defensive play from Chelsea prompted the first goal of the game. Petr Cech's short goal-kick to Oriol Romeu was pounced upon by Anderson, who presented Giggs with the chance to slide United into the lead.

A defensive error at the other end meant United's lead lasted just nine minutes, albeit a mistake forced by the blistering pace of Moses. The winger was sent sprawling by Alexander Büttner's rash challenge and David Luiz tucked his spot-kick past Anders Lindegaard to level the contest.

The Brazilian was then at fault as United regained the lead, losing possession to Rafael inside the United half and vacating an area soon filled by Chicharito, who took Anderson's pass, stumbled, but still managed to fire a clinical left-footed finish past the onrushing Cech to ensure the Reds reached the interval in front.

Half-time substitute Nick Powell almost made an immediate impact with a snapshot from distance which tested Cech, but Gary Cahill soon rose to power home a corner and draw Chelsea level – despite Rafael's valiant attempt to clear the ball before it could cross the line. As the game continued to oscillate wildly, United took the lead for the third time with the evening's finest goal. Slick interplay between Anderson and Nani culminated in the Portuguese winger dinking a delightful finish over the onrushing Cech to send the travelling supporters wild.

Though Chicharito spurned the chance to make it 4-2 by firing off-target, Chelsea piled on the pressure throughout the game's late stages. Lindegaard thwarted Moses, Azpilicueta headed over from close range and Juan Mata had a strong penalty appeal ignored, even though his shot struck Keane's arm. Referee Lee Mason did, heartbreakingly, oblige in the final moments of injury time when Wootton careered into Ramires. The inevitable penalty was rolled coolly down the middle by Hazard and Mason prepared both sides for another half-hour instalment of a thrilling game.

Chelsea were dominant in the early exchanges of extra time, with Sturridge twice going close before he pounced on Wootton's weak back-header, rounded the stranded Lindegaard and slid home a simple finish. United appeared dead and buried. Luiz hammered a free-kick against the bar and Moses was denied by Lindegaard, only for Hazard to unlock the Reds' creaking defence with a dazzling piece of skill to tee up Ramires for Chelsea's fifth.

Time remained for Azpilicueta to bundle Chicharito to the ground inside the Chelsea area, giving Giggs the chance to cap a staggering personal display with a second goal of the game, but ultimately it was insufficient to prevent an early cup exit. That aside, there remained plenty of positives for Reds young and old after pushing a strong Blues side all the way.

The Teams

CHELSEA: Cech, Azpilicueta, Bertrand, David Luiz, Cahill, Romeu (Oscar 71), Mata, Mikel (Ramires 46), Moses, Sturridge, Piazon (Hazard 55)
SUBS NOT USED: Hilario, Ferreira, Marin, Saville
BOOKED: Luiz, Romeu, Mikel, Oscar, Ramires

MANCHESTER UNITED: Lindegaard, Rafael, Büttner (Powell 46), Wootton, M.Keane, Anderson (Tunnicliffe 81), Giggs, Nani, Fletcher, Hernandez, Welbeck (Macheda 99)
SUBS NOT USED: Johnstone, Lingard, Brady, Vermijl
BOOKED: Keane, Wootton, Nani, Giggs

'It was a tie I enjoyed, actually,' says Ryan Giggs, looking back on his superhuman 120-minute outing. 'It was a great game to be a part of. Obviously, it was a tough game and we went down with a team which was a lot weaker than Chelsea's. We had a lot of young players – particularly the two centre-halves – and players who hadn't perhaps played a lot, and I was really pleased with the way we played, we just couldn't quite get over the finishing line in the last minute.

'Even extra time was a great experience for the players who played, and one they can learn from and enjoy, even though we went out. I think the manager was genuinely pleased with the way we played and the performances. Chelsea's substitutions were a credit to the way we played. They had to bring on the big guns to see them over the line, while our manager kept faith with the young players, even bringing on Nick Powell and Tunners [Ryan Tunnicliffe], who were brilliant when they came on.

'You're not going to get any tougher test than Stamford Bridge against a more or less full-strength Chelsea side, and it was a good night. Even though you're disappointed, it was a good night for the players' development. Personally, I found it a good game to be involved in. Obviously I got the two goals and I enjoyed the performance, I enjoyed helping the young lads and the way they played. It was probably – even though we don't normally say that when we've lost – a real high point in the season for me.'

'Ryan is an example to all the players on that pitch, including the Chelsea players,' marvelled Sir Alex. 'In Ryan we saw a player of absolutely unbelievable proportions in terms of playing one hundred and twenty minutes when he's thirty-nine next month. He was absolutely magnificent and is a real credit to himself and the game.

'In terms of the game, we were in complete control of the match, playing really good football and all we needed to do was see the game out and keep possession. Nani decided to try and beat a player, lost the ball and we ended up conceding a penalty kick. It's disappointing. Some of our football was terrific. Our counter-attacking was very good, but if you are winning three-two in the final seconds of the game then you should see it out. We only have ourselves to blame, really. From a spectator's point of view, it was a terrific game of football. You're getting your money's worth with nine goals, there's no doubt about that!'

October had been a chest-pounding, thrill-a-minute month, and there would be no let-up as November hoved into view.

5

November

As United prepared to kick off November with the visit of Arsenal, one player predictably dominated all pre-match discussion: Robin van Persie. With nine goals and a spate of key contributions in his first dozen Reds appearances, the ex-Gunners skipper would meet his former side for the first time since his sensational summer switch to Old Trafford. For Arsène Wenger, though van Persie's instant integration to his new side made him the man for his side to fear, he insisted that his former talisman should not be rebuked by the Gunners' travelling support at Old Trafford.

'I hope the reception for him is a respectful one, because he has played for us for eight years, he has done very well for us,' said Wenger. 'You want him to be respected.'

At his pre-match press conference, Sir Alex Ferguson echoed those sentiments. 'I think Arsène has laid his seed for his supporters in terms of respecting him,' said the United manager. 'If you think about all the former players who come back to Old Trafford, they always get a warm applause. I don't think that will be a problem; I think the fans will recognise the eight years he gave them and that will be nice.'

In the wider issue of the game in which van Persie would be playing, the manager was braced for a stern test from the Gunners, who had undergone wholesale changes over the summer – not least due to the sales of van Persie and Alex Song. 'Every game against Arsenal is always a big one,' he insisted. 'It won't be any different tomorrow. They have proved defensively this year that they're a stronger, more physical team and it'll be a hard game.'

Barclays Premier League

Saturday 3 November | Old Trafford | Attendance: 75,492

MANCHESTER UNITED 2 Van Persie (3), Evra (67)
ARSENAL 1 Cazorla (90)

Inevitably, Robin van Persie haunted Arsenal with the opening goal as United strolled to victory against the Dutchman's former employers.

Van Persie needed less than three minutes to lash in his tenth strike for the Reds, after a mistake by Gunners centre-back Thomas Vermaelen. The Arsenal defence was found wanting again early in the second period when Reds captain Patrice Evra nodded home Wayne Rooney's cross.

United's number ten missed a penalty between those two goals, while the Reds spurned several other chances to embellish the scoreline, before Santi Cazorla's impressive late strike salvaged some pride for the Gunners, who were reduced to ten men by Jack Wilshere's pair of bookings.

Virtually all pre-match chatter had concerned van Persie's form against his previous club, and the Dutchman didn't waste any time in bagging the goal that had appeared inevitable. Less than three minutes had elapsed when Rafael's early cross was inexplicably shanked away by Vermaelen, falling perfectly for van Persie to bludgeon a first-time, right-footed effort across Vito Mannone.

As Old Trafford writhed in jubilation, van Persie cut an unmistakably muted figure beneath his giddy colleagues, opting not to celebrate against the club that had brought him to England. Nevertheless, he was doing little to help them in open play. It took a solid stop from Mannone to fend away the Dutchman's 21st-minute effort, who also headed straight at his former colleague from Ashley Young's accurate cross.

Mannone saved from Rooney's drilled effort as the one-way traffic continued, and just before the break the United striker was handed a golden chance to double the Reds' lead. Cazorla clearly handled Young's cross inside the area, giving referee Mike Dean a simple award, only for Rooney to drag his shot wide of Mannone's right-hand post. Another miss from the Reds followed almost immediately after the restart. Vermaelen was robbed by van Persie, who raced down the right and crossed for Antonio Valencia, but the unmarked Ecuadorian failed to connect properly from six yards out and skewed the ball horribly wide.

Olivier Giroud turned and fired just wide of David De Gea's right-hand post to remind United of the perils of passing up so many presentable openings, but there was still time for van Persie to half-hit a shot at Mannone after springing the Gunners' creaking offside trap before the second goal finally arrived.

Rooney played a short corner to Young before receiving the ball back and curling an inviting cross into the box where Evra nipped between defenders to stoop and nod a finish inside Mannone's right-hand post. Those celebrations had barely subsided when United were further boosted as Wilshere collected his second booking for treading on the Frenchman's foot.

Van Persie and Anderson had further goals ruled out for offside, but Cazorla cracked home a fine individual effort with the last kick of the game to give the scoreline an unfathomably misleading appearance of closeness. The corresponding game in 2011-12 had finished 8-2 to United, but one could argue that the gulf between the two sides had grown in light of van Persie's switch to the team which now – by virtue of Chelsea's draw at Swansea – topped the Premier League table.

The Teams

MANCHESTER UNITED: De Gea, Rafael, Evra, Ferdinand, Evans, Valencia (Nani 82), Carrick, Young, Cleverley (Anderson 61), Rooney, van Persie
SUBS NOT USED: Lindegaard, Wootton, Powell, Scholes, Hernandez
BOOKED: Cleverley, Young, van Persie, Rooney, Anderson

ARSENAL: Mannone, Sagna, Mertesacker, Vermaelen, Santos, Arteta, Wilshere, Ramsey (Walcott 52), Cazorla, Podolski (Arshavin 81) Giroud
SUBS NOT USED: Koscielny, Coquelin, Jenkinson, Chamakh, Martinez
BOOKED: Arteta, Wilshere, Arshavin
SENT OFF: Wilshere

'It was a special day,' admitted Robin van Persie, of his maiden meeting with a previous club. 'I played there for eight years. I had a fantastic time there and I respect the fans, the players, the manager and the whole club. So that's why [I didn't celebrate]. It was the first time I have ever played against my former club because I only have three. It was a special day, but in the end it is about the game, which we won so I am pleased with that.

'In the end it was quite a game; I think we played well. We were a bit sloppy with chances and should have scored two or three more –

I should've scored two, but I am happy with one. In the end, we are happy with three points because that is all that matters.'

While van Persie's opening goal had appeared a formality, the appearance of Patrice Evra on the scoresheet for the second time in a month required double-takes all round. 'Accidents can happen and it's happened twice now this season!' the Frenchman joked.

'I'm really happy to score again, but the most important thing is the three points. We're a little bit disappointed we didn't keep a clean sheet, but in the end it was an important win and that's what everyone was looking for before the game. It's been a terrific week for us.

'The expectations are very high here. When they are so high you can sometimes forget that you've beaten a team like Arsenal. It's a big game we have won. We've won at Liverpool, at Chelsea and now we have beaten Arsenal. Last season we didn't do that and that's why as a team we know we have the potential and the quality to win the league. The reason we are not really happy is because we didn't score more goals, but in the end it has been a terrific week for Manchester United. The confidence is really high in the team.'

Rio Ferdinand, however, had an ominous message for the rest of the Premier League. 'Yes it's been good, but we're aiming for better,' warned the defender. 'I don't think we have hit a real purple patch yet, which we are really searching for. We played quite well today as a team and we defended well. But getting it all in one package and doing it all in a ninety minutes at the right times, we're still aiming for that and it will come soon, don't worry.'

The next shot at perfection came in Portugal, where victory over SC Braga would extend an unblemished Group H record and tie up qualification for the knockout stages of the Champions League with two games to spare. Though Braga had established a two-goal lead before succumbing to a United fightback at Old Trafford, Sir Alex

Ferguson – fresh from picking up the Barclays Manager of the Month award for October – was in confident mood ahead of his side's trip to the Estadio AXA.

'With nine points from the first three games, we really should be kicking on and make sure we confirm the number one spot,' said the manager. 'That's the important thing. It's always good to win your group. After the experience of last season, we're showing that we're paying more attention to team selection in the sense that we've used a big proportion of experienced players.

'At Old Trafford, Braga attacked us straight from the kick-off, we lost two early goals and Braga weren't in a hurry at two-nil up. Against our diamond, it was easy for them to get the ball out to the wide positions and control the game that way. In the second half, we had to kill off Braga's width so they couldn't get out. We really did play well in the second half. In general it was a good attacking performance and we played some really good football in the game.'

Sir Alex included Chris Smalling in a 20-man travelling party and confirmed that the England defender would play some part and get some competitive minutes on board for the first time since the penultimate game of the 2011-12 campaign. Both Darren Fletcher and Paul Scholes were omitted from the party, however, and the manager was quick to play down their absence.

'Fletcher got a little bit of a cold on Sunday, and there's no point taking him travelling with a cold,' reasoned Sir Alex. 'Scholesy . . . for the last few games I've been resting him to freshen him up a little bit. I'm just taking care of an old man, that's all! My team selection for Braga will reflect the game we play afterwards, Aston Villa away, so I'll change the squad around. If we win, we're through to the next stage. Obviously, I hope I can pick the team that'll do that. I know Braga's record in Europe is good – particularly at home they can be a big threat. I think it will be a hard game but hopefully we can manage it.'

UEFA Champions League

Wednesday 7 November | Estadio AXA | Attendance: 15,388

SC BRAGA 1 Alan (49 pen)
MANCHESTER UNITED 3 Van Persie (80), Rooney (84 pen),
Hernandez (90)

Manchester United marched into the Champions League knockout
stages, negating a largely lacklustre display with a late comeback
against SC Braga in Portugal.

Robin van Persie's smartly taken leveller, Wayne Rooney's penalty
conversion and a close-range finish from Chicharito gave the Reds a
fourth straight Group H victory, after Alan's spot-kick early in the
second period had given the hosts a deserved lead.

The Reds' late rally came completely without warning in a game
unexpectedly enlivened by a ten-minute stoppage for floodlight failure. Home goalkeeper Beto had been troubled more by the teeming
rain than by the visitors for 80 minutes, while David De Gea, conversely, needed to make three sharp saves and was also rescued by his
woodwork.

A rejigged United side had looked out of sorts for long periods
amid taxing conditions. Chris Smalling made his first outing of the
season, named alongside Jonny Evans from the off, with Rio
Ferdinand dropping to the bench. Rafael joined Ferdinand in reserve
as Antonio Valencia started at right-back. The changes continued
throughout the team, with Robin van Persie, Michael Carrick and
Tom Cleverley all named as substitutes as Sir Alex Ferguson opted to
field Ryan Giggs and Anderson in midfield, with Wayne Rooney
dropping off lone striker Chicharito and flanked by Nani and Danny
Welbeck.

There was a disjointed look about United's opening, while

Braga began with greater cohesion at both ends of the field. Yet, in a first half largely devoid of talking points, the only clear opening fell to Eder, who thudded a diving header against the base of De Gea's post.

United had defended relatively comfortably in the first period, but fell apart three minutes into the second half as a loose clearance allowed Custodio to charge into the area and crash into Evans, prompting referee Felix Brych to award a penalty, which Braga skipper Alan emphatically roofed to send the Estadio AXA wild. Shortly afterwards, the pitch was plunged into darkness as floodlight failure caused a ten-minute delay in play. When the game resumed, Ferdinand was immediately introduced in place of Evans.

Subsequent changes saw van Persie come on instead of Welbeck, and Rafael for the limping Nani, and slowly United began to wrest control of the game. With ten minutes remaining, goalkeeper Beto needlessly charged from his line to try to reach Giggs's pass ahead of van Persie, then changed his mind and then watched on helplessly as the Dutchman bent a superb early finish into the unguarded goal.

Incredibly, United were ahead just four minutes later. After Chicharito's shot had been saved by Beto, Rooney was felled by Coelho and, after consulting his assistants, referee Brych awarded the kick. Though he slipped as he took the kick, Rooney's effort sailed into the roof the net to put United's travelling support into rapture.

Braga were spent and immediately looked susceptible to late counter-raids, which transpired in injury time as Chicharito was found by Rooney's neat flick. Though he needed to fashion time and space before having a shot blocked on the line, the little Mexican slid in to put the ball into the roof of the net. Rarely did it look on the cards, but United had wrapped up progress to the last 16 of the Champions League, as group winners, with two games to spare.

The Teams

SC BRAGA: Beto, Nuno Andre, Echiejile (Ze Luis 90), Douglao, Ruben Amorim (Barbosa 86), Ruben Micael, Leandro Salino, Custodio, Viana (Mossoro 86), Eder, Alan
SUBS NOT USED: Quim, Baiano, Ismaily, Djamal
BOOKED: Custodio, Eder

MANCHESTER UNITED: De Gea, Valencia, Evra, Evans (Ferdinand 58), Smalling, Anderson, Giggs, Nani (Rafael 73), Rooney, Hernandez, Welbeck (van Persie 64)
SUBS NOT USED: Lindegaard, Carrick, Young, Cleverley
BOOKED: Smalling

Through to the knockout stages of the Champions League already, United had come a long way in the space of a year on the European stage. 'We were all disappointed with last season,' admitted Ryan Giggs. 'It wasn't good enough. We knew we had to do something about it and we have. We hope this continues now. We're in good form, both in the league and the Champions League, so we have to carry it on now.'

The Reds scaled the heights only in the final ten minutes in Portugal, but still crammed three goals into that short spell of dominance to overturn Braga's lead. For Wayne Rooney, winning ugly was no bad thing. 'There have been games this season where we've been fantastic and there have been games where we've had to grind out results,' said the striker. 'Tonight we had a difficult night and we weren't at our best, but we won the game and that's all we can ask.

'We've topped the group and that's the main thing. We're happy with that. We're in a good position and we know we can play better football. Now we have a run of games where we feel we can get maximum points, so hopefully we can do that. Anyone can go on a run and win the tournament. We have to make sure we're at our best and you need to be a bit lucky in the draw for the early rounds of the knockout stages, but we're ready and with the final at Wembley it's a great incentive for us.'

The injury-enforced withdrawal of Nani and Jonny Evans ensured that victory came at a cost in Portugal, but for Chris Smalling, posting his first outing of the season represented a major boon for the remainder of the campaign.

'It was a really frustrating time for me, especially over the summer when I had to work hard while the lads were on pre-season, and then had a breakdown again,' admitted the England international. 'I had been looking at this period of October and November for being able to come back and make an impact. I've been able to train over this last week or so and I feel ready. I'm hoping I can stay away from injuries now because I think I'm due that. I feel good after playing the game, so bring on Saturday.'

Smalling's involvement became likelier as the game drew closer, with Sir Alex troubled by ongoing defensive concerns. 'We're monitoring the situation with Jonny,' he confirmed. 'If he doesn't make it, then Chris will have to play. It's asking a lot for him to play Wednesday and then Saturday. The great thing is that he's back and there are no issues with him at all. He did very well on Wednesday – we were pleased with that. Nemanja Vidic is a long way off. We can forget about him until after Christmas, I think. Phil Jones trains with the first team on Monday with the football side, which is good, and he should be available maybe ten days after that, so things are looking better that way.'

Short on defensive numbers, it was to the manager's benefit that he could draw on so many attacking options for an unexpectedly tricky trip to the struggling Villans.

Barclays Premier League

Saturday 10 November | Villa Park | Attendance: 40,538

ASTON VILLA 2 Weimann (45, 50)
MANCHESTER UNITED 3 Hernandez (58, 87), Vlaar (63 og)

Chicharito was the hero of the evening as United roared back from two goals down to win a breathless encounter at Villa Park.

Andreas Weimann struck either side of half time to hand Paul Lambert's team a shock two-goal advantage, but Chicharito's introduction from the bench tipped the game United's way. The Mexican halved the arrears, forced an own-goal from Ron Vlaar and then converted a late diving header to procure three points when, for almost an hour, the Reds had seemed set to take nothing home. It meant another evening of mixed emotions for Sir Alex Ferguson, who saw worrying trends in his side's play for long periods of the evening, only to have them all negated by the spirit on show in his troops.

Villa goalkeeper Brad Guzan was virtually unemployed in the first period, fielding only a routine Michael Carrick header and Wayne Rooney's ambitious long-range shot in the 44th minute. That came shortly before the hosts' first effort of note, one which led to the deadlock being broken. Christian Benteke used his bulk to lever Chris Smalling out of play on the left flank, then picked out Weimann for a thunderous, side-footed finish past David De Gea.

The half-time interval prompted Sir Alex to introduce Chicharito in place of ex-Villan Ashley Young, but Villa went further ahead in the 50th minute. Benteke's clever dummy allowed Stephen Ireland to switch the ball to Gabriel Agbonlahor, who advanced on goal and smashed a low ball across the six-yard box for the onrushing Weimann to convert at the far post.

Finally stung into life, United set about retrieving the apparently lost cause. Paul Scholes's delightful ball over the top of the Villa defence released Chicharito, who clipped a clinical finish under Guzan for his seventh strike of the season. Five minutes later, it looked as though the Mexican had swiftly extended his tally to eight, but instead the equaliser was credited as a Vlaar own goal. Rooney beautifully picked out the run of Rafael and, when Hernandez met the Brazilian's cross at the far post, the ball cannoned into the net off the Dutch defender.

With 25 minutes remaining and United suddenly rampant, only one outcome appeared likely. But, after Guzan dived to palm away a Rooney attempt, Villa showed they were still very much in the mix with Weimann denied a hat-trick only by a superb stop from De Gea following a Barry Bannan centre.

The Reds came agonisingly close to going ahead when Robin van Persie hit the bar twice inside a minute, first smashing a header against the woodwork from a Rooney corner and then producing a wonderful attempt that curled past Guzan but thudded to safety off the crossbar.

Instead of taking the headlines, however, the Dutchman would – for once – play a support role in United's latest comeback. After Anderson had won a free-kick, van Persie's teasing delivery dropped perfectly for Chicharito to dive and nod an unstoppable finish inside Guzan's far post, sending the travelling Reds feral with delight and wrapping up yet another come-from-behind victory.

The Teams

ASTON VILLA: Guzan, Vlaar, Clark, Stevens, Lowton, Ireland (El Ahmadi 79), Westwood, Bannan (Delph 87), Agbonlahor, Benteke, Weimann (Holman 80)
SUBS NOT USED: Given, Albrighton, Bowery, Williams
BOOKED: Ireland

MANCHESTER UNITED: De Gea, Rafael, Evra, Ferdinand, Smalling, Valencia, Carrick, Young (Hernandez 46), Scholes (Cleverley 71), Rooney (Anderson 79), van Persie
SUBS NOT USED: Lindegaard, Büttner, Fletcher, Welbeck
BOOKED: Carrick

The Premier League's Dubious Goals Panel would later confirm that they viewed United's equaliser as a Ron Vlaar own-goal, but Chicharito insists he will forever view the game as the one in which he scored his first Reds treble. 'For me, I say it's my first hat-trick,' smiles the Mexican. 'I've got my ball in my house. You see decisions all the time, they're getting them right, getting them wrong, so I think it's always a controversial thing. For me, it was very special, I scored my first hat-trick and it was very special to come from the bench, but I wasn't the hero people say because it was a group game and every player does their best to help the team. That game I was very lucky because I scored the three goals.'

Whether a scorer of two or three goals, Chicharito had already picked himself for United's next outing at Norwich City, according to Sir Alex. 'He'll be playing next week,' said the manager. 'He does his natural thing. He's fantastic in the penalty box with his movement, his quickness and being in space and that has got him three goals today. It's an absolutely magnificent result for us, it was a magnificent game; I must say that. Aston Villa played fantastic, they've run their socks off and you have to feel sorry for them, with the effort they put in. But we never give in. We hit the bar twice. Once we lost the second goal, we came alive. It was a fantastic game.

'The supporters were fantastic. This is one of the local games for us now, in a way. You saw them today – they were great. We were inspired by that. There's no doubt that with great support like that you get inspired and you do something for it. The second half today showed we never give in. We can come from behind [and win] against anyone, which is something we've done eight times this season. That's encouraging. Anybody who plays against us knows they have to play until the ninety-fifth minute.'

For all the positives in another comeback triumph, however, the manager could not overlook the sluggish 50 minutes of play which had gone before it.

'We were careless in the first half, with no real tempo to our game,' he said. 'We hadn't had a shot on goal, so we had to improve on that and we did. I was disappointed to lose the second goal like that, when a player goes unmarked into your penalty box, but I started to think if we got a goal we could change the game and, once we scored, it did.'

While Chicharito had already been pencilled in for action at Carrow Road a week on, Wayne Rooney's involvement had been cast into doubt after he hobbled off with an ankle injury in the 79th minute at Villa Park. The 27-year-old was quickly withdrawn from England's squad for a midweek friendly against Sweden but, after regaining fitness, succumbed to an untimely bout of tonsillitis.

For Sir Alex, pre-match preparations not only involved the nervy procedure of awaiting those players returning from international duty; he also felt a warning was required after a worrying trend in his side's displays had continued unabated.

'Certainly after last Saturday's experience we don't want to lose two goals and be having to fight back all the time,' warned the manager. 'That's certainly an Achilles' heel this season. The fact we've got players who can change the course of the game is certainly a big advantage to us. When Chicharito came on last week, the game changed completely.

'You actually don't expect it. You don't expect to be behind by two goals. That's the part that you always find difficult. It's not that we underestimate anyone – it's just that we don't expect a Manchester

United team to be behind. You've got to go into games believing you're going to be two goals ahead rather than two behind. But it has happened a few times this season. We've been two goals behind against Tottenham and we were a bit unlucky not to come back. But it won't happen all the time. It's not definite that you'll come back from two-nil down. And this is the area we are going to improve on. We are going to defend better. We don't want to lose the advantage of what we've experienced last week.'

Sadly for all concerned, the manager's warning would go unheeded as the Reds travelled to Norfolk.

Barclays Premier League

Saturday 17 November | Carrow Road | Attendance: 26,840

NORWICH CITY 1 Pilkington (60)
MANCHESTER UNITED 0

United slipped to second spot in the Barclays Premier League after losing to Norwich City in an insipid encounter at Carrow Road.

Anthony Pilkington's header just before the hour mark was the outstanding moment of quality in a game largely conducted at a sluggish tempo, while the hosts' well-drilled defence restricted United to a handful of half-chances. Robin van Persie had the Reds' best openings, but even the prolific Dutchman had to feed off scraps when little went right for the visitors, who now sit a point behind reigning champions Manchester City.

As expected, Wayne Rooney and Jonny Evans missed the trip to Norfolk through injury, while David De Gea was a surprise omission as he recovered from having his wisdom teeth removed earlier in the week. Anders Lindegaard deputised in goal, while Chris Smalling continued in central defence and Sir Alex Ferguson made good his vow to start Javier Hernandez up front, just ahead of van Persie.

The Dutchman was quickly involved in the play, taking little more than two minutes to force John Ruddy into an alert save with a low, curling effort from just outside the area. Collectively, United's early play carried plenty of intent, with the hosts penned back but quick to look for counter-attacks.

The first such break happened after eight minutes, as Robert Snodgrass intelligently released Pilkington, only for the winger to fire comfortably wide of the target after diligent covering from Antonio Valencia.

An Ashley Young free-kick from distance prompted a straight-forward save from Ruddy and Wesley Hoolahan's 25-yard effort received similar treatment from Lindegaard, before Patrice Evra almost completely missed a free header from Young's pinpoint corner. Snodgrass made more substantial contact when Hoolahan whipped in a fine left-wing cross, but the ex-Leeds midfielder's header drifted comfortably wide of Lindegaard's far post. Not long after, Javier Garrido fizzed a dangerous, low cross through a similar course, only to see it evade target man Grant Holt.

The hosts were increasingly menacing in attack – though they did waste a presentable opening when Smalling's scuffed clearance cul-minated in only a blocked shot from Bradley Johnson – and it took a superb sliding clearance from the United man to stop Holt from turning in Snodgrass's cross.

Shortly before the break came United's clearest chance of the half, only for van Persie to get himself in a tangle in trying to reach Ryan Giggs's beautifully flighted ball through the middle. That opening sparked a late spell of pressure from United, and Ruddy produced a superb reaction save to fend away Young's half-volley through a crowded penalty area. Nevertheless, the interval arrived with the points still in touching distance for both sides.

As in the first period, United began the second half brightly. Young's well-weighted pass released van Persie and, though he took two attempts to bring the ball under control, the Dutchman brought a solid save from Ruddy with a low, near-post effort. Norwich hit straight back and pressured Lindegaard with a deep free-kick from Snodgrass, but in open play both sides continued to serve up a dearth of excitement until just before the hour mark, when Garrido's superb cross was expertly guided past Lindegaard by Pilkington.

The goal prompted Sir Alex Ferguson to introduce Paul Scholes and Danny Welbeck in place of Chicharito and Valencia, and Welbeck came close to levelling when his header drifted just past Ruddy's upright.

United's general play improved under the dawning realisation of the situation's gravity, but Norwich's resolve redoubled with every passing moment. Two yellow-and-green-clad banks of bodies steadfastly protected Ruddy, crucially keeping calm and sticking to their task under the mounting pressure.

Norwich passed up a glorious chance to double the margin of victory when Jonny Howson dragged an inviting chance wide, and were indebted to Ruddy's heroics as he tipped over Sebastien Bassong's errant header, then clutched substitute Anderson's low effort under heavy pressure from Scholes. Having produced an inordinate number of rousing late comebacks already in 2012-13, United finally returned to the well to find it empty.

The Teams

NORWICH CITY: Ruddy, Whittaker, Bassong, Turner, Garrido, Johnson, Pilkington, Hoolahan (Howson 83), Tettey, Snodgrass (E.Bennett 90), Holt (Morison 83)
SUBS NOT USED: Jackson, Tierney, Bunn, R.Bennett

MANCHESTER UNITED: Lindegaard, Rafael, Evra, Ferdinand (Anderson 83), Smalling, Valencia (Scholes 69), Giggs, Carrick, Young, Hernandez (Welbeck 69), van Persie
SUBS NOT USED: Johnstone, Jones, Fletcher, Cleverley
BOOKED: Rafael

'We're disappointed to lose the game, obviously, but we have to give credit to Norwich for the way they fought and battled for every ball on the pitch,' admitted Sir Alex. 'They defended fantastically well and their goalkeeper had a really good night also. It's disappointing. They deserved the win just because they worked so hard for it.

'We had a lot of possession and one or two half-chances without having any great chances, but it just wasn't our night. The players we've got are used to making comebacks, particularly in the last minutes of matches. We're always a threat. We were in some respects tonight also, but they defended really well and the goalkeeper's made two or three really good saves at vital moments.'

A sapping run of four successive away games would lurch from Norwich to its final stop in Istanbul, as the Reds returned to Champions League action at Galatasaray. Though United's qualification as Group H winners was already assured, and the trip counted for few tangible benefits, the Turks coveted a major scalp in order to prolong their own hopes of qualification. Those ambitions were boosted by the naming of United's squad – eight of the 21 players who travelled to Turkey arrived without a previous European appearance to their name. A predictably boisterous welcome awaited the squad, with the Reds' travelling party undergoing a last-minute change of terminal after hundreds of Galatasaray fans descended on the building.

No stranger to such welcomes after United's previous visits to Turkey, Sir Alex remained unruffled for the pressure-free tie. 'We don't consider the young players a gamble,' said the manager. 'What we do consider is our reputation and we have to be fair to the other teams in the group. When we discussed the team for tomorrow, we had to give serious consideration to how the media and the public would react, so we had to think hard about the team we picked.'

Among those quickly pencilled in for involvement was Phil Jones, who had recovered from injury and was in line for his first outing of the season. 'It's a big day for Phil,' admitted Sir Alex. 'He's been out all season, but he's done enough training now to make sure his fitness is okay. I'm looking forward to bringing him back. Phil's had different types of injuries in his United career so far. He had concussion, he had a rib injury . . . But he's young so he's still to develop physically in terms of his body. He's only twenty years of age so there's plenty of time for him.'

Perched alongside his manager at the press conference, Darren Fletcher cut another wise old figure, even at the comparatively tender age of 28. 'I'm one of the most senior players in the squad,' laughed the Scot. 'But it's a role I'm used to with Scotland – you talk to the younger players, give them encouragement.

'I appreciated that sort of thing when I was young. I had a little word in my ear – nothing much, you don't want to force too much information – but I really appreciated those words of advice. Hopefully these guys will as well when I do it. We're expecting a really hostile atmosphere. But if you want to play at this club you have to play in big matches and you have to experience and deal with atmospheres like the one we're going to have here.'

UEFA Champions League

Tuesday 20 November | Turk Telekom Arena | Attendance: 50,278

GALATASARAY SK 1 Burak (53)
MANCHESTER UNITED 0

Beaten but not bowed, United suffered a first European setback of the season as Sir Alex Ferguson handed several of his younger squad members an invaluable Champions League outing at Galatasaray.

The Turkish champions kept themselves in the frame to qualify behind the Reds – already through as group winners – thanks to Burak Yilmaz's 52nd-minute header, but the way many of United's younger players comported themselves in a bruising match amid a simmering atmosphere augured well for the future.

From the off, the din generated by the vast majority of the 50,000-strong crowd seemed to have little effect on the travelling Reds. Free of the pressure which weighed on the hosts' display, United almost moved ahead through Tom Cleverley's stinging effort from range.

Semih Kaya was fortunate only to be booked for a two-footed lunge on Alexander Büttner and Hamit Altintop took a blow to the ribs to round off an action-packed first ten minutes. Yilmaz was then guilty of spurning two headed opportunities as Galatasarary began to stamp their authority on the match.

The Reds continued to give as good as they got, remaining calm in possession and keeping cool despite the hosts' physical approach to proceedings. Phil Jones came close to nodding in from a corner, before the impressive Nick Powell came even closer by powering a header against the crossbar from close range.

After the break, however, Galatasaray took charge in a key period. Lindegaard was twice called into action, holding well from former Liverpool and Manchester City left-back Albert Riera's volley and then spectacularly turning over Felipe Melo's bullet header from ten yards. From the resulting corner, Burak succeeded in nodding the hosts into the lead. Yet, soon after, United looked certain to equalise after a high-speed counter-attack, only for Melo to hurl his body on the line to block Chicharito's effort just when the Mexican seemed certain to level the scores.

Galatasaray's experience and top-level fitness began to tell in the dying stages as United gradually committed more bodies to forcing an equaliser. Lindegaard produced an athletic stop from Emmanuel Eboue, but then topped that with a staggering fingertip save to turn Altintop's blockbuster onto the underside of the bar with 12 minutes remaining.

Sir Alex threw on Federico Macheda, Ashley Young and Joshua King in the closing stages, but couldn't avoid dropping points for the first time in the Champions League. Despite following defeat at Norwich with another setback, there was no cause for concern in the Reds' ranks. Amid all the flares and colour in Turkey, United's future looked indisputably bright.

The Teams

GALATASARAY SK: Muslera, Dany Nounkeu, Kaya, Eboue, Altintop, Inan, Elmander (Baytar 63), Melo, Riera, Yilmaz (Bulut 90), Amrabat (Colak 81)
SUBS NOT USED: Ceylan, Cris, Birinci, Kurtulus
BOOKED: Kaya, Burak

MANCHESTER UNITED: Lindegaard, Rafael, Büttner, Jones, Carrick, Anderson (Young 74), Cleverley, Fletcher, Powell (Macheda 74), Hernandez, Welbeck (King 85)
SUBS NOT USED: Johnstone, Wootton, Vermijl, Cole
BOOKED: Rafael

'It's disappointing to lose the game because we don't like losing games,' conceded Michael Carrick. 'But there were a lot of positives, especially in the first half. We played some good football at times, it was just that the final ball didn't fall for us as we could've easily scored. The way the younger lads went about it with the crowd and whole occasion, it didn't affect them, and I'm sure they would have gained from that and we can move on and be better for it. Of course, in many ways the main work was done to get us through. We're still disappointed coming away not getting anything from the game but, at the end of the day, we're through and we need to kick on with our league form.'

In a match soundtracked by a deafening din, the home supporters were the talk of the away dressing room afterwards. Phil Jones labelled the atmosphere: 'The best I've ever played in,' while Anders Lindegaard admitted: 'It was quite a special atmosphere to play in: very hectic, very noisy and loud. You can't really communicate on the field by yelling and talking. You need to be more visual. At times, obviously it was very difficult.'

For the Danish stopper, however, the bigger picture was bleaker than the colour and noise delivered by the Galatasaray supporters. 'We've lost two games in a row,' he stated. 'I played two games in a row and we've lost both. It's very hard to find smiles about anything or a positive side. We have an important game on Saturday against QPR and need to get back on track.'

After four games on the road, the Reds could finally look forward to some home comforts at Old Trafford, where Queens Park Rangers would be the next visitors. The struggling Hoops limbered up for the game by replacing manager Mark Hughes with Harry Redknapp, who would watch his first game at the helm from the stands. While the Loftus Road board had opted to rejig their set-up in the hope of preserving their top-flight status, they would arrive at a stadium furnished with a testament to longevity and stability, with a statue of Sir Alex Ferguson unveiled the day before the game.

At a star-studded unveiling ceremony, the great and good of United's past were either in attendance or paying tribute via video for a man who had passed a staggering 26 years at the Old Trafford helm. 'He's a born winner,' said David Beckham, via video. 'He's unique, especially in the modern day,' added Jose Mourinho, while fellow Real Madrid figurehead Cristiano Ronaldo conceded: 'He's like a father in football . . . I really miss him.'

'It's fantastic, a really proud moment,' Sir Alex told the thronging assembly. 'Normally people die before they see their statue, so I'm out-living death! I've had an incredible journey at the club and I've had so many great players, some of whom are here today. They should build this statue for them all, because they've been absolutely marvellous.'

For those in attendance, the gravity of the afternoon was not lost. 'That was a big moment in the club's history,' says Danny Welbeck. 'The manager had the unveiling of the Sir Alex Ferguson Stand and then the statue, so it was a great moment and a privilege to be in and around it. It was so great for him and it's a statue of success for him to show what he has done. But his will to win doesn't stop there, and he has a great determination that rubs off on the whole club. He has a statue outside of Manchester United's football ground and he is still hungry for success. That is so motivational to see.'

The manager's next task was to see off the division's bottom team, and his quest to do so would be aided by the return from tonsillitis of Wayne Rooney, while Jonny Evans joined training just in time to confirm his own availability to face a team boasting just four Premier League points from a dozen games.

'Hopefully, we can get back on track tomorrow after the disappointment of last week,' said the manager. 'If you analyse things a little bit more closely, it's probably a lesson to everyone that changing a team and bringing eleven new players in to the Premier League is not easy. But I am surprised they've only got four points. I didn't expect them to immediately set a blazing trail or be up at the top of the league or anything like that with eleven new players to bed in. But they've only four points and of course that creates its own headlines.'

Having sustained successive setbacks, United would have to beware the shock of the new against the struggling visitors.

Barclays Premier League

Saturday 24 November | Old Trafford | Attendance: 75,603

MANCHESTER UNITED 3 Evans (64), Fletcher (68), Hernandez (71)
QUEENS PARK RANGERS 1 Mackie (52)

After two successive defeats, United bounced back to winning ways in customary form: by coming from behind after spending the majority of the game shredding the nerves of Reds everywhere.

Jamie Mackie's close-range opener put table-propping QPR on the brink of a stunning upset, only for a quickfire burst of three goals in seven minutes to send United strolling through to victory, despite long periods of frustration at Old Trafford.

The Reds initially carried plenty of purpose, but found themselves kept at arm's length by a side being watched from the stands by their new manager, Harry Redknapp. It took 16 minutes to carve out a first opening, but Shaun Derry got an important toe to the ball to thwart Paul Scholes, before Robin van Persie turned Danny Welbeck's cross into Julio Cesar's side-netting.

As the rain cascaded down at Old Trafford, QPR showed minimal attacking ambition but defended in numbers and with plenty of organisation and aggression. United's best attempt of the opening half hour came when Ashley Young lashed wide after Scholes' neat tee-up. Cesar was increasingly busy as the half wore on. Patrice Evra fired straight at the Brazilian after a one-two with van Persie, before Cesar blocked a pair of efforts from Wayne Rooney. At the other end, Mackie served notice of the visitors' sporadic threat when he dived to head past Anders Lindegaard, only to have his goal correctly ruled out for offside.

Though United survived that scare, there would be no reprieve shortly after the interval when Rangers caught the Reds napping at a corner. Adel Taarabt returned the ball to unmarked taker Kieron Dyer, who cut in past van Persie to centre dangerously. Lindegaard could only palm the ball into the path of Mackie, who gratefully opened the scoring.

Sir Alex's swift retort was to introduce Anderson and Javier Hernandez for Young and Scholes, and the move soon worked. The scores were levelled following a Rooney corner on the left as Welbeck won a header at the far post and, although Hernandez was unable to reach it, Evans flung himself at the loose ball to send it into the net.

Old Trafford was instantly lifted, and the anticipatory air made way for bellows of delight when the hosts soon moved into the lead. Another Rooney corner dipped perfectly onto the head of the onrushing Fletcher, who powered the ball past Cesar for his first goal in almost a year. With momentum firmly behind United, however, there was no let-up. Three minutes later, Anderson cut the visitors apart with an electrifying burst of acceleration and a precise pass to release Chicharito, who took a touch before steering his finish beyond the exposed Cesar.

Job done, United were able to power down over the final few minutes, even if Rafael did need to show his alertness in clearing Clint Hill's header off the line. While hardly the emphatic rediscovery of form that many had hoped for beforehand, the result – and the manner of its achievement – did represent a timely return to character for Sir Alex's masochistic side.

The Teams

MANCHESTER UNITED: Lindegaard, Rafael, Evra, Ferdinand, Evans, Young (Anderson 59), Scholes (Hernandez 59), Fletcher, Rooney, Welbeck (Powell 79), van Persie
SUBS NOT USED: De Gea, Jones, Smalling, Cleverley
BOOKED: Scholes

QUEENS PARK RANGERS: Julio Cesar, Traore (Ferdinand 61), Hill, Nelsen, Derry, Taarabt (Hoilett 73), Dyer, Faurlin (Granero 84), M'bia, Cisse, Mackie
SUBS NOT USED: Green, Diakite, Wright-Phillips, Ephraim
BOOKED: M'bia

Sir Alex Ferguson enthused about Anderson's performance after the Brazilian came off the bench to help spark another United comeback. 'I thought Anderson changed the game,' said the boss. 'We played for about ten or fifteen minutes, that was the sum total of a real performance for Manchester United. Queens Park Rangers had a surge of determination and belief, they worked really hard and that's what you expect when a team loses its manager. We saw that again today.

'Of course it is frustrating to keep conceding first and you have to be concerned about it. The one thing about it is their goal sparked us off. From that moment on, we really got at them and played with great determination and speed and it made a difference. Ando laid the third goal on a plate for Chicharito but it was a great first touch and a great finish. In that period, we really looked fantastic but, once we went three-one up, we just idled and saw the game out. We had opportunities to get four or five, but there were one or two careless passes at the end of the moves which would have made it a far better day.'

Conventional thinking might have suggested that the day

couldn't have gone much better from Darren Fletcher's perspective. But, despite the personal boost of scoring his first goal in a year, the Scot demanded better after the Reds' unconvincing victory.

'We're very frustrated,' said the midfielder. 'It shouldn't take going a goal behind for us to start playing. The only positive thing we can take from it is that every time we do it we seem to respond. But we can't keep making a habit of it. We want to go on a run of winning games now and not keep conceding first. After the defeats at Norwich and at Galatasaray, it was important we got a win today. Hopefully now we can kick on and see an improvement in our performances.

'The biggest thing my goal meant was that it put us in the lead. It didn't mean anything personal to me – it got us back in the game. It's great to be back and to score goals, but it has to be in winning teams. That's what made today special. It wasn't great to go a goal down in my first league game back. I was thinking: "Here we go," but the lads always respond and the most pleasing thing for me about my goal was that it put us two-one up.'

It also helped keep United ahead of Manchester City and Chelsea, who ground out a goalless draw at Stamford Bridge the following day. The Reds would soon have the opportunity to keep setting the title race pace, with West Ham due at Old Trafford for a midweek encounter. Paul Scholes collected his fifth booking of the season against QPR and would miss the visit of Sam Allardyce's side, and Sir Alex was wary of facing a Hammers outfit helmed by his close friend.

'Big Sam went to Upton Park a year and a bit ago and the cynics said he's not a West Ham manager as he doesn't play football,' the boss said. 'What was his mandate? To get them up into the Premier League as quickly as possible and he got them up within a year. Tell me someone else who could've done that? He's very underrated, it's as simple as that.'

As he prepared for battle with the former Blackburn manager, Sir Alex had to check on the availability of Antonio Valencia – who had been nursing a hip injury for a fortnight – but was able to confirm that Anderson's game-changing cameo against QPR had thrust him into a starting berth against the Hammers.

'Ando's performance was outstanding,' confirmed the manager. 'He took the game by the scruff of the neck and he was so positive and determined in his play that he picks himself on Wednesday. Chris Smalling and Phil Jones were on the bench on Saturday and they're available. It's good to have them as back-up and in the back four things are much healthier. We've got plenty of options.'

Barclays Premier League

Wednesday 28 November | Old Trafford | Attendance: 75,572

MANCHESTER UNITED 1 Van Persie (1)
WEST HAM UNITED 0

Robin van Persie scored after just 31 seconds at Old Trafford to preserve United's position at the summit of the Barclays Premier League and overcome a dogged display from Sam Allardyce's Hammers.

The Dutchman's deflected strike was enough to swing the game United's way, while a rare but promising clean sheet ensured a three-point haul for the Reds. There were plenty of positives from the hosts' performance, including outstanding showings from Brazilian pair Anderson and Rafael. The former made just his second league start of the season after his great performance against QPR, but it was fellow midfielder Michael Carrick who teed up the opening goal half a minute into the game.

The England international fizzed an incisive pass through to van

Persie, whose exquisite first touch cushioned the ball over Winston Reid and teed up a side-footed shot which struck James Collins and looped high over Jussi Jaaskelainen before dropping into the Scoreboard End goal.

While the tone had been set for a comfortable evening for United, West Ham had other ideas. Kevin Nolan came close to equalising on 11 minutes when he only just failed to reach Matt Taylor's dangerous free-kick at the near post, while Andy Carroll twice blazed over after the ball had dropped to him in promising positions.

While Anders Lindegaard was largely kept on the game's periphery by his well-drilled defence, Jaaskelainen was again called into action to smartly block Chicharito's powerful 20-yard drive. The visitors largely coped well with United's forward raids, however, and were firmly in the game when the interval arrived.

United's lethargic start to the second period presented half-chances to both Mohamed Diame and Carroll before the Reds sparked into life and Tom Cleverley sent a half volley whistling over the crossbar. Van Persie hit a free-kick straight at Jaaskelainen after being upended 20 yards out by Joey O'Brien. Then Wayne Rooney drew a full-length save from the Finn when he curled an effort towards the far post and West Ham somehow managed to avoid conceding from the resulting corner when both Javier Hernandez and Jonny Evans went close during a frantic goalmouth scramble.

When Anderson stung Jaaskelainen's palms with a scorching effort from 25 yards, the Old Trafford crowd grew increasingly restless at the narrow state of the scoreline – and that mood almost spilled over into blind panic when Lindegaard produced a point-blank save to deny Carlton Cole an equaliser in the dying stages. Instead, Sir Alex's men hung on to claim a hard-earned three points on an evening when the Reds profited from two of the season's rarities: a quick start and a clean sheet.

The Teams

MANCHESTER UNITED: Lindegaard, Rafael, Evra, Evans, Smalling, Anderson (Jones 84), Carrick, Cleverley (Young 66), Rooney (Welbeck 78), Hernandez, van Persie
SUBS NOT USED: De Gea, Büttner, Ferdinand, Fletcher
BOOKED: Carrick

WEST HAM UNITED: Jaaskelainen, Reid, Tomkins, O'Brien, Collins, Demel, Nolan, Jarvis (Maiga 70), Taylor, Diame (O'Neil 76), Carroll (Cole 62)
SUBS NOT USED: Spiegel, Spence, Moncur, Lletget
BOOKED: Nolan

On a night when the attacking heights were rarely hit, United's defensive discipline attracted the majority of the post-match plaudits, with midfielder Michael Carrick ruefully admitting: 'It was by far not a classic. Obviously we weren't at our best and the flowing football that you want to play and the chances that you want to create didn't quite happen. But we got a clean sheet, which was quite pleasing, and I thought we defended well.

'They had a couple of opportunities and when they put balls into the box like they did, those can fall to anybody. But overall I thought we defended well – we didn't play as well as we could have, but we won the game and managed to keep a clean sheet. A clean sheet is the biggest plus that we can take from tonight. That gives us something to build on in the future.'

With little to dwell on from an unremarkable victory over the Hammers, attentions soon switched to the final month of 2012. December promised a packed fixture list littered with a variety of challenges – most tantalisingly the first Manchester derby since City had taken their first title in 44 years.

6

December

'December is generally a good month for us,' mused Sir Alex Ferguson. 'We usually get ourselves to the New Year in a challenging position, and that's where you want to be. When you have the second half of the season in front of you, you know full well that pressure can affect everyone, there's no question about that. We tend to do not too badly.

'The start of the month, with City away, is a hard one, but then we've got Sunderland, Reading, Swansea, West Brom – we've got a reasonable programme, so we should be expected to gather some points there.'

The Reds' bid to start the month with a three-point haul at Reading's Madejski Stadium was hit by the news that their approach would need to be narrow, with Nani and Antonio Valencia sidelined through hamstring and hip injuries respectively. Nevertheless, with Paul Scholes back from suspension and Ryan Giggs expected to shake off a hamstring strain, the manager was counting his blessings. 'It's quite late for Scholesy to get a suspension – it's usually about

October!' he quipped, before adding: 'It's amazing that we've had defensive injuries for such a long period and now we've got the defenders back we've got two wide players injured. That's the game for you. Everyone else is fine.'

It was a surfeit, not a shortage, of talent that was giving the manager a selection headache in choosing his starting goalkeeper, with Anders Lindegaard's form keeping Spanish youngster David De Gea on the fringes. 'I don't think Anders has done anything wrong since he came into the team. That's what is keeping him in,' the manager told his pre-match press conference. 'I am going with Anders at the moment because he has not let me down. It's good that you've got two competing for a position – that applies to anywhere in the team. I am not happy to rotate all the time – I don't think that creates consistency.

'David is fine. He is still young. He had a tooth infection and had to have two teeth out, which meant his jaw was quite badly swollen. We gave him that time off. But Anders has come in and done well. It is one of those situations where there is no actual reason to leave Anders out in terms of form. Hopefully, David understands that – there is no long-term issue there.'

Addressing issues at the opposite end of the field, the manager insisted he had no problem with Wayne Rooney's relatively meagre return of three goals in 14 games. 'Wayne is going through a period like all strikers do,' he said. 'It will change once he starts to score reasonably regularly. Then it will become better for him. Also, he has missed bits of games. Wayne is the type of player who can't miss games. He needs to play all the time.'

Having seen his side slip up at unfancied Norwich in November, the boss was mindful of underestimating the promoted Royals, and warned his players to be on their toes. 'I think away games are getting more difficult in the Premier League,' said Sir Alex. 'Our game at Norwich is a good example of that. Norwich fought like tigers. They were really organised and motivated and made it a difficult day for us and I think we can expect the same at Reading – a really difficult game.'

Barclays Premier League

Saturday 1 December | Madejski Stadium | Attendance: 24,095

READING 3 Robson-Kanu (8), Le Fondre (19), Morrison (23)
MANCHESTER UNITED 4 Anderson (13), Rooney (16 pen, 30), van Persie (34)

United and Reading conspired to serve up a thrilling, occasionally ludicrous, encounter as the Reds twice came from behind to edge a flabbergasting game in which all the game's talking points were confined to a madcap first period.

Hal Robson-Kanu lashed home the opener, then Anderson cracked in an equaliser and Wayne Rooney slid home a penalty, before Adam Le Fondre and Sean Morrison quickly headed in from corners to have the hosts 3-2 up by 23 minutes. For all the nightmarish defending on show from the visitors, however, their attacking play was just as irresistible, and Rooney clinically turned in Patrice Evra's cross to level again, before turning provider for Robin van Persie to spring the hosts' offside trap and beat Adam Federici.

The tone was set for a breathless evening after only eight minutes. For the tenth time in 15 Barclays Premier League games, the Reds fell behind when Jonny Evans's clearing header fell perfectly for Robson-Kanu to take a touch and rifle a finish high into Anders Lindegaard's net.

With United renowned for overturning deficits and Reading known for surrendering leads, both sides' form hinted at what would subsequently unfold, yet few could have imagined how quickly the

110

game would be turned on its head. The Royals led for less than five minutes before United drew level in stunning fashion. A sweeping move involving van Persie and Anderson culminated in Ashley Young feeding a pass through for the Brazilian, who unleashed a stinging effort which flew off the inside of Federici's post and into the roof of the net.

The visitors' tails were up, and when Evans was needlessly barged to the ground by Jay Tabb, referee Mark Halsey had no choice but to award a penalty. Rooney duly sent Federici the wrong way to put United ahead for the first time, but just when it appeared a familiar script was being penned, the game was once again subverted as Reading struck twice in four minutes amid scenes of ghastly defending from the Reds.

Nicky Shorey's whipped deliveries provided the problems, dipping into dangerous areas where the Royals had all too easily found space. First, Le Fondre was completely unmarked and nodded between Lindegaard and van Persie, then Morrison escaped Evans to power home a thunderous effort.

United were rocked and looked liable to further concessions with every forward foray from the hosts. Yet, by the time Sir Alex introduced Chris Smalling in place of Rafael, who had been booked for a foul on Jobi McAnuff, the Reds had drawn level once again. Evra fed Young and raced onto the winger's neat flick, then slid a superb ball back into the path of the onrushing Rooney for a simple side-footed finish. Three minutes later, the goalscorer turned provider with a beautifully faint flick which released van Persie – played onside by Shorey – for a clinical, right-footed finish past Federici.

The Dutchman then seemed to have bagged his second goal in the 40th minute, but the officials failed to spot that his close-range finish had been cleared from behind the line by Adrian Mariappa. As a breathless first half drew to a close, Anderson limped from the fray with a hamstring injury.

Inevitably, both sides began the second half with greater caution, with chances at a premium. After firing over the near post, van Persie had a glaring opportunity to establish a two-goal lead when he pounced on Federici's dally, only to blaze wide of an open goal. That miss left Reading with a glimmer of hope, but they came no closer to a share of the spoils than when Morrison's downward header was comfortably tipped over by Lindegaard in the first minute of injury time.

Instead, United's defensive improvement – with Evans and Rio Ferdinand more imposing and controlled, while Reading's steady supply of crosses was curtailed – secured a victory which just about blended a favourable cocktail of the good and bad of the Reds. Following on from Manchester City's home draw with Everton, United would go into the following weekend's derby with a three-point lead at the top of the table.

The Teams

READING: Federici, Shorey, Mariappa, Morrison, Cummings, Leigertwood, McAnuff (McCleary 79), Tabb, Robson-Kanu (Hunt 83), Le Fondre, Roberts (Pogrebnyak 69)
SUBS NOT USED: Taylor, Pearce, Harte, Guthrie
BOOKED: Tabb

MANCHESTER UNITED: Lindegaard, Rafael (Smalling 31), Evra, Ferdinand, Evans, Anderson (Jones 45), Carrick, Young, Fletcher, Rooney, van Persie (Welbeck 74)
SUBS NOT USED: De Gea, Giggs, Hernandez, Cleverley
BOOKED: Rafael

'It was crazy, to be honest,' understated Wayne Rooney, 'but we dug in there. In the first half, with the goals we conceded it wasn't good enough defending at set-pieces and it could have cost us. In the second half we wanted to be more solid. It gave them a bit of easy possession, but we wanted to make sure we were solid and we thankfully got the three points. When you look back it is enjoyable, but when you're playing you don't know what's going to happen. It's end-to-end, a bit like a basketball match, but I'm sure the fans and the neutrals will be delighted to watch it.'

Sir Alex Ferguson was not among their number. The United manager was vexed by another bitter-sweet victory in which his side's defensive fragility exposed itself.

'I thought it was going to be a record score in the Premier League at half time,' said the boss. 'It was unbelievable. It was really bad defending and the worst we've been this season. We need to sort that out. Every time the ball came near our box you were just praying! We never competed for a cross, but in fairness to Reading they have great deliverers of the ball – Nicky Shorey whips in fantastic crosses. But we should have been doing better. We could have been battered today, but thankfully we are always scoring goals and that is rescuing us every time. In the first half, I said to myself that it would be a miracle if we win this one. I'm just glad that we did.

'It is not a question of our character at all, not with these boys. It's down to us and if you make mistakes like that when you are defending, you are going to have to perform rescue jobs every week and today was yet another rescue job. There were still a lot of plus points in the sense that the boys never gave in and they showed a great determination to get over the line. And that's what it was about today – getting over the line.'

The manager's mood was hardly helped by the loss of Anderson, whose impressive run of form was curtailed by a hamstring injury which threatened to sideline the Brazilian for a number of weeks. 'He's been playing really well and scored a great goal today,' sighed Sir Alex. 'I'm very disappointed for him.'

As the Reds prepared to round off their Champions League qualifying programme with a dead-rubber visit of CFR Cluj to Old Trafford, it was defending which topped the agenda at Carrington –

though more for the looming Manchester derby than the visit of Romania's finest.

'Teams like City will definitely punish any slack defending, so we are going to have to be really on top of our game,' warned Darren Fletcher. 'It is becoming a concern, although I think, particularly at set-pieces, it is individual mistakes which we can try to sort out. Everybody knows and sometimes you can focus in on the bigger games and make sure mistakes don't happen.'

The Group H finale against Cluj would not be a proving ground for the derby, with changes expected throughout the team. Nemanja Vidic was pencilled in for a return, only to sit out the game on the player's say-so. 'He feels he needs another few days' training so he won't be available,' revealed Sir Alex. 'He's not far away. He's training well now, but I think another few days will bring him on better. I wasn't considering Nemanja for Sunday anyway. Playing tomorrow would have been a bonus, but Sunday would have been too soon.

'We'll rest some players, as we did against Galatasaray. But we have to be fair to all the teams who are trying to reach important positions – whether that's the Champions League or the Europa League. In that respect, we'll play a team that we expect will win. But there will be changes.'

UEFA Champions League

Wednesday 5 December | Old Trafford | Attendance: 71,521

MANCHESTER UNITED 0
CFR CLUJ 1 Alberto (56)

United's proud European home record sustained an unlikely blemish as CFR Cluj sprung a huge upset against a much-changed Reds side at Old Trafford.

114

In a largely forgettable game, the Romanian side took the spoils through a blistering goal by Luis Alberto to inflict only the ninth victory for an away side at Old Trafford in European competition.

Cluj goalkeeper Mario Felgueiras was by far the busier goalkeeper in the second half, often besieged at the Stretford End by the likes of Wayne Rooney, Ryan Giggs and Paul Scholes, but his work was ultimately in vain as Galatasaray overcame Braga to take Group H's second qualifying berth behind United.

Sir Alex Ferguson's squad rotation was most keenly felt in defence, with a first Champions League start for centre-back Scott Wootton and another outing for Alexander Büttner at left-back. Meanwhile, Marnick Vermijl, the young Belgian, watched from the bench in the hope of making his European bow. The remainder of the team comprised a blend of youth and experience, demonstrated as 22-year-old Danny Welbeck glanced a header fractionally wide from 39-year-old Ryan Giggs's right-wing corner. Teenage talent Nick Powell also looked to make the most of a rare opening, chancing his arm from range on several occasions.

Cluj needed a victory to prolong any hopes of progressing, and regularly mounted offensives of their own. Firstly, Wootton matched Modou Sougou for pace and blocked his shot with a brilliant challenge, while David De Gea saved from Felice Piccolo's powerful header. Felgueiras denied both Welbeck and Rooney in the same spell of United pressure shortly before half time, acrobatically palming away the former's header and then the latter's chip, but the Cluj stopper was left relieved when Chris Smalling nodded off target from Chicharito's dangerous cross.

United rejigged at the end of the first half, when Scholes replaced the injured Tom Cleverley, but it was Cluj who duly broke the deadlock in devastating fashion. When the Reds lost possession inside the centre circle, Luis Alberto seized the initiative, surged forward and despatched a sensational shot that swerved past De Gea before flying in off the right-hand post.

Another game, another deficit for United, but overturning Cluj's lead over the ensuing 35 minutes proved an insurmountable task. Kiko Macheda was introduced in place of Powell to become the fourth Reds striker on the field, but clear-cut chances proved elusive. Felgueiras had to parry a free-kick from Giggs and clutch Rooney's rising shot as United toiled in vain, while events in Portugal ultimately negated a victory which Cluj closed out in relative comfort.

While the Romanians could only contemplate life in the Europa League, United could revise the lessons learned and look ahead to February's return of the Champions League.

The Teams

MANCHESTER UNITED: De Gea, Jones, Büttner, Smalling, Wootton, Giggs (Fletcher 86), Cleverley (Scholes 45), Powell (Macheda 73), Rooney, Hernandez, Welbeck
SUBS NOT USED: Lindegaard, Rafael, Young, Vermijl
BOOKED: Scholes

CFR CLUJ: Felgueiras, Ivo Pinto, Muresan, Piccolo, Cadu, Rada, Bastos (Maftei 78), Luis Alberto, Rui Pedro (Aguirregaray 71), Camora, Sougou (Kapetanos 90)
SUBS NOT USED: Stancioiu, Sepsi, Godemeche, Bjelanovic
BOOKED: Felgueiras, Cadu

Though inexpensive in terms of the Champions League, United's Premier League hopes looked to have taken a knock in the shock defeat, with Tom Cleverley limping from the fray and immediately casting doubt over his involvement in the Manchester derby. 'We'll assess Tom in the morning,' a grim-faced boss told reporters at his post-match press conference. 'He felt his calf a little but it's not good news. We'll see what he's like in the morning.'

There were still positives, however, for the manager in his side's display. 'We achieved what we wanted to achieve, without getting the result,' he reasoned. 'It's a fantastic goal they scored to beat us. We gave players game time and brought young players back in. The more game time Chris Smalling and Phil Jones get can only help us. I thought Phil was outstanding tonight. Getting him and Chris back is a big plus-point. I think all our defenders did their job pretty well.'

Despite his tender years, Jones showed perspective when dissecting the defeat, and opted to look ahead to the chance to kick on in the Premier League. 'We were probably missing a little bit of urgency in the first half,' admitted the defender. 'But I think we had that in the second half. Cluj were difficult to break down but we created enough chances, enough to win two games, and we put enough balls into the box. We just couldn't stick our chances away, while it was unfortunate they scored a wonder goal. These things happen. We all are up for the derby. We know it's a big game for both clubs and hopefully we can come out on top. We're aiming to extend our lead.'

In order to do so, United would have to inflict City's first Premier League defeat at the Etihad Stadium for almost two years. But, while no team had beaten the Blues on home turf in the league since Everton in December 2010, United's FA Cup win in January 2012 demonstrated that it could be done. Still, Sir Alex did not attempt to sugar coat the task at hand.

'It's going to be a massive game and if we defend like we did at Reading we'll be in trouble,' he said. 'If we win, it will be one of our best-ever results, because they're a really good, powerful team with massive players. It won't be easy.'

In order to procure a positive result, a positive attitude was required. For Patrice Evra, a sea change in United's mental preparation for the derby would prove key. 'This year, compared to last year, we prepared much better for the game,' says the Frenchman, looking back. 'When we prepare, it's not about the things the staff are doing, it's just mentally. I think this year we didn't talk about Manchester City before the game; we just spoke about us, where we were going to get the ball, what we were going to do to hurt them.

'Last year it was more about: "Be careful of this player or this player," and more about our defending ways. We are Manchester United and that's not how we should think. This year I've not heard a lot of people talking about who City are playing next, because we don't care. Last year that was the problem: we cared too much about City and what they were doing, who their next game was against, and that's why this year in the derby we went into it a little bit arrogant, but in a good way. We respect them a lot, but we just wanted to show them that we are Manchester United, we want to be the number one team, we are the ones with nineteen titles and I think now every year we have to show them.

'We have fought a lot with Chelsea, with Liverpool, with Arsenal, now City is coming, but I always say that the most difficult opponent for Manchester United is Manchester United. It's not because I'm playing here, it's because it's the truth. It was an example last year. A lot of people criticised us last year and said we didn't play well, but in the end we lost the league just by goal difference. That's why I was confident going into this year, I said if we were playing well, playing the Manchester United way, then we can win the league. That's the name of the game since I came here and I can't deny that. It's not being arrogant, it's just the truth. We didn't think as much about City going into this game.'

Boosted by the news that both Tom Cleverley and Antonio Valencia would be fit enough to start at the Etihad – though he kept those particular cards close to his chest when addressing the press – Sir Alex was in jovial mood ahead of the game. Reminded of his September 2009 interview when he labelled City United's 'noisy neighbours', the manager joked: 'They're screaming now!'

Going on to address the latest silverware rival to emerge in his epic reign at the United helm, Sir Alex stressed: 'Challenges are what we're made of. I've been lucky that, in my time here, I've been involved with great competitions against individual teams: Liverpool, Arsenal, Chelsea and now City. It's fantastic. There are no dull moments. This season we've responded to City's challenge by adding van Persie and Kagawa. Kagawa is on his way back from injury now, but van Persie has been unbelievable. He's scored thirteen goals already. His intelligence and maturity definitely bring an improvement to the attacking side of our game.'

With van Persie on board and on song, and positivity oozing out on the training field, Ryan Giggs admits he had high hopes going into the 164th Manchester derby. 'I was confident going into the game,' the veteran recalls. 'In training I felt that the week leading up to it we had really good preparation, the lads were hungry, the lads obviously had what happened last year at the back of their minds and we knew it was a big, big game and we needed a result.

'Probably not many people fancied us to go there and get that result because of the record that City had, and the so-called stop-start that we'd had to the season, but I was really confident that we'd go there and win. I went into it probably as positive as I have for a long time for a derby game. I just felt we had what it took to beat them.'

Sure enough, Giggs's instincts proved accurate.

Barclays Premier League

Sunday 9 December | Etihad Stadium | Attendance: 47,166

MANCHESTER CITY 2 Y.Toure (60), Zabaleta (85)
MANCHESTER UNITED 3 Rooney (15, 28), van Persie (90)

A last-gasp winner from Robin van Persie tipped a thrilling derby United's way, putting the Reds six points clear of City and ending the champions' long unbeaten home record in the Premier League.

Wayne Rooney's first-half pair capped a fine counter-attacking display from the Reds but, after Ashley Young's goal had been incorrectly chalked off, City roared back to level. With the game beautifully poised going into stoppage time, van Persie sealed an unforgettable win for the visitors with a free-kick which deflected off Samir Nasri and dipped beyond the dive of Joe Hart.

That dramatic denouement provided a fitting climax to a contest which United just about shaded, largely by virtue of a well-executed tactical plan of containment and countering in the first half.

The game's first chances fell to Mario Balotelli, as his ambitious free-kick was helped wide by David De Gea before the Italian could muster only a wild slash at a Gael Clichy cross, but United's first forward foray resulted in the game's opening goal. Young headed Patrice Evra's ball down the line on to van Persie, whose chest-pass returned it to the winger and sent him scampering into space. Young advanced and fed Rooney, who meandered into the City area before half-hitting a shot back across goal, past the wrong-footed Hart and inside the England goalkeeper's right-hand post.

City's disappointment was compounded when captain Vincent Kompany had to come off due to injury, with Kolo Toure taking his place. Before long, Hart had to race from goal to prevent Young from reaching a van Persie through ball, and a second United goal arrived just before the half-hour. Almost unchallenged by the hosts, Michael Carrick and Antonio Valencia combined to release Rafael down the right, and Rooney advanced onto the Brazilian's pull-back to sweep another clinical finish wide of Hart.

A furious response was expected but, aside from a scare when Gareth Barry fluffed his shot from the edge of the area just before the break, the Reds looked assured as the half ended. When that state failed to change in the early minutes of the second period, Roberto

Mancini introduced Carlos Tevez in place of the ineffective Balotelli. Sir Alex Ferguson, meanwhile, made the injury-enforced trade of Jonny Evans for substitute Chris Smalling.

City began to pose more questions of their visitors, but United's menace remained in plain sight, and a three-goal lead should have been established on the hour as van Persie arced a superb right-footed effort against the inside of Hart's post and Young turned home the rebound. The goal was incorrectly disallowed for offside, and in the next passage of play City halved the arrears when De Gea saved superbly from Tevez and David Silva, but was beaten by Yaya Toure's follow-up.

As the hosts threw more at United's largely untroubled defence, more counter-attacking openings arose. Evra was frustrated to be denied a penalty after apparently being clipped by Kolo Toure inside the box, while van Persie headed wide from Tom Cleverley's measured cross. City's response was led by Silva, who wound his way towards goal before firing a point-blank effort against De Gea's shoulder and onto the crossbar.

That relief was short-lived, though, as City levelled in frustrating circumstances. A Tevez corner was cleared only as far as Pablo Zabaleta, who was inexplicably unmarked and allowed to charge onto the loose ball and drill home an unstoppable finish.

The tide had turned and it seemed certain that if there was going to be a winner, it would come from the hosts. De Gea had to be alert to save from Silva and Tevez, as City sought three points, but the introduction of Danny Welbeck for Cleverley confirmed that Sir Alex was also hell-bent on hogging the spoils.

As vindication for that bold move, Welbeck recovered possession deep in City territory in a passage of play which culminated in United winning a free-kick, 25 yards from the hosts' goal. After a lengthy debate with Rooney, van Persie struck a shot which deflected off Nasri and nestled in Hart's net via the inside of the post, sending United's travelling supporters wild with delight.

Unsavoury scenes followed as Rio Ferdinand was struck by a coin thrown from the home support and then confronted on the field by a City fan, but that epilogue could not detract from a sensational tale. The Reds had sent out a message to the rest of the division, but nowhere was it understood more keenly than within the confines of Manchester.

The Teams

MANCHESTER CITY: Hart, Zabaleta, Clichy, Kompany (K.Toure 21), Nastasic, Nasri, Barry, Silva, Y.Toure (Dzeko 84), Aguero, Balotelli (Tevez 52)
SUBS NOT USED: Pantilimon, Maicon, Garcia, Lescott
BOOKED: Nasri, Y.Toure, Tevez

MANCHESTER UNITED: De Gea, Rafael, Evra, Ferdinand, Evans (Smalling 48), Valencia (Jones 84), Carrick, Young, Cleverley (Welbeck 87), Rooney, van Persie
SUBS NOT USED: Johnstone, Giggs, Hernandez, Scholes
BOOKED: Ferdinand, Rooney

'It was a big game,' recalls Michael Carrick. 'We drew a lot of confidence from going to Liverpool and winning, going to Stamford Bridge and winning, so to go to City . . . it was a huge game anyway, but to win like we did in the last minute, it gives you an extra-special feeling. Being in the position we were, at two-nil, it shouldn't have come to that, but it was a special day. When you look back on those big games, it's vital that you come out on top, and especially with it being away from home it was a great day for us.'

'The first half couldn't have gone more to plan,' adds Tom Cleverley. 'We played how we prepared to play and I think if the disallowed goal had been allowed to stand then we could have gone on to get one of our best wins in a long time. Unfortunately, they got back in the game and I was actually on the bench when the winner went in. I just remember grabbing Eric Steele and Jonny Evans and going mad when Robin's free-kick went in. It was a really big win, but we didn't celebrate too hard because we knew there was a long way to go.'

Given the positioning of the dugouts, which are within touching distance of the home support, overly vociferous celebrations are never too advisable at the Etihad Stadium. Jonny Evans, however, spotted one Red flaunting that notion deep into enemy territory.

'When we got the winner it was just unbelievable,' says the defender. 'We were right behind it, myself and Tom Cleverley, and we had a great view of it. We just started going ballistic, hugging each other. If you can't celebrate in your own dugout then there's something wrong, but to be fair there was a fella and his little girl sat right behind the dugout, and he was going nuts for United. I thought: "He's a brave man." I think he left about five or ten minutes early so he missed the final goal, but I guess he just wanted to get out safely!'

As the dust settled on a massive victory for the league leaders, the bravery of Sir Alex Ferguson drew plaudits, largely for the decision to remove midfielder Cleverley to introduce striker Danny Welbeck despite letting a two-goal lead slip, a move which paid spectacular dividends.

'Even though Welbz was only on for five or ten minutes, he made a big impact,' admits Cleverley. 'He helped win the free-kick that got us the winner, so it was a brilliant substitution.'

'It was a brave move to put on a striker and that did win us the game,' adds Ryan Giggs. 'That's the way it is at this club. We don't hang on for two-two draws, we go for it. If we get beaten in the process, so be it. I think we've got the philosophy that by doing that, we'll win more than we lose.'

This particular win, if attained, had been identified pre-match as one of the Reds' greatest under Sir Alex, so it was little wonder that the boss revelled in a 'special' victory. 'This was special simply because they hadn't lost at home for two years,' he said. 'Both of us are contenders at the top of the league and it was an incredible game, you couldn't take your eyes off it.

'The intensity, passion, competitiveness . . . everything was there. And you've got to give credit to City for the way they keep going and for scoring late goals. Fortunately, we got the last one that counted. You know Robin's capable of that. It took a little deflection, but it was a wicked hit and I'm really delighted it's flown in.

'I think we played very well. I thought the game should have been out of sight in the second half with the number of chances we had. It's a funny game, football – it would have been three-nil with a goal that was perfectly onside. Instead, they go up the park and score within minutes. That's the kind of game football is, it can kick you in the teeth that way.

'City kept fighting, they kept battling and they've got this great record of scoring late goals. City scored a second goal and they deserved it. But up to that point, I thought we were far better than them. When you count the points up in May, I hope it is significant.'

The afternoon's sole negative was undoubtedly the unsavoury incident in which a home supporter confronted Rio Ferdinand, who seconds earlier had been coined for celebrating van Persie's winner in front of the away support. Manchester City quickly issued a public apology and the Football Association confirmed they were investigating the incidents, but the damage had been done.

'It could have taken Rio's eye out and you've seen the cut on his head,' lamented Ashley Young. 'When Wazza was taking a corner there were so many objects being thrown onto the pitch as well and, on another day, if the pitch had not been so wet, the fan who came onto the pitch wouldn't have slipped over and could have attacked Rio. It's not nice to see that and hopefully it'll be dealt with.'

There was little time to dwell on the events at the Etihad Stadium, with Sunderland due at Old Trafford just six days later. As with the derby, the fixture was laced with flashbacks to the gut-wrenching climax to the 2011-12 campaign, when Black Cats supporters revelled in United's misery with a mocking 'Poznan' celebration in tribute to Manchester City. At the time, Sir Alex had instructed his players: 'Remember this day,' so it was inevitable that the added motivation of revenge would be brought up ahead of the Wearsiders' visit to Manchester.

'I don't think revenge will come into it,' Sir Alex speculated. 'It was disappointing, actually, when you think of the number of players we've given Sunderland over the years. I think we gave them the players that got them promoted: Evans and Simpson. But I don't think it was malicious; it was them enjoying the moment. I don't think it was anything against Manchester United, really. Winning the game is more important to us. And given the impetus we got from last week, hopefully that will be a decider for us. It's time for us to really kick on.'

The manager could finally call upon his captain, Nemanja Vidic, in time to lead that charge. The Serbian was fit enough to rejoin the match-day squad – a timely boost after Jonny Evans' hamstring injury ruled him out of the clash with his former loan club – and Sir Alex was delighted to welcome back his defensive lynchpin.

'Having Vida back in the squad is a big, big one for us,' he stressed. 'His experience, his ability to head the ball, his offensive qualities are well renowned now and he's our captain. Whether I start him or not, that's another issue. But it's great to have him back. We hope we've given him the proper rehabilitation. Coming back from the last injury, we gave him a long rehabilitation and I thought it was a good one. But unfortunately he suffered another injury. In fact, in the last year and four months or so, I think he's played only about ten games. So it's an issue and we're hoping that he sails through it. We'll give him a chance and there will be opportunities for him because he brings that great experience, that warrior-type defending he's renowned for.'

It was decided that Vidic would be introduced midway through the second period if United were in a position of authority against the Black Cats. They wouldn't have to wait long to establish one.

Barclays Premier League

Saturday 15 December | Old Trafford | Attendance: 75,582

MANCHESTER UNITED 3 Van Persie (16), Cleverley (19), Rooney (59)
SUNDERLAND 1 Campbell (72)

Only profligate finishing prevented United from running up a handsome victory in a one-sided meeting with Sunderland, who never recovered from the hosts' storming start to the game.

The Black Cats were unable to match the Reds' breathless early tempo, which yielded goals from Robin van Persie and Tom Cleverley inside the first 20 minutes. A spate of chances came and went before Wayne Rooney finally struck to lend the scoreline a touch more realism, though that was later dashed by Fraizer Campbell's consolation goal on his return to Old Trafford.

United's control and attacking intent in the first half were impressive to watch. Michael Carrick was supreme in a first 45 minutes in which he dictated the game's tempo and orchestrated attacks as teammates buzzed around in front of him. A wane in United's tempo coincided with his withdrawal at half time.

A pre-match scene had been set in which United, seeking revenge against the visitors following the final day of the 2011-12 campaign, would take charge and the hosts' early play certainly boasted the vim and vigour previously reserved for high-stakes encounters with fellow title challengers.

In the second minute, Simon Mignolet was quick off his line to cut out Phil Jones's sliding cross, and the tone was set for a busy afternoon for the Belgian. Ashley Young then had a shot deflected wide on six minutes and, after the resulting corner, forced a fingertip save from Mignolet.

Following another corner shortly after that, Patrice Evra found himself unmarked on the penalty spot with the ball at his feet, but he blazed his shot over the bar. Parity didn't last long, however, and in the 16th minute Young engineered space with a sharp turn and cross which Sunderland captain John O'Shea shanked straight to van Persie, who needed one touch to control, another to sweep the ball into the top corner.

Van Persie almost grabbed a swift second when his header from Jones's deep cross was turned around the post by Mignolet. United continued to pour forward and Tom Cleverley doubled the lead in style with his first league goal at Old Trafford, playing a neat one-two with Carrick and arcing a fine shot into Mignolet's far corner.

Rooney volleyed over from van Persie's headed knock-down as United continued to run riot, but James McClean did call David De Gea into action with a powerful near-post effort after robbing Rio Ferdinand. When Rooney struck the bar from close range shortly after the restart and Young fired over at the second attempt, it seemed little would change in the second half. However, minus Carrick's control, United were increasingly pegged back and Craig Gardner quickly forced a low save from De Gea, who then had to smother Stephane Sessegnon's rebound.

Van Persie artfully teed up Rooney for a simple tap-in to put United three goals ahead, but Sunderland were undeterred and on 72 minutes got their reward as Sessegnon crossed to the far post for substitute and ex-Red Campbell to nod home from close range. It was fair reward for their efforts, but nevertheless the Black Cats could consider themselves fortunate to have escaped

Old Trafford without the hiding United's display had threatened to mete out.

The Teams

MANCHESTER UNITED: De Gea, Jones, Evra, Ferdinand (Vidic 68), Smalling, Valencia, Carrick (Scholes 46), Young, Cleverley (Giggs 73), Rooney, van Persie
SUBS NOT USED: Lindegaard, Hernandez, Welbeck, Fletcher

SUNDERLAND: Mignolet, O'Shea, Bramble, Cuellar, Larsson, Gardner, Colback (McFadden 85), Johnson (Campbell 68), McClean, Sessegnon, Fletcher (Wickham 46)
SUBS NOT USED: Westwood, Saha, Kilgallon, Vaughan

'It is difficult when you stop playing, then play, stop playing and then play again,' recalls Nemanja Vidic, looking back on his second comeback of the season. 'I had that two or three times. It is always hard when you have a long injury and you can do so much physical stuff, but when you come on the pitch it is different. You have to pick up the form very quickly, because it is the middle of the season and that is hard. But I worked hard in the gym, physically, knowing that in time I would heal and pick up the form. This is something you do not worry about, but it something that you want to happen quickly. I think I did well.'

There would be no contradiction from Sir Alex Ferguson, but the manager's post-match attentions were directed largely towards his side's wastefulness in front of goal. 'A lot of our football was fantastic and some of our interchange play was terrific,' he lauded. 'I don't know if we relaxed when we went three-nil up, or if Sunderland got a grip of the game, but towards the end they played very well and could have scored two or three goals.

'Some of our play was fantastic and we should've scored more. Tom Cleverley's goal was a marvellous piece of interchange play, a first-time finish and a really superb goal which epitomised the way we were playing at that point. I'd no complaints for an hour and it was wonderful to watch.

'We don't pick out Robin van Persie's runs as well as we should – his movement is great and he kept them on the back foot. But Wayne could've scored three of four goals, he hit the bar and missed two or three chances in the first half. We should have scored more.'

Such charity in front of goal irked the manager, but with Christmas fast approaching, the victory preceded the season of more palatable goodwill at Carrington. The Reds would travel to Wales to face Michael Laudrup's Swansea City two days before Christmas, but first would enjoy two festive traditions: the Academy players' pantomime and a trip to hand out presents at the Royal Manchester Children's Hospital. For Patrice Evra, both events are a huge part of Christmas.

'The panto was very funny,' he smiles. 'There were not a lot of the lads because some of the players were away on a trip, so there were only around six players involved this time, but we love that because there were a lot of jokes about the senior players. Now they enjoy killing Anderson and Ferdinand, but it's funny and we have a lovely time. We all have a nice meal together and then afterwards there's the show, but I say "well done" to the kids because it's a lot of pressure to handle, being in front of everyone, but they make us laugh and well done.

'With going to hospitals, it's so important. I know many clubs are doing this. It's like a tradition in England, but in France they never do these kinds of things. In Monaco, sometimes I'd go myself to the hospital to see kids and give out presents, but that was just a personal thing I liked to do. When I came here and we started doing it, I was really surprised and so happy, because I think it's so important to put a smile on the faces of those kids. They aren't feeling well and just seeing us can sometimes give them extra hope.

'It's so important and I love to do it, I really give it one hundred per cent because I think doing that kind of thing is more important than football. You realise how lucky you are to be at Manchester United, especially the young players, because you could be that kid in a hospital bed and you just feel lucky for yourself. You have to come out and enjoy your life more. You see life differently because it gives you perspective and it's so important that we do everything we can for them.'

'It's so special,' adds Chicharito, who also handed out presents to ailing patients. 'It's unbelievable. To go and try to give some happiness or warmth to patients in the hospital is a very good feeling, just to go over there and give them some gifts. We try to help them, but it's more special for us being in that type of place because they have real problems, those people. Sometimes our problems are that we're not playing or we're losing games, but they're fighting for their lives, so that's another very good part of our life to try to be a part of things with them. To even be with them for five minutes, to speak with them and try to help them in any way is such a good feeling.'

Having made so many new acquaintances on their charitable visit, United's players soon learned that they would be seeing a familiar face back at Old Trafford when they were drawn against Cristiano Ronaldo's Real Madrid in the second round of the Champions League. The Portuguese had spent six years with the Reds prior to his world-record move to the La Liga giants, and his impending return created a buzz around Carrington.

'I had that feeling that we were going to get Madrid,' reveals Evra. 'I can't explain why, but a lot of players thought the same. We knew it would be a big occasion for us – it's a long time since we had a big occasion like this at Old Trafford. We've been to finals, played big games against Chelsea and Arsenal in the Champions League, but they were still games against English teams. To play against another big European team, a Spanish team in Real Madrid, what more could you ask than that? You just think back to when you were a child and you dream about playing in that kind of game.

'Of course, I was in touch with Ronnie after the draw. I was sending him love – you have to kill him with the love for that game, no making him angry! Just messages like: "You are the best!" This is his house and we knew he would get a great ovation.'

Among those looking forward to trying to stop Ronaldo and the rest of Jose Mourinho's side was Jonny Evans, who ensured a positive climax to his own impressive year with a new contract extension. 'I'm delighted to sign my new contract,' he beamed. 'I am so proud to play for such a great club, and there's no better feeling than playing football in this team and winning games. Even when I was nine or ten years old back home in Northern Ireland, clubs asked me to go on trial, but I didn't go because I knew that Manchester United was the place I wanted to play football. I would love to play here throughout the rest of my career.'

The good news kept coming. Evans had sufficiently recovered from his hamstring injury to rejoin the squad which would head to Swansea – a timely boost for Sir Alex in his plans to shackle the Premier League's surprise package: Michu. The Spaniard had been picked up by Michael Laudrup for just £2 million and arrived in England with little reputation, yet stood alongside Robin van Persie at the head of the division's scoring charts.

'Michael Laudrup is cherry-picking and the boy Michu was a first-class piece of business,' said the manager. 'I'd never really heard of him. I should have a word with my scouting department! The fact he's done it early gives us an opportunity to look at him better and assess his qualities. He can play up front but tends to drop into the middle of the pitch too, so it gives them the problem of do they play him off the front or bring Danny Graham back? We have to be aware of it anyway. He's shown good finishing. He's got that bit of composure, but hopefully we can deal with it.'

Doing so in theory was more manageable than doing it in practice, it would prove.

Barclays Premier League

Sunday 23 December | Liberty Stadium | Attendance: 20,650

SWANSEA CITY 1 Michu (29)
MANCHESTER UNITED 1 Evra (16)

United's club record run of 27 games without a draw came to an end as Swansea withstood an impressive Reds display to take a share of the spoils at the Liberty Stadium.

Patrice Evra powered home a Robin van Persie corner with a fine header, only for Michu to quickly level by turning home the rebound after Jonathan De Guzman's shot had been parried by David De Gea.

Sir Alex's men then dominated second-half proceedings and twice hit the crossbar through van Persie and Michael Carrick. But, despite a string of half-chances, the Reds couldn't force a winner and had to settle for a first draw since the previous April's tie with Everton.

Swansea had lost at home only twice all season and made a confident start to the afternoon, with Michu and Wayne Routledge both chancing their arm in the opening stages. United's swift riposte was to bring smart stops from Michel Vorm through efforts by Wayne Rooney and Ashley Young.

The second of those – a reflex stop down to Vorm's left after Carrick's pass had released Young – led to the corner from which the game's opening goal arrived on 16 minutes. Van Persie's whipped in-swinger perfectly picked out Evra, who rose amid a cluster of home defenders to power a header between the upright and Swans mid-fielder Leon Britton.

United's play took on added swagger thereafter, only for Swansea to hit back and level out of nothing when Michu pounced to tap in from close range after De Gea had stopped De Guzman's stinging effort. The equaliser rocked the visitors and galvanised the hosts, who embarked on a spell of sustained pressure until the interval, even though the final chance of the half came United's way when Rooney's half-hit shot was kept out by Vorm.

After the break, the game resumed on an even keel, with Young's shot well blocked by Ashley Williams, and De Gea forced to make two fine saves – first from distance, then from close range – as Kemy Agustien and then Routledge let fly with powerful efforts.

Rooney shifted to the left side of midfield as Sir Alex brought on Javier Hernandez for Antonio Valencia and Young switched to the right flank. The change almost brought immediate dividends, as van Persie volleyed against the crossbar from Rooney's tantalising cross. The woodwork was also struck by Carrick, whose near-post header from a van Persie corner was brilliantly tipped onto the crossbar by Vorm, before van Persie and Young both saw goalbound efforts blocked in a frantic passage of play.

In an increasingly fractious game, tempers boiled over when Williams needlessly booted the ball against the head of a prone van Persie after the Dutchman had tumbled to the ground, with both players booked after the ensuing skirmish. Time remained for one more half-chance, with substitute Ryan Giggs lobbing wide of an untended goal from 45 yards after Vorm had dashed from his line, and the Reds were left to rue a rare share of the spoils as Manchester City reduced the league leaders' advantage to four points with their late win over Reading.

The Teams

SWANSEA CITY: Vorm, Chico, Williams, Tiendalli, Davies, Britton (Ki Sung-Yeung 62), Michu, Dyer, Routledge, De Guzman (Moore 70), Agustien (Shechter 87)
SUBS NOT USED: Tremmel, Graham, Monk, Richards
BOOKED: Flores, Williams

MANCHESTER UNITED: De Gea, Jones, Evra, Evans, Vidic, Valencia (Hernandez 61), Carrick, Young, Cleverley (Scholes 85), Rooney (Giggs 78), van Persie
SUBS NOT USED: Lindegaard, Büttner, Fletcher, Welbeck
BOOKED: Jones, Rooney, van Persie, Scholes

Sir Alex was left bemused by his side's inability to convert possession and goalscoring chances into three points after a frustrating stalemate in South Wales. 'How we didn't win the game is the question of the year really, because we absolutely battered them,' he lamented. 'We created a lot of chances and hit the post, the bar and there were a few scrambles in the box.

'In criticism, you would have to say that sometimes our final ball wasn't good enough. In the second half it was an absolutely brilliant performance. But I've got to be disappointed with that result. We should have won the game by quite a margin really.' The boss also vented his ire towards Ashley Williams for his part in the incident with Robin van Persie, insisting: 'Robin is lucky he wasn't killed today.' But he and his players quickly set their sights on the Boxing Day visit of Newcastle.

'We now have three games in the next nine days,' outlined Nemanja Vidic. 'Obviously we have a few players who are coming back from injury and they will be important for that period. We had a few chances, but you have to give Swansea credit as well; they fought well and gave everything to get a point out of the game. Swansea is a tough place to come, but we're disappointed we didn't go home with three points.'

'I felt that we deserved to win at Swansea and that is why I am really confident for the rest of the games we having coming up over Christmas,' added Patrice Evra. 'We have to move on from the draw and focus on our next game against Newcastle. It is important to win and it is important that we keep playing well. We face Newcastle at home, let's make sure we get three points. After that, it is West Brom and we must make sure we get three points then, too. This is an important part of the season and it is an opportunity to get a lot of points. I'm not worried; I am really confident for the games coming up at Old Trafford.'

That confidence came in spite of the news that Wayne Rooney would be missing for the remainder of the festive period, having strained a ligament behind his knee during the Reds' Christmas Day training session. It would prove a nightmare before Boxing Day for Sir Alex, who also lost Ashley Young to injury in the same session, while Danny Welbeck succumbed to illness in the team hotel. Allied to Phil Jones also picking up an injury at Swansea and Nemanja Vidic's ongoing comeback being carefully managed, the boss had to fall back on his squad's depth and hope for the best against Alan Pardew's Magpies.

Barclays Premier League

Wednesday 26 December | Old Trafford | Attendance: 75,596

MANCHESTER UNITED 4 Evans (25), Evra (58), van Persie (71), Hernandez (90)
NEWCASTLE UNITED 3 Perch (4), Evans (28 og), Cisse (68)

United snatched a staggering last-gasp victory over Newcastle at Old Trafford, coming from behind three times before Chicharito

slid home an injury-time winner to cap an unforgettable Boxing Day encounter.

The Reds were rarely at their best against a brave Newcastle side, who exploited the hosts' uncertain defending in rain-sodden conditions before succumbing to United's improved second-half display.

After James Perch's early opener, Jonny Evans levelled from close range, but quickly scored an own-goal. Patrice Evra hammered home a second equaliser, Papiss Cisse thrashed Newcastle back into the lead and Robin van Persie put United back on terms almost immediately, before Chicharito slid in Michael Carrick's pass to send Old Trafford wild. Incredibly, Manchester City's defeat at Sunderland allowed the Reds to build a seven-point lead at the head of the Barclays Premier League table, on an afternoon when Sir Alex Ferguson's side looked set for a desperate setback.

Once again, the Reds went about their task the hard way. In just the fourth minute, Demba Ba advanced on goal and chanced his arm from 25 yards. David De Gea parried away the low effort, but the ball fell perfectly into the path of the onrushing Perch for a simple tap-in.

United's endeavours to get back into the game were met not only by the emboldened visitors, but the teeming rain and an increasingly slickened playing surface. There was much bluster without end product but, as soon as United located the target, parity was restored. Van Persie's in-swinging free-kick was flicked on by Ryan Giggs and the ball became stuck among a ruck of players. Chicharito was the first to react, quickly firing off a shot which Tim Krul brilliantly saved, only for Evans to reach the rebound ahead of Danny Simpson and slide home the leveller.

Yet, just three minutes later, the Northern Irishman had inadvertently restored the visitors' lead amid scenes of confusion. The ball was worked wide to Simpson, who advanced into space and smashed in a cross-shot which Evans, under pressure in his attempt to intercept, could only divert inside De Gea's post. The goal was initially chalked off for offside, but referee Mike Dean consulted his assistant and duly concluded that Evans had applied the finish, rather than the lurking Cisse.

Having so quickly surrendered a position of promise once again, United's game retook an uneasy air, while Newcastle were seemingly first to every ball. Matters almost worsened for the league leaders when Sylvan Marveaux curled a free-kick against De Gea's crossbar, but the interval arrived with a one-goal deficit reflecting kindly on United's display.

For United, the second period began with greater promise than the first, but it still took a bolt from the blue to level the scores shortly before the hour-mark. Van Persie's cross was tamely headed away by Perch, straight to Evra. The skipper took a touch and fired a venomous low effort through Ba's legs and underneath the finger-tips of Krul, bagging the Frenchman's fourth goal of a relatively bountiful season.

United's dander was up and the mood inside Old Trafford was dramatically lifted, yet Newcastle would not be deterred. Substitute Gabriel Obertan took advantage of yawning space down United's right flank, slid a ball across the area and the onrushing Cisse powered home an unstoppable finish.

The game's see-saw nature continued, as the Reds drew level just two minutes later. Antonio Valencia powered down the right flank and crossed for van Persie, whose powerful effort was beaten away by Krul. Carrick alertly stabbed it back to the Dutchman for a low, drilled finish past the Newcastle stopper.

An enthralling game had taken another twist and, tantalisingly, had over 15 minutes remaining. Chicharito rounded Krul but ran out of space, van Persie brilliantly volleyed just wide and Chicharito then headed against the outside of Krul's post from Valencia's fine cross. To serve a reminder of the game's capricious nature, substitute

Sammy Ameobi's trickling effort rebounded off the inside of De Gea's post and bounced back to the relieved Spaniard.

When Chicharito headed Giggs's cross straight at Krul from close range, and van Persie nodded past the top corner, a thrilling game looked set to end all-square. Then, just as the clock reached 90 minutes, Chicharito sent Old Trafford into delirium. The little Mexican timed his run perfectly to be level with Simpson, reaching Carrick's superb lofted pass to slide a perfect finish past Krul.

It was a huge dose of festive cheer for all of a Red persuasion – particularly in light of City's shock setback at Sunderland – but once again Sir Alex's men had left it late before delivering the perfect Christmas gift.

The Teams

MANCHESTER UNITED: De Gea, Smalling, Evra, Ferdinand, Evans, Valencia, Giggs, Carrick, Scholes (Cleverley 69), Hernandez (Fletcher 90), van Persie
SUBS NOT USED: Lindegaard, Vidic, Wootton, Büttner, Tunnicliffe
BOOKED: Evans, Valencia, Hernandez

NEWCASTLE UNITED: Krul, Coloccini, Santon, Simpson, Williamson, Perch, Anita, Bigirimana (Obertan 65), Marveaux, Cisse (Sammy Ameobi 79), Ba (Shola Ameobi 71)
SUBS NOT USED: Elliot, Tavernier, Ferguson, Campbell
BOOKED: Simpson, Williamson, Cisse

'It was a very crazy game,' laughs hero-of-the-hour Chicharito. 'Every time we went down, we'd score, then they'd score. We always try to come back and fortunately we scored in the last minute – that type of game is always special. We don't always want it to be like that, because we play with a lot of emotion when we score late like that, but sometimes we might prefer to be winning two or three-nil and not conceding goals. It's maybe better than always going through the agony and the nerves of going into the last five minutes needing goals, but when that happens it's always very special! Thankfully the goal was OK and was very, very important for us.'

Jonny Evans still looks back with a rueful smile on one of the more eventful evenings of his career, having scored at both ends in controversial circumstances. 'It was crazy,' echoes the Northern Irishman. 'They've scored the goal, I've equalised and then scored an own-goal which obviously provoked a massive debate. Once I'd seen that the referee had gone over to speak to the linesman, I thought they had a real chance of turning it round and getting the goal, which is what they did.

'I think it could have gone either way. It probably set things up for fantastic game, probably one of the best at Old Trafford in the last few years in terms of excitement, goals, the slippery pitch, it was around Christmas time, it was just a fantastic game to be a part of – even though you're a defender conceding three goals – you still don't mind scoring four! As a player, you just want to go into the lead and sit and chill out, but obviously for the fans ... We were playing the game and the feeling you get from it is unreal. You don't really think about the consequences, you just think: "Let's win this game," and you do everything you can to win it.'

Even at the time, there was no mistaking the feeling that United had secured a key result in the season. 'It was really important to get the win, no matter how we did it,' said Rio Ferdinand. 'We seem to make sure the punters get their money's worth when they come to the ground at the moment, but it was a great show of character from the lads at the start of a really busy schedule. The manager has got that never-say-die sprit and it filters down through the club – we take it out on the pitch and reflect that.'

'I wish this was the last game of the season!' Sir Alex joked. 'What this tells you about is the courage of our team. Fantastic courage. The players never gave in and that's a great quality to have. I'm pleased that we came back three times after going down three times and then scoring the winner. Chicharito deservedly got the winner, his movement and courage were unbelievable. He and van Persie were absolutely phenomenal, I thought.

'It's a really significant result for us. It puts us in a good position. As I always say of December, it's a month that tells you everything. And when we come to the end of the Wigan game on 1 January, we'll still be top of the league.'

One more game remained before the turn of the year, with Steve Clarke's impressive West Brom due at Old Trafford, and Sir Alex's plans were boosted by the return of Danny Welbeck, Ashley Young and Shinji Kagawa. It would be the return of Nemanja Vidic, however, which would have the most telling influence.

Having spent months on the sidelines and watched on amid United's spate of concessions – including the gung-ho horror show which ultimately did not prove costly against Newcastle – the Serbian was able to identify problems and help fix them upon his return to the starting line-up.

'When you watch the games, everybody has an opinion – which is normal,' says Vidic. 'I have an opinion and sometimes I will see something and have an idea about how to solve a problem, but we always believe in the coaches will find a way, which I think they did, because we stopped giving away so many chances to the opponents anymore and we started conceding fewer goals.'

The visit of the Baggies would coincide with a defensive tightening which would prove key to United's ambitions for the remainder of the season.

Barclays Premier League

Saturday 29 December | Old Trafford | Attendance: 75,595

MANCHESTER UNITED 2 McAuley (9 og), van Persie (90)
WEST BROMWICH ALBION 0

An early own goal by Gareth McAuley and Robin van Persie's late strike proved decisive as United ended 2012 on an ideal note, with a workmanlike shift to see off a spirited show from the Baggies.

Crucially, after the Boxing Day defensive fiasco against Newcastle, Sir Alex Ferguson's side kept just their fourth Premier League clean sheet of the season, showing the kind of defensive fortitude required of champions. The afternoon's action had been in doubt, pre-match, after sustained rainfall prompted a pitch inspection. United started slowly on the sodden turf, with Baggies striker Shane Long particularly troublesome in the opening exchanges.

Before long, however, United forged ahead. Ashley Young worked a one-two with Shinji Kagawa and the England winger drilled in a cross that deflected off Gareth McAuley and past former Reds keeper Ben Foster. Suitably buoyed by the early lead, United continued to take the game to the visitors. Danny Welbeck was only just unable to reach a long ball by Tom Cleverley, and then worked Foster from a Kagawa pass. Welbeck's cross was then headed over by Young, who was soon thwarted by a brilliant save from Foster, who somehow turned the winger's close-range shot onto the bar.

From the resulting corner, Nemanja Vidic poked the ball back to Michael Carrick following a scramble, but the midfielder's effort was blocked by Gabriel Tamas. From another set-piece, Vidic headed wide as the home support began to grow uncomfortable with their side's wastefulness. Albion mustered a moment of danger when Peter Odemwingie broke into the box and dragged his shot wide, before

Foster's clearance rebounded off the hustling Welbeck and flew just past the post.

After the interval, the visitors improved markedly. Chris Brunt fired a fierce drive straight at David De Gea and Carrick cleared from McAuley from a dangerous free-kick to the far post. United's increasingly fragmented play dropped in production, prompting the introduction of van Persie in place of Kagawa. Steve Clarke made a change of his own by introducing Chelsea loanee Romelu Lukaku to the action.

Sir Alex restructured his side in a bid to hold on to the lead, with Antonio Valencia dropping to right-back and Chris Smalling switching to the middle to form a five-man defence. That left United short on attacking numbers, but van Persie still managed to bring a sharp stop from Foster before wrapping up the points in the final minute of the game.

The Dutchman picked up possession on the right side of the area, worked his way infield and bent a brilliant effort over Foster to confirm that United would end 2012 with a victory and a seven-point lead at the head of the table.

The Teams

MANCHESTER UNITED: De Gea, Smalling, Evra, Evans, Vidic, Valencia, Carrick, Young, Cleverley (Scholes 82), Kagawa (van Persie 65), Welbeck
SUBS NOT USED: Lindegaard, Ferdinand, Giggs, Hernandez, Büttner
BOOKED: Valencia

WEST BROMWICH ALBION: Foster, Ridgewell, McAuley, Jones, Tamas, Brunt (Morrison 75), Thorne, Dorrans (Fortune 83), Rosenberg (Lukaku 67), Long, Odemwingie
SUBS NOT USED: Myhill, Jara, Dawson, El Ghanassy

After the drama of Boxing Day, Sir Alex was pleased to see his side record a rather more straightforward home win over the Baggies, although he did find cause for concern in the state of the Old Trafford playing surface.

'The pitch was a problem for us with the way we pass the ball – it slowed our game down a bit,' he said. 'We did well in the first half, we dominated at times, but you must give credit to West Brom, who had more of the game in the second half and were a threat with their crosses. They were very resilient and stubborn and worked really hard when it came to defending.

'They had quite a bit of possession into the second period, so we decided to bring on Robin and Paul Scholes just to settle us down a bit and they did that well, and of course Robin scored a fantastic goal. It's a good result considering how heavy the pitch was – that's two games in four days on it and it's not easy. The slowness of it killed our speed really.'

Having teed up the Reds' opening goal with a vicious delivery, Ashley Young sought to pay tribute to the league leaders' much-maligned defence after an invaluable clean sheet. 'We defended brilliantly,' said the winger. 'The back four and the keeper were fantastic. Every one of them at the back was fantastic and deserve a pat on the back and a clean sheet for how much work they put in.

'It wasn't an easy pitch out there today. It was boggy and everybody will be tired tomorrow because they put in a good shift. I don't think we wanted that drama again after the other night against Newcastle. We wanted to get off to a good start and we managed to do that.'

Nemanja Vidic was a figurehead for the victory over West Brom, and his fitness would prove influential in the Reds' defensive displays over the remainder of the season. The club captain was delighted to have his side end the year seven points clear at the head of the table, but experience had warned against complacency.

'It is good to have this advantage,' he said, 'but we have to be careful. There is still a long way to go. We have the experience of last year when we were eight points in front and in the end it didn't finish well. I think this season is different. We are more mature. We have young players who have the experience from last year. That is a big help for the team. With the experience we have already, we can do well, I think.'

Seven points clear at the top of the table, with a mouth-watering Champions League tie and a fresh assault on the FA Cup to come, the skipper's cautious optimism for 2013 was well warranted. So far, so good.

7

January

New Year, new start? More of the same, more like. With a handsome advantage in the Barclays Premier League to press home and an FA Cup third-round trip to West Ham to factor in, Sir Alex was keen for little to change as 2013 began. As such, the boss was quick to play down suggestions of mid-season transfer dealings. 'Don't hold your breath waiting for us to jump through the transfer window when it opens,' he said. 'If you believed everything you read in the media, we would have the biggest squad in Europe, not to mention becoming bankrupt!

'It's been open season to link us with a stack of players, admittedly some very good ones, but it just isn't going to happen. You can never say never in football, because you don't know who might become available but, speaking generally, I am not looking to do any serious transfer business in January. I don't have to because I am more than satisfied with the players I have in my squad, a group as good as any I have had in my time at Old Trafford.

'So we won't be dashing around in a panic. Of course, as always, we will be on the lookout for young players of potential who we can develop. We have always done that and it's the main reason why we never have to buy out of desperation. We always work for the future as well as trying our best to produce winning teams for the present. Clearly, serious injuries can upset your plans and force you to go out for a replacement but, by and large, I think we are well covered to cope with the normal absence of players.'

The manager was still without a handful of players for the Reds' New Year's Day trip to Wigan Athletic, but could at least call upon the returning Rafael, while Robin van Persie, Chicharito, Paul Scholes and Ryan Giggs had all been rested against West Brom to preserve their fitness for the short trip to the DW Stadium. With Wigan fresh from a 3-0 win at fellow strugglers Aston Villa, however, the boss was wary, insisting: 'It'll be a hard game.' His players quickly confounded those concerns.

Barclays Premier League

Tuesday 1 January | DW Stadium | Attendance: 20,342

WIGAN ATHLETIC 0
MANCHESTER UNITED 4 Hernandez (35, 63), van Persie (43, 88)

United sent out an ominous statement of intent by beginning 2013 with a comfortable 4-0 victory at the DW Stadium.

Strike partners Javier Hernandez and Robin van Persie shared the goals for the Reds, who were rarely troubled by the overrun hosts throughout a one-sided encounter. Despite a sluggish start from both sides, United were first to emerge from the New Year slumber as Chicharito began posing problems for the home defence. The Mexican had a goal correctly chalked off for offside after 12 minutes, having already forced Ali Al-Habsi into a routine save.

Ashley Young was denied a penalty after he and Jean Beausejour tumbled on the edge of the box, but United – inspired by the excellent Ryan Giggs – began to turn the screw as the hosts repelled a series of fine crosses and Al-Habsi just about managed to fend away a drive from Rafael.

With 35 minutes on the clock, the breakthrough duly arrived courtesy of the ever-alert Hernandez. Rafael won a header to find Tom Cleverley and the former Wigan loanee helped the ball down the line to Jonny Evans. The centre-back's measured cut-back was initially mis-kicked by Patrice Evra, but the Frenchman's second attempt yielded a shot which Al-Habsi could only parry to Chicharito for a simple tap-in.

Wigan's defence continued to creak under United pressure, and a calamitous collision between two Latics defenders allowed Michael Carrick's pass to find Hernandez in space. The Mexican decided to pass to his strike partner, and van Persie twisted and turned to leave Ivan Ramis on his backside before guiding a right-footed finish wide of the motionless Al-Habsi.

There was still time for Hernandez to find the net again before the half-time whistle, following more fine work in midfield by van Persie, but the lively forward was again rightly flagged offside when prodding the ball under Al-Habsi. The same fate befell Arouna Kone's strike on the hour mark, when he finished Franco Di Santo's centre from an offside position, but United struck quickly to nip in the bud any notion of a Wigan fightback.

Again van Persie and Chicharito were involved, as the former's free-kick deflected off the wall and into the path of the latter, who sharply despatched an unstoppable shot past Al-Habsi. Turning on the style, van Persie powered his way through to sweep just over the top as the game descended into a procession.

Substitutes Chris Smalling and Shinji Kagawa enjoyed a run-out at the expense of the flawless Rio Ferdinand and Carrick, before

Danny Welbeck replaced Young. The changes in personnel seemed to affect United's rhythm and Smalling caused a nervous moment with a back-pass before being booked for a foul on Kone. Jordi Gomez's free-kick flew just wide of David De Gea's right-hand post.

The final words belonged to United, however, and fittingly it was van Persie who rounded off the scoring. Rafael's flick led to an error by Beausejour, which allowed Welbeck to unselfishly tee up the Dutchman. The leading scorer stretched to send the ball back across Al-Habsi and wrap up a convincing victory for the league leaders.

The Teams

WIGAN ATHLETIC: Al-Habsi, Caldwell (Stam 69), Boyce, Ramis, Figueroa, McCarthy, Maloney (McManaman 86), McArthur, Beausejour, Kone, Di Santo (Gomez 70)
SUBS NOT USED: Pollitt, Jones, Boselli, Golobart
BOOKED: Caldwell

MANCHESTER UNITED: De Gea, Rafael, Evra, Ferdinand (Smalling 68), Evans, Giggs, Carrick (Kagawa 68), Young (Welbeck 78), Cleverley, Hernandez, van Persie
SUBS NOT USED: Lindegaard, Valencia, Vidic, Scholes
BOOKED: Smalling

'This is a special team,' beamed Robin van Persie. 'Defenders are working their socks off for the midfielders, the midfielders are working for the strikers . . . Everybody wants to run and everybody has one target in their mind. We have to look at it game by game, but everybody wants to be champions. I feel that I'm surrounded by champions. They know how to win and that makes it really easy for me.

'Everybody's helping each other and everybody wants to share the goals. Look at the last goal – Danny wanted to give the ball to me so I could score. Everybody's like that – I'm like that, Chicha is like that. Everybody wants to share the goals and that, in my opinion, is the way to score heaps of goals. Hopefully we can keep it going. We've had a couple of games where we've had high scores, but we want to score even more goals because that could be vital come the end of the season.'

While the Premier League's leading scorer was quite rightly in upbeat mood after a resounding victory, his manager was staying cautious. The mistakes of the 2011-12 campaign remained fresh in his mind, not least because it was at the DW Stadium where a timid defeat had prompted the late-season collapse which handed Manchester City the title.

'There are seventeen games left and we have a seven-point lead. It's not what I would say is a healthy lead, but it is a lead and it gives us something to kick on with,' said Sir Alex. 'We just don't want to make the mistakes we did last year.' The boss also reserved praise for his goalscorers, each blessed with different attributes, but both equally devastating against the Latics.

'Chicha, as we've known since the day he came, is a penalty-box player,' he said. 'He's tremendous in the way he latches onto things and reacts to things brilliantly. Robin is a completely rounded footballer with his ability to make and take goals. His first goal was an absolutely magnificent bit of football, with his balance in turning the defender and then, no drawback, he just side-footed it into the net. It was a really good goal.

'We knew we were getting a top player, a major player, who was going to make the difference to the team. Those were my thoughts when we went for him. I knew he would make the difference because he's got maturity, great international experience and he's played for Arsenal for seven years. He's come to us at the very peak of his career, which we're delighted at.'

'Chicha and Robin were brilliant today, and it wasn't only about their goals,' continued Ryan Giggs. 'Their work-rate and the way they defended from the front and closed players down made it so much easier for the midfielders to put pressure on their players. They'll get the plaudits for their goals, but their work-rate was also important for us.'

Wayne Rooney's bid to further bolster the Reds' striking department stuttered as his recovery from a knee injury showed little sign of sufficiently accelerating to thrust the England international back into contention for the forthcoming FA Cup trip to Upton Park or, more gallingly, the Premier League visit of Liverpool.

'It's a surprise as he was meant to be back training now,' conceded Sir Alex. 'So he'll be out for longer than we thought and I don't think he will be fit for the Liverpool match. The injury is nothing serious. He just got clipped behind his knee. Nothing shows in the scan but he's still feeling it. Hopefully in two weeks it'll be sorted but nonetheless it's a loss.'

Though shorn of Rooney's services and faced with a growing list of setbacks in recent FA Cup campaigns, the manager insisted that he and his players were determined to end a barren run in the competition that stretched back to 2004. Though the Reds remained the competition's record winners, with 11 successes in total, the dearth of FA Cup winners in the United squad now rankled the manager.

'Rio has been with us ten years and never won the cup – it's amazing,' Sir Alex said. 'We'll have to do something about it. The cup is a tournament where form doesn't necessarily win games. Luck has a lot to do with it. We've had some hard draws – twice away to Liverpool, away to City and a home tie with Leeds, when I rested a few players and we were caught short. I think with a club like ours, the closer we get to Wembley, the better we become.'

Chris Smalling, whose only club-level experiences of Wembley had come in Community Shield triumphs over Chelsea and Manchester

City, echoed his manager's sentiments and set his sights on an increasingly elusive winner's medal. 'We need to make sure we get back on track in the competition,' said the defender. 'Especially as the league is going well and we're into the Champions League knockout stages. We want to do well in the cup as well. The FA Cup has always been a massive competition. We've not got an easy game, but I'm sure it'll be a good, competitive one. We expect a tough game. When I saw the draw I thought it wasn't the easiest one we could have had, but it'll be a good atmosphere and Upton Park is always somewhere I've enjoyed playing. Hopefully we can put on a good show at Upton Park.'

The FA Cup

Saturday 5 January | Upton Park | Attendance: 32,922

WEST HAM UNITED 2 Collins (27, 59)
MANCHESTER UNITED 2 Cleverley (23), van Persie (90)

One of the goals of the season preserved United's interest in the FA Cup, after West Ham had looked set to spring a comeback upset against Sir Alex Ferguson's Reds.

With United trailing in injury time, Ryan Giggs launched a staggering, pinpoint 45-yard pass towards substitute Robin van Persie. The Dutchman's silken touch beautifully cushioned the pass, before his pace and power teed up a clinical right-foot finish past Jussi Jaaskelainen to prompt wild celebrations among the travelling support and on the away bench.

The visitors' neat attacking play had warranted a first-half lead through Tom Cleverley, only for towering Hammers centre-back James Collins to head his side in front with carbon-copy goals in either half.

A United team bearing six changes from the Premier League win at Wigan began brightly at a vibrant Upton Park. After nine minutes, a sliding Chicharito couldn't quite connect with Chris Smalling's pass across goal, while West Ham quickly went up the other end and, from a corner, Paul Scholes cleared Alou Diarra's header off the line and Nemanja Vidic mopped up from the rebound.

United had the ball in the back of the net as the sprightly Shinji Kagawa picked out the run of Chicharito, who squared for Danny Welbeck to finish past Jaaskelainen, but the Mexican was clearly off-side and the goal was chalked off. As the Reds began to pile on the pressure, Vidic's header was cleared off the line by young Dan Potts.

The inevitable breakthrough arrived on 23 minutes, and in some style. Rafael and Chicharito combined down the right, and the latter's cross rolled invitingly for the onrushing Cleverley to steer the ball into the far corner of the net with an unstoppable finish. Yet, just as the game seemed to be settling into a promising pattern, United were pegged back. Just four minutes later, Joe Cole, playing his first game since rejoining the Hammers from Liverpool, crossed for James Collins to glance a header beyond David De Gea.

The interval arrived after much posturing from both sides, but little in the way of clear chances. Shortly after the break, Cleverley blazed over after impressive approach-play from Welbeck and Rafael to hint at a positive second period. Instead, the Reds were again undone by the combination of Cole and Collins in a goal of remarkable similarity to the Hammers' leveller. Lessons unheeded, United trailed with half an hour remaining.

Antonio Valencia and van Persie were duly introduced to add muscle and presence to United's approach, and the Dutchman soon got involved with a header that flashed wide of Jaaskelainen's post. It was the subsequent introduction of Giggs, however, which had the telling effect on the game. Mere moments after the veteran winger had seemingly headed United's final chance over the bar from Rafael's cross, Giggs half-volleyed an incredible pass to van Persie, who showed his predatory prowess to kill the ball and thud home a low finish to set up a replay at Old Trafford.

The Teams

WEST HAM UNITED: Jaaskelainen, Tomkins, Collins, Demel, Potts, Nolan, Collison, Diarra (Noble 73), J.Cole (Taylor 78), C.Cole, Vaz Te (Jarvis 61)
SUBS NOT USED: Spiegel, Reid, Spence, Lee
BOOKED: Collison

MANCHESTER UNITED: De Gea, Rafael, Büttner, Evans, Smalling (Giggs 78), Vidic, Scholes (Valencia 68), Cleverley, Kagawa, Hernandez (van Persie 68), Welbeck
SUBS NOT USED: Lindegaard, Ferdinand, Macheda, Young
BOOKED: Vidic, Scholes

'It was probably one of the goals of the season,' shrugs Ryan Giggs, looking back on Robin van Persie's flabbergasting leveller. 'We were going into the last minute, I got the ball and I just saw the movement of Robin. We probably didn't use Robin as much as we should have in regards to the runs he was making, which is only natural when he's come to a new club and he's a different sort of player, but his runs off the shoulder are so intelligent. As soon as I saw him, I knew where he was going, so I tried to put it in his path, which I did, but the touch and the finish were just clinical. He's been on – what? fifteen or twenty minutes? – one chance, bang, goal.

'It's something you do in training. Sometimes the pass comes off, sometimes it doesn't, but the special thing about it is that it came off in the game and it was such an important goal. He managed to finish it off. I've probably produced similar passes this season and they haven't been put away so they're forgotten about, but because Robin finished it off it makes it that much better. So, yeah, I was happy with the pass!'

At the time, any regret at having to shoehorn a replay into an already busy calendar was negligible, given the euphoric celebrations among United's players and supporters after nabbing parity at the last. Having twice succumbed to the Hammers' aerial aptitude, the Reds knew they would have to approach the rematch at Old Trafford with caution.

'They made this game hard,' admitted Nemanja Vidic. 'We always know that on set-pieces they are a tough team to play against, and eventually today they scored two against us from crosses. They scored from the second ball, which we should look at again, and we are definitely a bit disappointed. It's something to talk about. We have the height in the team, we should deal better with that, but most important is that we managed to stay in the game and I believe at home it's going to be a different game.

'It's a trophy we're looking to win. We showed today in how we celebrated the goal, and I'm hoping at home it will be a different game. I think we have a big squad and we can manage to have one more game. The goal is incredible. Robin's touch is magnificent and his finishing is top class. It's movement from the book, touch from the book, and goal from the book. It's something they can show to kids, how to move and finish in the last third.'

With the FA Cup saved and shelved for later in January, United's attentions could quickly move on. Robbie Brady was sold to Hull City for an undisclosed fee, but Sir Alex quickly insisted that another winger, Nani, remained a vital part of his plans, despite countless rumours suggesting that the Portuguese trickster would be leaving Old Trafford at some point in the coming months.

'We need a Nani,' stressed the manager. 'He offers something different from the other players. He's an incredible talent; the boy's a great talent. Obviously his people have been negotiating with David Gill about a new contract, but I don't know what stage we are at with that. But we won't be letting him go. Why would I want to let him go?'

Nani had sufficiently recovered from a hamstring injury to be considered for the ever-enthralling visit of Liverpool to Old Trafford, but Jonny Evans had sustained a similar injury in training and was out for a fortnight, while Anders Lindegaard succumbed to flu on the eve of the game. As he pondered his selection, Sir Alex conceded that whoever he opted for had to be able to help attain a positive result: the only thing that matters in such fiercely contested local derbies.

'It never changes. It's always an immensely important game and also intense and emotional,' said the United manager. 'Everything you can think of in a derby game will probably be there. Derby games are very tricky affairs – they always have been. I'm quite happy to play badly and win this one! At least we go into the game in reasonable form.'

'Reasonable' was something of an understatement for Robin van Persie, who warmed up for the game by picking up the Barclays Player of the Month award. Having bagged the winner in his first taste of the fixture at Anfield earlier in the season, the Dutchman would again look to exert his influence in a major fixture. But, with Liverpool marooned in mid-table and United locked in another title battle with rivals Manchester City, the build-up to the game raised an increasingly relevant question: which is the greater enmity – United v Liverpool or United v City?

'I think United-Liverpool was the top one for quite some while,' opined Paul Scholes. 'Liverpool probably haven't done as well as they'd have liked over the last few years – and they'd probably admit that. But it's definitely still right up there, it'll always be right up there. Whether Manchester City have overtaken Liverpool now, I don't know. It'll probably take years for City to create what Liverpool have done. But Liverpool historically are our biggest rivals; they're always the biggest games and the best atmospheres.'

Such occasions only feel like the biggest and best when the result is positive. Fortunately for United, that's exactly how the occasion panned out.

Barclays Premier League

Sunday 13 January | Old Trafford | Attendance: 75,501

MANCHESTER UNITED 2 Van Persie (19), Vidic (55)
LIVERPOOL 1 Sturridge (57)

Having appeared in a position of total comfort, United withstood an unexpected surge of second-half pressure to register a victory over Liverpool in a typically competitive clash at Old Trafford.

Robin van Persie slid home a well-worked opener midway through the first period to herald the start of United's dominance, and when Nemanja Vidic unwittingly deflected home Patrice Evra's header, victory appeared assured for the Reds. Daniel Sturridge almost immediately reduced the arrears with a close-range finish, however, to provoke a jittery atmosphere inside Old Trafford as the improved visitors took a stranglehold on proceedings and almost forced an unlikely draw.

Old Trafford's first match of 2013 got off to a quiet start on the pitch despite the wall of noise being generated from the stands. Both teams struggled to make an impact, but the Reds gradually began to take control of the game, and forged ahead with their first clear sight of goal. A neat interchange between Tom Cleverley and Danny Welbeck ended with the ball finding its way to Evra, whose low, drilled cross sped perfectly to the feet of van Persie for a crisp, swept finish past Pepe Reina.

The goal knocked the visitors out of their stride and galvanised the hosts. Van Persie fired over after an intelligent run infield from Ashley Young, while the impressive Welbeck had a shot blocked by

Daniel Agger and then rifled a left-footed effort over from a tight angle. But, while the England striker's finishing was off, his breathless all-round game meant a harrowing afternoon for Brendan Rodgers' defence.

Aside from a wild Luis Suarez volley, Liverpool never threatened David De Gea's goal in the first period. United, conversely, should have been further ahead by the break as Cleverley's superb volley sped narrowly by the upright, before van Persie's impudent backheel was blocked on the line and referee Howard Webb declined to award a penalty when Shinji Kagawa was prevented a tap-in by a hefty shove from Glen Johnson.

The half-time introduction of new signing Sturridge in place of Lucas changed the game's complexion, with Liverpool quickly carrying more attacking threat but leaving greater gaps in midfield. Andre Wisdom slashed a finish woefully wide after a lightning counter-attack from the visitors, and that miss was punished after 54 minutes. Martin Skrtel flattened the onrushing Welbeck as the striker sprinted to reach Evra's measured pass, giving van Persie a dangerous position from which to deliver a free-kick. The Dutchman's back-post delivery was met powerfully by Evra, whose goalbound header glanced off Vidic's face and nestled in the Stretford End goal.

Just as that appeared to be that, however, Liverpool hit back. Steven Gerrard pounced on uncertainty in the United midfield and motored towards goal, before unleashing a low shot which De Gea did well to reach, only for Sturridge to react first and tap home the simple rebound. A flare went off in the away end; Liverpool's fans considered the contest wide open again.

United had chances to wrap up the points – most notably when Reina impressively clawed away Kagawa's curling effort – but Liverpool began to enjoy the clearer openings, as Sturridge fired off target from Suarez's cross-field pass and substitute Fabio Borini volleyed wide after lax defending from the Reds.

Sturridge blazed over from a promising position with Liverpool's final chance of note, while an athletic back-heel from van Persie required alert fielding from Reina as the game wound towards its likeliest conclusion – but not before a nervy final half-hour for Sir Alex Ferguson and his players.

The Teams

MANCHESTER UNITED: De Gea, Rafael, Evra, Ferdinand, Vidic (Smalling 79), Carrick, Young (Valencia 46), Cleverley, Kagawa (Jones 77), Welbeck, van Persie
SUBS NOT USED: Amos, Anderson, Giggs, Hernandez
BOOKED: Evra

LIVERPOOL: Reina, Johnson, Wisdom, Agger, Skrtel, Gerrard, Downing, Lucas (Sturridge 46), Allen (Henderson 80), Sterling (Borini 62), Suarez
SUBS NOT USED: Jones, Carragher, Shelvey, Robinson
BOOKED: Skrtel, Agger, Johnson, Lucas

'People were talking about the Liverpool game and the points difference between us in the league, but you can pretty much guarantee that if you put anybody in a Liverpool shirt to play Man United then they'll give you a tough game,' says Michael Carrick. 'In some ways it's more of a cup tie than a league game in the way that the teams go at it. They're always tough games. They're not the prettiest of games, but it's just about getting the result and getting those three points.

'To get the six points off Liverpool like we did this season is great. It doesn't have to be the prettiest. We fought and scrapped for the one at Anfield, managed to get the win and we were hanging on for the win at Old Trafford, but we'd put ourselves in a position to win the game with the way we played before that.'

Central to that performance was Danny Welbeck – 'He was

fantastic,' purred Sir Alex – and the Longsight striker appreciated the relevance of the result in both immediate and historical senses.

'Liverpool are our all-time rivals and it is a great occasion for both cities,' said the striker. 'Obviously I know what it's like, being a Manchester lad growing up through the ranks. It's been drilled into us ever since I was a little kid. Beating Liverpool is really big for us and I'm delighted to get the three points. We had our game plan set up and I think it really worked well in the first half. In the second half, Liverpool got into it towards the back end of the game. It was tense. We could feel the pressure they were putting us under for the last ten to fifteen minutes. The main thing was to stay compact, get behind the ball and defend well as a team. I think in the end that's what we did. I think we dug in really well and it was a great team performance.'

Amid the collective gains, one divisive issue remained: who exactly had scored United's second goal?

'I'm claiming it because, to be fair, it's my header, and as soon as I touched the ball I knew it was going in,' Patrice Evra continues to insist. 'It was only after the game when I saw the replay that I realised Vida had touched it. I can't deny that, but to be fair the ball was going inside the far post even if Vida didn't touch it. This is what I think, and a lot of people texted me telling me it was mine.

'Personally you want to get the goal, but if I don't get the goal then I get two assists instead, and it's not bad to get two assists against Liverpool. Robin told me we'd been robbed. He said: "Pat, make sure you get the goal," because he wanted another assist. In the end, the most important thing was the three points, though, but if this goal was for van Persie or Rooney, deciding the top goalscorer in the league, then one hundred percent it would be given to the striker!'

'To be fair, I am not complaining,' smirks Nemanja Vidic. 'Patrice was on the second post and headed the ball and just as it was on its way to the goal I felt the touch. At the end, they gave me the goal. I said to Pat: "If they give me the goal then I will not complain."

I don't think he is happy. He has to think about it in a different way – it's an assist for him!'

Vidic's involvement in the game had been curtailed by a second-half concussion, but he was well enough to resume training the following day in advance of the Reds' FA Cup replay with West Ham at Old Trafford. Nevertheless, the Serbian would be a risk and, with Jonny Evans sidelined, it soon became apparent that Sir Alex's central defensive options were limited. In attacking positions, however, the boss had an embarrassment of riches to ponder.

'Both Wayne Rooney and Nani will play,' he confirmed. 'Both are fit. There's Chicha and Antonio – we've got a strong squad, you know. There won't be many changes, really. Wayne coming back is good news. He's been training for a week and looking good. As for Nani, he came back from his spell abroad, having a break in Dubai, and is really looking very good. So I'm fine and will play a strong team.

'Of course, we've got a big squad, but it's also an important tie for the club. We want to try and have a go at this FA Cup. We haven't had a run for a long time, two or three years, as we had some bad draws, of course. We're at home and we have got to take advantage of that. If we get through, we have got another home tie against Blackpool or Fulham, so there's a big incentive for the club to make sure we get through.'

The FA Cup

Wednesday 16 January | Old Trafford | Attendance: 71,081

MANCHESTER UNITED 1 Rooney (9)
WEST HAM UNITED 0

Just as Robin van Persie's first-minute strike had settled West Ham's Premier League visit to Old Trafford, Wayne Rooney's

early goal accounted for the Hammers in a tense FA Cup third round replay.

In his first appearance since United's 1-1 draw against Swansea before Christmas, Rooney tapped home the only goal of the game just nine minutes in to earn the Reds a fourth round tie against Fulham. The striker also squandered a chance to put the game beyond doubt when he sent a penalty kick sailing over the bar on 79 minutes, ensuring a tense finale.

Sir Alex Ferguson made ten changes from the side that beat Liverpool three days earlier, with only right-back Rafael keeping his place, while West Ham boss Sam Allardyce also rotated his personnel in a number of positions.

Like Rooney, Anderson had been battling back to full fitness over the festive period, and the Brazilian played a major role in the game's only goal. His defence-splitting pass released Javier Hernandez, and the Mexican unselfishly drew Jussi Jaaskelainen from his goal before squaring to Rooney for a simple conversion.

Despite the quick breakthrough, the goal seemed to have little positive effect on the game. The Reds didn't threaten again until Nani's superb volley was blocked on the line by Daniel Potts, shortly before Chris Smalling met Rafael's cross eight yards out but could only head straight at Jaaskelainen. Before the break, Nani let fly with a speculative 25-yard effort, Rooney forced Jaaskelainen into a smart stop from similar distance and Anderson squandered a half-chance after linking well with Chicharito. In contrast, West Ham failed to test Anders Lindegaard at all in the first period.

The Reds should have been 2-0 up inside three minutes of the restart, but wayward finishing by Hernandez meant Alou Diarra's error on the edge of his penalty area went unpunished. There followed a spell of sustained West Ham pressure, although solid United defending – particularly from Phil Jones – kept the visitors at arm's length. Matt Taylor came close with a curling effort, then even closer with a cross-shot which Rafael repelled from his own goal-line, and the Brazilian then contributed at the other end by setting up Chicharito for an effort which Jaaskelainen bravely smothered.

Ryan Giggs, who was outstanding all evening, rolled back the years with a mazy dribble in the lead-up to the late penalty, won after the Welshman's cross struck young defender Jordan Spence on the hand. Rooney stepped forward to seal victory but blazed his kick over the bar. Ultimately, it didn't affect the final result; United hung on and remained on the road to Wembley. Next up, Fulham at Old Trafford.

The Teams

MANCHESTER UNITED: Lindegaard, Rafael, Büttner, Jones, Smalling, Valencia, Anderson (Carrick 67), Giggs, Nani (Scholes 77), Rooney, Hernandez
SUBS NOT USED: Amos, van Persie, Welbeck, Kagawa, Ferdinand
BOOKED: Scholes

WEST HAM UNITED: Jaaskelainen, Reid, Tomkins, Spence, Potts, Taylor, Diame (Collison 65), Diarra, O'Neil, C.Cole (Nolan 65), Vaz Te (Lee 78)
SUBS NOT USED: Spiegel, Jarvis, Demel, Lletget
BOOKED: Nolan, Spence

Beyond United's progress to another all-Premier League tie, much of the post-match debate was dominated by the incredible Ryan Giggs, who turned in another age-defying display to inspire the Reds' passage to the fourth round.

'He will play for another year,' Sir Alex confidently stated. 'There are no discerning signs of tiredness or weakness in his game, his quality is still there and he has fantastic balance. He has the appetite for it and he is just an incredible human being.'

Looking back, Giggs admits: 'I enjoyed the game, and like a lot of games this season I felt stronger as the game wore on and I think that's credit to the lads who keep you fit when you're not playing, and also credit to yourself for keeping yourself fit and being ready whenever you're called upon, because it can be tough. You build yourself up to maybe playing against Liverpool, get ready for that game and then you don't play, then you're getting yourself up for a game three days later. Mentally it's not a problem, it's just physically you need to be on that boiling point where you've got to be ready, match-fit, so it's hard to get your training in because you can't just be at the same high level all week, you've got to be up and down and make sure that you're peaking come the match.

'I want to obviously still contribute, I want to make sure this team wins things. I'm conscious of all those things, playing my fair share of games, so these are all matters that I take into account when deciding about carrying on playing and obviously the manager does as well. It's a two-way thing really, where if the manager wants me to carry on and I want to carry on then that's what we've done. It's obviously nice to hear praise from the manager, whatever age you are.'

At the opposite end of the age scale were Phil Jones and Chris Smalling – whose combined age was just four years greater than Giggs's. Nevertheless, their display against the Hammers at the heart of the United defence also drew commendations from Sir Alex.

'Jones and Smalling were fantastic, absolutely brilliant,' he said. 'The two of them were absolutely marvellous and I couldn't be more pleased. They have been injured for a while and needed games, so today would only help them. We have several other players who needed a game, like Nani, Rooney, Anderson and Büttner. So we had six players who had a run-out at a crucial time of the season with Real Madrid coming up and Tottenham on Sunday, so that is good news for us.'

The victory over the Hammers kept the Reds chugging along on three fronts, and the Carrington dressing room was abuzz as the season prepared to enter a hectic, but thrilling phase. Next up, the increasingly tricky trip to face Tottenham at White Hart Lane.

'The reason you come to United is to play in big games every week in different competitions,' said Phil Jones. 'As well as league games and FA Cup matches we've got two massive games coming up against Real Madrid and they're all matches that, if I'm involved, I'll relish. Personally, it was good to get another full game in against West Ham and good to be playing at centre-back, which is a position I always enjoy.

'I was just pleased to get a run-out. It's been so frustrating to be out injured – I'm a nightmare patient! But I feel fit and strong and hopefully I can get a good run in the side between now and the end of the season. It's great to come back into a team that's doing so well and playing so well. It's a nice feeling to be top of the league and hopefully we can keep things going this weekend.

'Spurs have done well this season. They've got some brilliant individual players and we'll have to be wary of them all. It'll be a test for whoever comes up against Gareth Bale – he's a great player. They have a lot of good individual players, but if we work collectively as a team hopefully we can stop him. The most important thing for us is to concentrate on what we're about and how we'll approach the game.'

While the journey south came too soon for Jonny Evans, the shock team news bulletin ahead of the game featured Darren Fletcher, who would miss the remainder of the campaign after undergoing surgery to resolve his ulcerative colitis condition. The procedure was carefully planned, and despite its severity a club statement stressed that the Scottish international was working towards a return for the 2013-14 campaign.

'This improves Darren's prospects of returning to his best,' explained Sir Alex. 'He had to change his game and he hasn't been the Darren Fletcher of three or four years ago in the games this season. Instead, he was sitting in front of the back four and he did well. That could be his role in the future. When he comes back, and I hope he does, it will be in a different role.

'It was something we thought would happen anyway. He tried his best to cope with the condition with the treatments he was using but, in the last couple of weeks, it's come back. This operation will hopefully solve the situation and we expect him to be back in July. It's a blow for the boy, but given he's been dealing with the condition for a few years, it's just another step for him. He has fantastic character, he's a brilliant boy. He'll do his best, no doubt about that. He always does.'

In the short term, however, the manager needed to address the considerable task of facing Tottenham. 'I've watched quite a few of their games and their form has been consistent,' he warned. 'They're in good form and I think they'll challenge for the top four. Villas-Boas has Spurs in the way he wants them and I think there are signs they're playing how he wants them to play. That's what a coach wants to do – get his philosophy across.

'We have a fantastic record there, though. It's a stadium that's old-fashioned, football-wise, like Aston Villa and Everton. There's always a good atmosphere and we enjoy playing there. But we can't take anything for granted. We have a hard game on Sunday. We have to perform.'

Barclays Premier League

Sunday 20 January | White Hart Lane | Attendance: 35,956

TOTTENHAM HOTSPUR 1 Dempsey (90)
MANCHESTER UNITED 1 Van Persie (25)

A last-gasp equaliser from Clint Dempsey undid an afternoon of sterling resistance from United, snatching away two points after

Robin van Persie had seemed set to give the Reds an impressive away victory.

The Dutchman's superb header had the visitors ahead midway through the first period, and the lead was only preserved by a solid defensive display from the entire United side – David De Gea in particular – before Dempsey turned home a leveller in injury time to send a snow-swept White Hart Lane wild.

The snow blanketing North London had initially cast doubt on the game going ahead, but referee Chris Foy gave the green light after a pitch inspection an hour before kick-off. In the opening exchanges, neither side seemed to fully get to grips with the conditions, with possession see-sawing and chances at a premium. A glancing header from van Persie after ten minutes failed to trouble Tottenham keeper Hugo Lloris, and at the other end the lively Aaron Lennon forced a parried save from De Gea.

Just as Tottenham began to take control of proceedings, United forged ahead. Danny Welbeck neatly worked the ball out to Tom Cleverley on the right and the midfielder crossed perfectly for van Persie to head home from a tight angle at the far post. Deadlock broken, both sides were galvanised. United's play began to carry greater zip and purpose, but Spurs reminded the visitors of their perennial menace when De Gea had to improvise to save with his legs from Gareth Bale's right-foot shot from the edge of the area.

Andre Villas-Boas's side then piled on the pressure in the second half; just 30 seconds after the restart, Jermain Defoe engineered space for a shot but fired wide, then Bale curled an effort just over the bar, before Dempsey forced a world-class close-range stop, again with his feet, from De Gea.

United repeatedly had openings to counter-attack at pace, but each time the Reds' final ball was found wanting or the wrong decision was taken at a crucial time. Wayne Rooney was introduced in place of Shinji Kagawa, and the striker had been on the pitch for a matter of seconds when he had a strong claim for a penalty turned down after tangling with Spurs defender Steven Caulker in the area.

There was undoubted danger in the visitors' counter-attacking play, but still their lead remained a precarious one. Another forward surge from Lennon fed Defoe in the area, only for a superb piece of last-ditch defending from Rio Ferdinand to block the striker's effort as he appeared poised to level the scores. That appeared to be that, as United's well-marshalled defence rode out the storm until the final minute of stoppage time, when Benoit Assou-Ekotto's deep cross was punched by De Gea to Lennon, who had the awareness to square for Dempsey to slide home a leveller and undo so much resilient work from the league leaders.

The Teams

TOTTENHAM HOTSPUR: Lloris, Walker, Naughton (Assou-Ekotto 64), Dawson, Caulker, Dempsey, Lennon, Parker (Huddlestone 80), Bale, Defoe, Dembele
SUBS NOT USED: Friedel, Vertonghen, Sigurdsson, Livermore, Townsend
BOOKED: Dawson

MANCHESTER UNITED: De Gea, Rafael, Evra, Ferdinand, Vidic, Jones, Carrick, Cleverley (Valencia 74), Kagawa, (Rooney 62), Welbeck, van Persie
SUBS NOT USED: Lindegaard, Anderson, Giggs, Smalling, Hernandez
BOOKED: Rafael, Evra, Carrick, Rooney

'I think we played well and it is always a hard place to go,' reflects Nemanja Vidic. 'I think apart from the final five or ten minutes, we did well and didn't let them create many chances and didn't have anything to be scared of. In the end, we conceded that silly goal, but I thought it was a good performance from the team. Our shape was good and I thought we played a good game.'

At the time, the Serbian's manager was left with mixed emotions as he lamented a missed opportunity while also acknowledging a positive result. 'We had the opportunity to kill them off on the counter-attack but our final ball let us down,' said Sir Alex. 'We worked really hard, as did Tottenham. It was a really difficult, gruelling game but we dealt with everything they did.

'They kept pumping that ball in the box and we kept heading it out. Unfortunately, we didn't get that last one that really mattered, the last kick of the game. It's not an easy place to come to. There was a good quality to the match in terms of the commitment of both sets of players. It was a difficult game but unfortunately we didn't hold on for that extra minute. We've been to all the top teams' grounds now; we've just got Arsenal left. I think we can be pleased with the outcome and the points total in all of them.'

The boss also referenced the display of referee's assistant Simon Beck, and voiced his displeasure at the official's failure to award a penalty for a clear trip on Wayne Rooney. 'There was no way the linesman was going to give that – he gave them everything,' said Sir Alex. 'It was a clear decision. And he was ten, maybe twelve, yards away from the incident and he doesn't give it. And yet he gave everything else. I am disappointed with him – we have not had a good record with him. With Chelsea a couple of years back, he gave onside to Didier Drogba and he was three yards offside. You remember these things, because it is in important games and that was an important game.'

Before the month was out, the boss would be charged by the Football Association for his statement and, though he denied the charge, was subsequently fined £12,000 for his comments. By the time the FA imposed the charge, United had already jetted off for a mid-season training camp in Qatar, leaving behind the cascading snow for bone-warming sunshine in the Middle East.

'I think it will be an important break for us,' said Michael Carrick, before wryly adding: 'We can get the sun cream out hopefully, and get out on the beach and relax a bit! It's a busy season and there are busy times ahead. It's about recuperating and getting ready for the next game.'

Indeed, United were looking even further ahead, and in the absence of Sir Alex and his players, chief executive David Gill wrapped up the Reds' first and final foray into the January transfer market, signing Crystal Palace winger Wilfried Zaha and immediately loaning the youngster back to the Eagles until the end of the season.

Shedding light on United's pursuit and capture of the player, Gill reveals: 'He's a player we knew and Alex had been following. We'd seen him and we felt he was a young, English talent and we'd watched him when he played in the play-offs against Cardiff, for example. We were scouting him a lot in the Championship – a lot of teams were – and we just felt that because of his age, his potential and what he can bring to Manchester United it was the right thing to do – even if he's still quite raw in a lot of respects, as a young man.

'Seeing where our squad was at, it wasn't appropriate to bring him in in January; it was better for him to continue playing with Palace before joining us in the summer. So we did a deal and that was a precondition, really. We were very happy when we spoke to the chairman of Palace that it was only to be done on that basis. We've done that and it's going to be a big learning curve for him. I think he knows that and I think he's had ups and downs in form since the deal was announced.

'I think he's going to be an exciting Manchester United player; that's our view. He's something different. He can beat a man, he can play in the middle or wide. It's great for us. It's quite interesting that in a recent England game we had five players in the team, which is good for us. The backbone of Manchester United has always been this way. Matt Busby had it and Alex has nurtured it himself; this mix between British or English players and foreigners, and that's what this club is about.'

Having enlisted a new forward, Sir Alex's plans for the post-Qatar visit of Fulham in the fourth round of the FA Cup would include facing a former United attacker: Dimitar Berbatov. The Bulgarian's four-season stint at Old Trafford had ended with a summer transfer to Craven Cottage, where he had shone as the main man in Martin Jol's side.

'I think Berbatov is Fulham's best player,' stated the manager. 'I don't think he was a failure here. He did a great job here. He's a really good player, but the problem was that I had choices and it's never easy at his age to be a part of those choices if he is not play-ing. Therefore, we were happy enough that he wanted first-team football and we gave him the opportunity to go to Fulham. I think, at his age, it was the right thing to do. Fulham is a club that is ambi-tious. Some people like to see players run through brick walls all the time. Dimitar is not that type of player, but he is a very talented player and he had a decent goalscoring record here, we must remem-ber that.'

The manager was still unable to include Jonny Evans and Ashley Young in his plans to face Berbatov et al, but was in upbeat mood after a successful sunshine jaunt with his squad. 'We had a good week training in Qatar and it was a great time to go there,' he said. 'We couldn't have picked a better moment, actually, when you con-sider the weather we've had here. So it's worked out very well for us and hopefully we get the benefit from that. It was always the plan at some stage to do that this January. It couldn't have worked out better for us.'

Suitably sunned and revitalised, the Reds were ready to continue a three-pronged assault on silverware.

The FA Cup

Saturday 26 January | Old Trafford | Attendance: 72,596

MANCHESTER UNITED 4 Giggs (3 pen), Rooney (50), Hernandez (52, 65)
FULHAM 1 Hughes (77)

United eased into the last 16 of the FA Cup with a comfortable fourth round victory over Fulham.

Ryan Giggs opened the scoring in little more than two minutes, converting a penalty after Aaron Hughes's handball, while second-half strikes from Wayne Rooney and Chicharito – the latter bagging a brace – ended the resistance of Cottagers goalkeeper Mark Schwarzer and his colleagues. The Australian stopper performed first-half heroics for the swamped visitors, repeatedly denying Rooney and Nani, while the Cottagers' only other consolation was a late header from Hughes.

Rooney proved United's match-winner with an early goal in the Reds' third round replay against West Ham, and the England striker almost repeated the feat inside a minute after sloppy play from Steve Sidwell, who managed to deflect Rooney's shot into the side netting after gifting him possession. Fulham's reprieve was only brief, however, as the subsequent corner led to the opening goal. Rooney's inswinging cross was inexplicably flicked away from Chris Smalling by Aaron Hughes, and referee Mark Clattenburg had little option but to award a penalty.

Rooney, having missed his most recent penalty in the third round win over West Ham, stepped aside for Giggs to steer home from the spot, despite Schwarzer's valiant attempts to save. Fulham's keeper made sharp close-range stops to thwart Rooney and Nani, but his colleagues continued to contribute to their own downfall and Damien Duff was fortunate to avoid conceding another penalty when he nudged Giggs's pass out of play with his forearm while deep inside his own area.

Nani and Rooney continued to ask questions of Schwarzer in a one-sided contest, but the interval arrived with the outcome far from assured. If Sir Alex's half-time message to his players hammered home the need to quickly put the tie to bed, it certainly registered. Five minutes into the second half, Anderson, whose string-pulling had been a fruitful first-half outlet, released Rooney with a subtle angled pass which allowed the striker to race towards goal, cut inside Hughes's challenge and bash home a left-footed finish which hurtled past Schwarzer.

The game's second goal had a decisive air about it, and so it proved as Fulham's resistance crumbled and two quickly became three. Nani's cross to Chicharito was desperately cleared by Hughes, and the Portuguese kept play alive long enough to find Rooney, then helped on the striker's low cross for Chicharito to hook a first-time finish inside Schwarzer's post. The Mexican struck again with 25 minutes remaining. Phil Jones's dominant header found Giggs, whose threaded through-ball released Chicharito to advance, cut inside and unleash a shot which nicked Hughes, wrong-footed Schwarzer and nestled in the Stretford End goal.

Fulham, to their credit, salvaged a modicum of pride when Hughes escaped Rooney's attentions to powerfully head Ashkan Dejagah's corner past David De Gea, before Rooney had a late fifth ruled out for a perceived foul by Chicharito. However, that decision had little bearing on a contest which had long since been finished.

The Teams

MANCHESTER UNITED: De Gea, Rafael, Evra, Jones, Smalling, Anderson (Kagawa 71), Giggs (Valencia 71), Carrick (Scholes 61), Nani, Rooney, Hernandez
SUBS NOT USED: Lindegaard, Ferdinand, Welbeck, van Persie

FULHAM: Schwarzer, Riise, Hangeland, Baird (Karagounis 46), Hughes, Riether, Sidwell, Duff (Rodallega 61), Kacaniklic, Berbatov, Ruiz (Dejagah 70)

SUBS NOT USED: Etheridge, Senderos, Petric, Briggs

'We got the early goal, which is what you always want, but we didn't really kick on from there,' Ryan Giggs opined. 'We had a couple of chances and probably should have been a little bit more clinical, but then in the second half we were. We could have been a little better in front of goal, but we made up for that in the second half. The FA Cup means a lot. We've not done as well as we should have done in the last eight or nine years. There are a lot of players that are desperate to win it. With the history that we've got in the competition, we should be there – we should be getting to finals. Hopefully, this year will be the year.'

Rather than focus solely on righting wrongs in the FA Cup, another Reds midfielder, Anderson, instead openly cast a wide net. 'We want to win them all,' said the Brazilian. 'We have unbelievable players. I know the boss has two or three teams. He doesn't play eleven players all the time, he changes players and I think he has an unbelievable squad. I don't want to be the manager at this moment because there are a lot of quality players. The boss tries to keep everyone happy. Sometimes that's difficult, but that's the club; this is Manchester United.'

Sir Alex duly confirmed that his team selections were increasingly proving problematic, and the form of Javier Hernandez was a particularly recurring poser. 'It's a terrible dilemma when I've got that lad there,' sighed the manager. 'Sometimes I leave him out to bring in Robin van Persie, but as I explain to him, we regard him so highly.'

In planning for United's next outing, against Southampton, Sir Alex would have to factor in an unexpected variable: the shock installation of Mauricio Pochettino as Saints boss in place of Nigel Adkins.

'It's a horrible part of the game in football,' said the manager. 'It's the name of the game that you want to do well with your own personal contribution as an owner or a chairman, and they want to still be in the division. I don't know a lot about Pochettino, but I will have a chat with my brother Martin, as he's been scouting in Spain. It won't matter in this particular game as he's only just at the club, but they had a fantastic response against Everton in his first game.

'We're not taking anything for granted. These are big games, massive games. Teams will drop points in the title race. Not just us but Manchester City will drop points, absolutely; it's a certainty. The important thing is accepting the challenge that every game is just as difficult as the rest.'

Barclays Premier League

Wednesday 30 January | Old Trafford | Attendance: 75,600

MANCHESTER UNITED 2 Rooney (8, 26)
SOUTHAMPTON 1 Rodriguez (2)

Wayne Rooney's double overturned Jay Rodriguez's shock opener at Old Trafford, but the Reds were forced to scrap all the way for a narrow victory over Mauricio Pochettino's Southampton.

After edging an entertaining first period, Sir Alex Ferguson's side were penned back for long periods as the relegation-battling visitors put in a breathless shift of harrying and pressing.

Southampton set the tone for a difficult evening for the hosts inside three minutes. Michael Carrick intercepted a Morgan Schneiderlin pass, but his volley back to David De Gea allowed Jay Rodriguez to nudge the ball past the Spaniard and roll it into an empty net. Fortunately for United, parity was soon forthcoming as the self-inflicted wound was partially healed. Shinji Kagawa collected a deflected Carrick pass and threaded a superb through ball into the path of Rooney, who fired a clinical finish past Artur Boruc.

Tails up, the Reds tried to press home their time in the ascendancy. Rooney touched on a Phil Jones cross to Kagawa, and the lively Japanese schemer was unfortunate to hit the inside of Boruc's near post from a tight angle. Southampton would not succumb to the building United pressure, and Gaston Ramirez smashed a free-kick over the bar, but the hosts decisively moved into the lead shortly before the half-hour mark. Van Persie's far-post free-kick was intelligently nodded back across goal by the diving Patrice Evra, allowing a simple tap-in from Rooney from virtually on the goal-line.

Evra and van Persie both fired wastefully wide from similar positions as United began to dominate proceedings. Kagawa profited from a fine Rooney pass to release van Persie, who was uncharacteristically profligate when presented with a sight on Boruc's goal. The Pole was then equal to Danny Welbeck's powerful left-footed effort, taking his side into the interval just a goal behind.

Pochettino sought to haul his side back into the game with the introduction of substitutes Adam Lallana and Steven Davis, and the impact was immediate as Southampton bossed matters in a chastening 25-minute period for United. Rickie Lambert brought two saves from De Gea and Davis was twice off-target with half-chances, while the Reds' first opening of the second period took until the 71st minute to arrive, as Rooney's shot was easily claimed by Boruc.

Substitutes Rio Ferdinand, Rafael and Nani were sprinkled into play by Sir Alex, with a tactical rejig sending Phil Jones into midfield, and United gradually established a foothold in the half. Nani was quickly involved with a cross from which van Persie drew a staggering close-range save from Boruc. In the same passage of play, the Dutchman nodded home Rooney's cross but was marginally offside.

De Gea spectacularly fended away Lambert's free-kick with Southampton's final attempt of note and United squandered a smattering of chances to add a breakaway third goal, but when three added minutes of Saints pressure came and went without punishment, the Reds could reflect on three hard-earned points.

The Teams

MANCHESTER UNITED: De Gea, Jones, Evra, Smalling (Ferdinand 63), Vidic, Anderson (Rafael 68), Carrick, Kagawa (Nani 73), Rooney, Welbeck, van Persie
SUBS NOT USED: Lindegaard, Valencia, Cleverley, Büttner
BOOKED: Rafael

SOUTHAMPTON: Boruc, Clyne, Yoshida, Hooiveld, Fox (Shaw 78), Schneiderlin, Ramirez (Lallana 46), Cork, Puncheon (S.Davis 46), Lambert, Rodriguez
SUBS NOT USED: K.Davis, Lee, Richardson, Chaplow
BOOKED: Schneiderlin

'In my experience at the club, when we're going for championships there's always a game where you say to yourself: "We were a bit lucky," and I think this was one of those nights,' admitted Sir Alex. 'I thought Southampton, in the second half, gave the best perform-ance anyone's given here this season. I think they pushed right on top of us and didn't give us time to settle.

'In the second half, the players just found the pitch impossible. Once the pitch started to dry out, the players found it difficult to play a different way and it really required us to play the ball into the gaps, which we don't normally do. We can't use the pitch as an excuse, but it didn't help us. It's a worry. We've won the game and I think that's the one thing we can take out of it.'

Skipper Nemanja Vidic peered a little deeper for positives, high-lighting the determination on show in the way the Reds rode out an average performance and clung on to three points. 'We had to fight to win this game at the end,' the Serbian admitted. 'Sometimes it's important to win this type of game. Obviously, the performance in the second half, we're not really pleased with, but we have to be pleased with the result. We're in a good position now.'

And how. The Reds' late concession of two points at Spurs had been unpunished, with Manchester City and Chelsea both slipping to damaging draws themselves, at QPR and Reading respectively, and victory over the Saints took United's lead back up to a healthy seven points.

'It's important to win games, especially at this stage of the season, and every game now is important,' urged Vidic. 'We know that we have to forget the games that come before and always focus on the next ones. Nothing is finished yet. There is a long way to go, but we're in a good position.'

8

February

Well placed to contend on three fronts as the business end of the season hoved into view, United's players could direct their focus solely on football following the completion of the Carrington training complex. An extensive renovation, costing in excess of £20 million, had taken over a year to vastly enhance the complex, which had already been considered one of the leading training centres in the country. While steps had been taken to minimise disruption for all attendees to Carrington, there was inevitably a sense of respite among staff and players to finally lift the curtain on the new-look facility.

'It is a relief to have it finished after a year or so, and I think they've done a great job,' says Ryan Giggs, looking out over the balcony to the enhanced forecourt. 'We had all the builders and coming into a building site every day, but we knew that it was going to be finished and it was going to be a lot better environment to work and train in, so we're really pleased with it.'

'The club did it in a way which didn't really affect us too much,' adds Michael Carrick. 'The first-team changing room wasn't altered at all – that had been done already – so it was more just in and around the place, like the canteen. Instead, we used a canteen in the portakabins, so the food was just as good and it didn't change too much to be honest.

'They did a good job. It's nice to be finished so we can get back into the routine of being in the same building all the time, not having to go outside – especially in bad weather that little walk across to the portakabins was a killer – but now it's done and finished it's a good place to come and work. You can't complain about calling this place your office!'

While the training centre was in spruce condition, the same could not be said of the Old Trafford turf, which had suffered amid heavy rainfall, frost and general inclement weather throughout the winter. The Reds' victory over Southampton had highlighted the patchy state of the pitch, and while discussions between Sir Alex Ferguson and head groundsman Tony Sinclair allayed fears for forthcoming home games, plans were afoot to re-lay the turf at the end of the campaign.

'It's not good,' said the manager. 'We're changing the whole pitch in the summer. We're getting more sunlight now as well and that will help in terms of regenerating it. It's definitely a bit worn out, in my mind. On Wednesday there was a lot of water before the game, which helped us in the first half. But in the second it dried out and that made it difficult for us. The groundsmen work their socks off. Tony's as concerned as anyone and he's disappointed with how it is at the minute. It's not been the same since that game against Newcastle and the deluge of rain.

'We've had this pitch now for a number of years and it's been great. If you go back before that we had to renew it maybe once or twice a season. Although that helped, it was never perfect. The turf would lift out sometimes. We've declined to replace the turf at the moment because we believe Tony will get it right. We've got the artificial lights on it all the time. We also have to hope for better weather and a bit more sun. That really helps. The more light we get the better it is for the pitch.'

Sinclair and his army of groundsmen would be mercifully given time to work on the turf at Old Trafford while Sir Alex and his players made the Premier League trip to Fulham. Wayne Rooney, however, warned against reading too much into January's FA Cup cakewalk against the Cottagers, who are renowned for providing a substantially sterner challenge on their own ground.

'At home, Fulham are a different team,' said the striker. 'It's always a difficult game there. It's a smaller pitch and a compact stadium. That suits them. They've got players who can take the ball between the lines because the pitch isn't as big and then create chances. It will be a completely different game. They are down near the bottom so they will be fighting to get one or three points. We will need to make sure we are at our best to beat them.'

Having passed up the chance to take a penalty against the Cottagers in the FA Cup, deferring to Ryan Giggs so soon after his own miss against West Ham, Rooney also explained why he wouldn't be stepping up to the spot for the foreseeable future. After missing nine of 28 penalties in his Reds career, Rooney was handing duties to one of his colleagues.

'To be honest, it was my choice,' he said. 'It wasn't good enough. I went in to speak with the manager and said I'd spoken with Robin van Persie and told him he could take them. At a club like this, to miss two penalties like I did and not hit the target, it wasn't good enough.'

As far as Sir Alex was concerned, all he wanted was for his side to start killing off teams when presented with the opportunity. Be they chances missed from the spot or in open play, such profligacy had gone unpunished for long enough, in his eyes.

'It must be hard for our fans,' he admitted. 'It's the sadistic nature of our team. It was poor from us against Southampton, though. We should have been five-nil up at half time. A few times this season, we've been in comfortable positions but haven't dug our nails into the game. It's frustrating because I know we're capable of doing that. We've had opportunities to be better.'

With Manchester City set to host perennially tough opposition in Liverpool the day after United's trip to West London, however, a victory of any margin would be considered significant.

Barclays Premier League

Saturday 2 February | Craven Cottage | Attendance: 25,670

FULHAM 0
MANCHESTER UNITED 1 Rooney (79)

Some goals feel bigger than others, and Wayne Rooney's brilliantly taken late strike instantly bore the hallmarks of a huge moment in United's season as Fulham were narrowly overcome at Craven Cottage.

A hard-fought yet entertaining game had seemed set to end all-square, with goalkeepers David De Gea and Mark Schwarzer in inspired form, until Rooney pounced on defensive uncertainty from the hosts before coolly curling home a winner to send United's travelling fans wild.

The Reds almost took the lead after eight minutes as Nani's header from a Robin van Persie corner was saved by Schwarzer. Patrice Evra hit the bar from the rebound and Rooney followed that up with a shot that was cleared off the line. Seconds later, Evra had a shot stopped by Schwarzer, while at the other end De Gea pulled off two superb saves; first turning a long-range John Arne Riise effort over the bar, then brilliantly tipping Bryan Ruiz's low drive onto the post.

Inside a frenetic opening half-hour, Rooney unleashed a low shot that went just past the post, then thudded an effort against the upright from the edge of the box after good work from Nani and Tom Cleverley. When Brede Hangeland's skewed headed clearance looped onto the Fulham bar, the signs were beginning to suggest that United were in for a frustrating evening. Even the floodlights failed in a surreal interlude shortly before the interval, sucking the momentum from the visitors' game until the hour.

Having come close to breaking the deadlock for the hosts, Chris Baird blocked Nani's shot from six yards after van Persie's pull-back. Before long, Rafael cleared Ruiz's effort off the line as the game remained finely poised. Sir Alex introduced Ryan Giggs and Chicharito in an attempt to force the issue, but it was a combination between Jonny Evans and Rooney which ultimately made the breakthrough.

Philippe Senderos also contributed hugely, misjudging Evans's high ball forward and Rooney needed no second invitation to take up possession, advance menacingly into the area and curl a finish around Aaron Hughes, past Schwarzer and into the bottom corner before racing away in animated celebration.

The importance of victory was not lost on Rooney and his colleagues, who turned in a manful defensive display in the face of Fulham's stern last-gasp inquisition. Van Persie cleared a late Senderos effort off the line and Evans flung himself into a string of blocks to preserve United's advantage. Then Chicharito broke through and might have ensured a greater margin of victory in the dying stages, but Schwarzer saved smartly to preserve the scoreline, which was still just about enough to secure an invaluable three-point haul.

The Teams

FULHAM: Schwarzer, Riise, Senderos, Hangeland (Hughes 46), Baird, Riether, Karagounis (Emanuelson 68), Duff, Ruiz, Rodallega, Dejagah (Petric 82)
SUBS NOT USED: Etheridge, Frimpong, Davies, Kacaniklic
BOOKED: Baird

MANCHESTER UNITED: De Gea, Rafael, Evra, Ferdinand, Evans, Valencia (Hernandez 66), Carrick, Nani (Welbeck 84), Cleverley (Giggs 75), Rooney, van Persie
SUBS NOT USED: Amos, Smalling, Anderson, Kagawa
BOOKED: Rooney

'It's an excellent result for us and I'm very pleased with that,' reflected Sir Alex. 'Fulham have had a great home record over the years and that's a really important result for us. It was a fantastic, battling performance. There was a great determination about us. I thought they were really up for it, the players, making sure they weren't going to lose the game.

'When you look at our performance, you saw players who were prepared to put their body on the line. We blocked shots, had great headers out of the defence, it was a really determined effort by the players and we still played our football into the bargain. Fulham had some great chances, and our goalkeeper, Rio and Jonny were terrific. I think we've deserved to win, but it was a smashing game.'

Within moments of the final whistle, comparisons were already being drawn between Wayne Rooney's winning goal and a remarkably similar strike from Cristiano Ronaldo almost six years earlier. The Portuguese's goal – also a late winner – had been credited as a key moment in United's 2006-07 title win, and Rooney was hopeful of a similar significance being attached to his goal.

'It was obviously a little bit similar,' the England striker admitted afterwards. 'I think, after Ronaldo's winner, we went on to win the league and went on a great run that season. Hopefully that can happen again after today. I think, as you run through, that you always try and assess the situation and what you feel is best to do – if you feel you can score or if a team-mate is in a better position to score. But I fancied the shot and, thankfully, it's gone in. It did feel significant. It's a massive three points for us.'

Rooney also took time out to lend his voice to the chorus singing the praises of goalkeeper David De Gea, keeper of an invaluable clean sheet – a growing trend in United's season and the latest example of the Spaniard's glaring talent. 'He was superb,' stated Rooney. 'I think he's been great for us over the last few weeks as he's made some great saves. I know he got a little bit of criticism after the Tottenham game, but he made five or six world-class saves in that game and it wasn't the biggest mistake I've ever seen. We're all behind him and backing him. He's a great player for us and for the future as well.'

'He made some outstanding saves, especially the one from Ruiz, which he tipped onto the post,' echoed Jonny Evans. 'We're used to seeing that from him. We didn't necessarily think, "great save", because we're used to him doing that. I think people underestimate his shot-stopping ability.'

The importance of the Spaniard's heroics were further underlined when Manchester City unexpectedly drew with Liverpool, leaving the Reds nine points clear at the top of the table with the end of the season drawing ever closer. With some observers insisting that the title race was already becoming a procession, United's next fixture would prevent any such complacency from seeping into the Carrington camp.

Everton's previous visit to Old Trafford had been the Reds' penultimate home game of the 2011-12 campaign. With eight minutes to go, a 4-2 lead had the hosts on the brink of preserving a five-point lead over City with only three games left. Two goals in three minutes followed for the visitors, reducing that lead to three points which were subsequently wiped out and trumped by goal difference after defeat at the Etihad Stadium.

'I suppose you can go back through the whole league and look at games we slipped up on last year and say that game cost us,' admitted Jonny Evans. 'I suppose at the time of the season, that game came up just before the City game, although you could look at that one and say City cost us because we lost away there.

'The matches against Everton over the time I have been involved in the first team here have always been tough. They work really hard and put lots of balls into the box. They have played Marouane Fellaini up front and other powerful people like Nikica Jelavic and Victor Anichebe. You always know you are in for a physical game from a defender's point of view. We know it won't be easy.'

Sir Alex, meanwhile, was well aware of the threat posed by David Moyes's obdurate side. 'Everton are very experienced and, if you look at their record, they've only lost three games this season. They're obviously hard to beat. But the team is playing well, I'm pleased with their form and I'm pleased that the players we're changing around are buying into it well. They're all contributing in their own way and that gives us a better chance in terms of dealing with the various competitions we're in now.'

The players' understanding and acceptance of the situation stemmed from experience, according to Evans. 'In my first season after being on loan at Sunderland, we won the Carling Cup and the league and got to the Champions League final,' he recalled. 'That is what this squad is for. You generate momentum. At the time, I never thought there were so many games.

'We came through Christmas brilliantly. That is partly down to the squad and the manager being able to rotate the squad and having the confidence in the players so they don't feel as though they are fatiguing. They are always mentally prepared for all the games.'

Physical preparation could, however, be another matter. In addition to all the usual perils associated with a midweek break for largely meaningless international friendlies, Sir Alex also had to take into account Stuart Pearce's revelation that Phil Jones had suffered shingles – a condition similar to chickenpox – and would miss England Under-21 duty. While the media speculated about the probable length of the youngster's absence, the United manager could only bemoan the disclosure of such information.

'Phil Jones will hopefully be okay, irrespective of Stuart Pearce coming out and declaring he had shingles – which we thought was doctor confidence,' fumed the manager. 'We're disappointed in that, but it's not anything serious for the boy. It's a mild condition that has surfaced but he should be okay.'

Jones, like the rest of his team-mates, would be handed a further pre-match pick-me-up by another unexpected setback for second-placed City, who dropped points for the third game in succession with a convincing 3-1 defeat at Southampton. Against the same opposition who had blown apart the Reds' title charge a season earlier, United could move another huge step closer to title number 20.

Barclays Premier League

Sunday 10 February | Old Trafford | Attendance: 75,525

MANCHESTER UNITED 2 Giggs (13), van Persie (45)
EVERTON 0

Goals from Ryan Giggs and Robin van Persie moved United 12 points clear at the head of the Barclays Premier League table, as the Reds exploited Manchester City's shock slip at Southampton.

Against a predictably awkward Everton side, United looked for long periods like a side imbued with the right blend of attributes required to win silverware, rarely appearing in danger of surrendering a lead brought about by Giggs's opener. The veteran's close-range strike extended his record of scoring in every Premier League season since 1992-93, and preceded a well-taken second goal from Robin van Persie, who on another day might have plundered a hat-trick.

When, in the tenth minute, Wayne Rooney slipped a pass between two defenders and van Persie rounded Tim Howard, United looked certain to forge ahead. Instead, the Dutchman uncharacteristically smacked his right-footed shot against the upright. Three minutes later, van Persie atoned for his miss, latching onto Antonio Valencia's header and skipping past his marker before squaring the ball to Giggs, who controlled with his left foot before coolly side-footing home via the inside of the post with his right. Having scored in each of the Premier League's 21 seasons, Giggs could add another minor milestone to his mind-boggling collection.

In typically tigerish fashion, Everton responded well and Leon Osman's dipping 20-yard volley was well fended away by David De Gea. From the resulting corner, Nemanja Vidic made an exceptional block to deny Kevin Mirallas, and van Persie bravely flung himself in the way of a Darron Gibson rocket.

Sir Alex Ferguson had, however, taken steps to neutralise Marouane Fellaini, Everton's star man in taking four points from their previous two meetings with the Reds. Phil Jones was detailed with shadowing the Belgian, and the youngster carried out his duties expertly. For all Everton's posturing, their cutting edge was blunted. United's, conversely, was shown to be anything but in the final minute of the half.

Rafael ended a surging forward run with a perfectly timed pass into space behind the Everton defence, releasing van Persie. The Dutchman shaped to shoot but instead dragged the ball to the right of Howard and slid a finish between the post and the desperate lunge of Johnny Heitinga.

United's calm control of the game continued into the second period, although a rethink was required when an injury to Jones forced the introduction of Michael Carrick. Nevertheless, Jonny Evans twice went close to adding a third goal as his close-range header was kept out by Howard before his hooked follow-up was diverted from the goal-line by Nikica Jelavic.

Tom Cleverley was denied a spectacular volleyed goal from 20 yards when Howard stretched to his left and tipped the ball up and over the bar, and De Gea performed an equally impressive stop when he palmed out substitute Jelavic's long-range effort in his first meaningful contribution of the second period. With recollections of Everton's dramatic late comeback to pinch a 4-4 draw still so fresh in the mind, the final stages of the game were conducted amid a nervy atmosphere. Suitably educated by such memories, however, United stoically saw out the match to record a vital victory.

The Teams

MANCHESTER UNITED: De Gea, Rafael, Evra, Evans (Smalling 81), Vidic, Jones (Carrick 56), Valencia, Giggs, Cleverley, Rooney, van Persie
SUBS NOT USED: Amos, Anderson, Nani, Hernandez, Welbeck

EVERTON: Howard, Neville, Baines, Heitinga, Jagielka, Gibson, Osman, Pienaar, Fellaini, Mirallas (Naismith 70), Anichebe (Jelavic 57)
SUBS NOT USED: Mucha, Stones, Duffy, Oviedo, Hitzlsperger
BOOKED: Fellaini, Mirallas

'I was going to make about seven changes, but when I got the Southampton result, I felt this was a more important game for us because it could give us a comfortable lead,' revealed Sir Alex. 'We can make changes later on in the season. It is realistic; we knew that if we got a good result today then we'd be in a positive position.'

'We had to have the concentration: we knew what happened here against Everton last year, they're a tough side,' added Ryan Giggs. 'We knew that if we concentrated, we'd have a great chance. We played some good stuff. We had to really, against a very good Everton team. The main thing was obviously getting the result. The performance wasn't as important, but I think we played well. If we continue the good form and get the results, we'll be okay. We've been in really good form and we've got players on the bench or not even getting on the bench who would walk into any other team. The squad we've got at the moment is very strong.'

Having enjoyed an immaculate start to the month in domestic terms, United's players could now finally allow their imaginations to wander to the Champions League glamour trip to Spain to face the mighty Real Madrid. Los Blancos manager Jose Mourinho had been in attendance to watch the Reds' win over Everton and, having spent time with Sir Alex in the manager's office, admitted the tantalising tie was one to relish.

'We have to feel very privileged to play this match,' said the Portuguese. 'People think we're under pressure because one of the big teams will soon be out of the biggest competition. But Real Madrid and Manchester United staff, as well as the players, feel privileged. It's the kind of match you want to play and we have to prepare as best we can.

'It's such a big match. Everybody wants to play. Nobody will be tired. It's a match the world is waiting for. They are not waiting for other matches in the Champions League. So I hope we can give the world of football what they're waiting for. We've had so many matches between us, with Porto, Chelsea, Internazionale and now with Real Madrid. In every club I meet Sir Alex. I've won games, I've lost, I've drawn. I want to win and he wants to win. But I believe the loser, in the middle of being a bit sad, will have a little bit of space to feel a little bit happy because their friend has won.'

In contemplating the double-quick reunion with Mourinho, Sir Alex would have to consider the extent of injuries suffered by Phil Jones and Jonny Evans against the Toffees, after the former sustained a kick to the calf and the latter limped off with cramp. While United entered the tie buoyed by an increasingly handsome domestic position, Real trailed La Liga leaders Barcelona by 16 points – for Sir Alex, that put Madrid's focus firmly on success in Europe.

'I think their target is the European Cup,' he said. 'They got a bad start in the league and were chasing their tail a bit because Barcelona's form has been incredible. I think Jose has set his targets firmly on the European Cup, no doubt about that. It can be harder for us, but there's a bit of pressure for them, too. They play Barcelona next week and then again in a league game before we play them on the Tuesday at Old Trafford. So they've got a big programme them-selves. Maybe in Jose's situation he can make changes simply because the priority is the European Cup, but Real never want to lose to Barca, so he has to play a strong team in that game. But I think both teams are in a programme of playing game after game so it'll be interesting.'

The tie's most consuming subplot was unquestionably provided by Cristiano Ronaldo coming up against his former club. The Portuguese had gone from being the main man at Old Trafford to an equally prominent position for Real since his 2009 transfer to Spain, and his staggering goals return of fractionally more than one goal per game left United in no doubt of his danger.

'Ronaldo's form, I have to say, is pivotal to everything Real Madrid do,' said Sir Alex. 'His goal tally – one hundred and seventy-nine goals in a hundred and seventy-eight games – tells its own story.

He's a fantastic player and I knew he would do well and improve tremendously in Madrid. He was still youngish when he left us and it was obvious he was going to be a top player in the world, no doubt about that. When he first came, he was a boy who wanted to display all his tricks and technical abilities but, bit by bit, he overcame all the little flaws in his game because he's an absolutely rounded player.'

Ronaldo warmed up for United's visit to the Estadio Santiago Bernabeu with a hat-trick against Sevilla, but Patrice Evra warned against the perils of concentrating purely on the threat of the former Reds winger – even though he had been in contact with his ex-colleague ahead of the Reds' trip to Spain.

'We have already been texting each other,' said the Frenchman. 'I hope he will get a great ovation from our fans, because what he did for United was unbelievable. I miss him, too. We have played against Ronny many times in training, and me and Rafa know what he can do. He is a top-class player. For me, he is the best player in the world. He will be a tough opponent, but we have to make sure we are friends out of the pitch, and enemies on it! It will be emotional for Ronny because he loves Manchester United. I hope the emotion will get to him. That will be perfect for us.

'But you can't concentrate on pressure. Everyone dreams of playing in games like this. You just have to be a kid. Not on the pitch, of course! But before you start the game, you have to be like a kid who's dreamed of playing this game and so you don't want to miss your chance to do well. When the game comes, you have to be focused and concentrate because it will be difficult and we will have to fight to win. And when it's time to face Madrid, we will be ready when the referee blows the first whistle.'

UEFA Champions League

Wednesday 13 February | Estadio Santiago Bernabeu | Attendance: 85,454

REAL MADRID 1 Ronaldo (30)
MANCHESTER UNITED 1 Welbeck (20)

United established a slight first-leg advantage over Real Madrid after a captivating 1-1 draw which could easily have ended in a comfortable victory for either side.

Danny Welbeck opened the scoring with a deft header from Wayne Rooney's corner, only for Cristiano Ronaldo – who else? – to soar above Patrice Evra and power Real Madrid level within ten minutes. Thereafter, both sides were indebted to fine displays from their goalkeepers, with both David De Gea and Diego Lopez making a string of impressive stops to leave the tie tantalisingly poised ahead of the return leg at Old Trafford.

Sir Alex Ferguson managed to shoehorn Welbeck, Shinji Kagawa, Wayne Rooney and Robin van Persie into an attacking line-up, with Phil Jones and Michael Carrick providing an invaluable defensive shield behind the forward line. United's defence was creaking in the opening minutes, however, as Sami Khedira dragged a shot wide, Angel Di Maria flashed a 20-yard effort just past the post and David De Gea performed a breath-taking fingertip save from Fabio Coentrao's low, curling drive. Monstrous teenage defender Raphael Varane then headed over from a Mesut Ozil free-kick before, against the odds, United broke the deadlock.

A Rooney corner from the left flank was met perfectly by Welbeck, who rose above the static Sergio Ramos to head inside Lopez's left-hand post, before embarking on wild celebrations in front of the 4,000 jubilant travelling Reds.

Impressively, Jose Mourinho's side appeared undeterred by the shock of Welbeck's goal, and continued to pressurise the visitors before drawing level within ten minutes. After Di Maria had stung the palms of De Gea and Ronaldo had flashed a low drive just wide, the pair combined to draw Madrid level, with Di Maria crossing from the left flank and Ronaldo powerfully nodding beyond the helpless De Gea. The former Red kept his celebrations low-key as the Bernabeu exploded with noise.

In an exceptionally open game, the Reds still posed a strong threat in attack, with van Persie and Welbeck looking particularly sharp. The duo almost conjured up a second United goal on 34 minutes, as Welbeck saw his poked effort from van Persie's cross bounce off Lopez's back and drop just wide of the far post. Rooney dragged a low shot narrowly off-target from the resulting corner.

De Gea produced an excellent parry from Ozil and Ronaldo thundered an effort over from 25 yards just before the interval, which gave United the chance to regroup and shore up their approach in the second period. Welbeck was detailed with nullifying Xabi Alonso's influence in midfield, and the United striker did the job manfully, cutting off Madrid's deep-lying threat and forcing them to rely on the individual brilliance of Ronaldo and Di Maria.

The latter sent an impressive shot inches wide of the post with De Gea motionless, but United increasingly appeared in a position of comfort. Referee Felix Brych inexplicably opted not to punish Varane for hauling down Evra as the United left-back raced towards goal, a decision which not only denied the Reds a goalscoring opportunity but also the boon of a red card for the Madrid defender.

Seconds after Gonzalo Higuain had replaced Karim Benzema, De Gea spectacularly saved with his feet after Coentrao had skidded in at the far post to meet Khedira's dangerous centre. United's first substitution introduced Ryan Giggs in place of Kagawa, and the Welshman was afforded a warm welcome from the home support.

They were hushed, however, midway through the second period as van Persie was denied twice in agonising fashion. After his right-foot drive was pushed onto the bar by Lopez, the Dutchman scuffed a second effort past the goalkeeper from an inviting position, only for Alonso to save the hosts with a last-ditch clearance off the line.

As the game wound to its climax, both sides increasingly sought to land a damaging blow. Ronaldo blasted a trademark free-kick onto the roof of the United net and then, with the final kick of the game, van Persie almost snatched victory for the Reds with a shot well saved by Lopez. After a performance curiously tinged with both relief and regret for both sides, the deciding chapter of the tie promised to be a spectacular encounter at Old Trafford.

The Teams

REAL MADRID: Diego Lopez, Arbeloa, Varane, Ramos, Coentrao, Khedira, Ronaldo, Ozil, Alonso (Pepe 83), Di Maria (Modric 75), Benzema (Higuain 60)
SUBS NOT USED: Adan, Carvalho, Kaka, Essien

MANCHESTER UNITED: De Gea, Rafael, Evra, Ferdinand, Evans, Jones, Carrick, Kagawa (Giggs 64), Rooney (Anderson 84), Welbeck (Valencia 73), van Persie
SUBS NOT USED: Lindegaard, Smalling, Cleverley, Hernandez
BOOKED: Rafael, Valencia, van Persie

'I think if you'd said we would play out a one-one draw before the game, most of us would take it,' admitted Robin van Persie. 'Away from home it's a good result. For the people who watched that game, they've seen chances on both sides and I think it was a great game to watch. I had three chances in the second half, especially the one just after I hit the bar. That was a big chance: I should have put that one in. I just slightly mis-kicked it, didn't hit it properly. With a bit of luck, it could have gone in but it didn't and in the dying seconds the keeper made a really good save – I was counting on that one to go in.'

While van Persie could consider himself unfortunate not to have beaten Lopez, one man crucially had. Though it was only his second goal of the season, Danny Welbeck's header against one of the game's greatest teams was a moment that would provide him with memories to savour in the future.

'It is not something I think about at the moment, though,' the Longsight lad insists, looking back. 'In twenty years it will be something that I might look back on and think that was class to do that at the Bernabeu in the big game: Real Madrid v Manchester United. At the time, playing in the game, it was just another step. I will always remember [under-18s coach] Paul McGuinness, when I was preparing for massive Youth Cup games; he just said you need to play the game and not the occasion. Everybody always used to emphasise that when I was growing up. So I played the game and not the occasion, so it wasn't something I thought about. It was just like any other game, really. You go on the pitch and want to do what you normally do. You don't want to do complicate things, because football is a simple game and it is easy to complicate. I try to keep it simple.'

The outcome of the tie was far from clear-cut, however. Welbeck's goal had given United tangible reward for an impressive tactical display, but Sir Alex Ferguson and his staff could highlight positives and negatives among their players.

'I think it was an interesting match,' said the manager. 'There were chances at both ends. We sat back off them too much in the first half and they had a lot of play around the edge of our box which is not healthy or good to watch. It was unlike us in many ways, but we changed it around in the second half and put Danny Welbeck around Xabi Alonso. It made a great difference and the ebb of the game definitely changed. I've got to be pleased. The players dug in and got the result. It takes us back to Old Trafford with a great chance.'

Inevitably, much post-match debate centred on the goalscoring display of Cristiano Ronaldo, whose mixed outing yielded his side's leveller. The Portuguese admitted: 'I didn't celebrate because I played in Manchester for six years and it was very emotional for me,' while Sir Alex concurred: 'It was difficult for Cristiano playing against us, his old team. Maybe there was a little bit of emotion attached to it, but he was still a big threat for them.'

Ronaldo was unable to hog all the headlines, however, following David De Gea's superb display. While the quietly spoken Spaniard merely told the post-match mixed zone – a gauntlet of international press which every player must run – that he was 'very happy' with his performance, members of the British press managed to coerce goal-keeping coach Eric Steele into a more expansive conversation about the Reds' number one.

'He was born in Madrid, played for the enemy. There were all these different pressures on him – but you wouldn't have known,' smiled Steele. 'That [save from Fabio Coentrao] was the one. If we go one-nil down to Real Madrid after five minutes at the Bernabeu, that makes things a lot harder. He saw it late – one of their boys might have been offside in front of him – but he got a finger to it. Some goalkeepers may have had the anticipation; David also had the speed of the first-step movement and that great long reach to get enough on it. That's the fine line for a goalkeeper. That's why a goal-keeper can be a hero one moment and zero the next.

'There have been dark moments [during his time at United], but he has his family close to him. He doesn't read the press. Trust me; he's very mature for his age. He's had to be because you're not just replacing a goalkeeper in Edwin [van der Sar], you're replacing a legend. It's not just about the shot-stopping. There's more to it. Put it this way: if you think about what David has been through, he has to have inner strength. He has dealt with it. And he's such a likeable lad. He hasn't come in swearing and squeaking. He's just got on with his job.'

The improvement in De Gea's game proved yet more validation of United's longstanding policy of trusting young talents. While long-termism inevitably sustains setbacks, the rewards, ultimately, are often worth the wait, and at Sir Alex Ferguson's next meeting with the press, ahead of the Reds' FA Cup fifth-round meeting with Reading, he championed the performances of his twinkling talents against La Liga's finest.

'We're always patient with young players,' he stated. 'We're patient with Tom Cleverley. We sent him out on loan on four different occasions and he's matured. Now he's an important member of the squad. You have to show patience. If you think they have the ability then you have to be prepared to wait for that.'

Patience would be rewarded for several players ahead of the Royals' visit to Old Trafford. With three competitions still in United's sights, everybody would get their chance to contribute, and Sir Alex compared his squad with the most successful he had ever managed: that which had swept the board in 1998-99's Treble campaign.

'The squad I had then is not nearly as strong as the squad I have got today,' he insisted. 'But the reality is that we should not get carried away. There's a good spirit in place and they're all contributing. Whatever side I pick, we're expected to qualify. That's what happens at United: whatever team you play you're always expected to win. I went to see Reading last week and they're a team who are showing plenty of fighting qualities at the moment, as you'd expect given they're down the bottom of the league.

'We'll take nothing for granted. In the FA Cup, you always expect the unexpected. It happens so many times. You just hope you're not a casualty or a shock. We've had a few over the years. But I can't be more pleased than I am at the moment with the form and spirit in the place.'

The FA Cup

Monday 18 February | Old Trafford | Attendance: 75,213

MANCHESTER UNITED 2 Nani (69), Hernandez (72)
READING 1 McAnuff (81)

Second-half goals from Nani and Chicharito sent United into the quarter-finals of the FA Cup after a tense, attritional victory over Reading at Old Trafford.

Brian McDermott's Royals stifled United for long periods, but Nani, on for the injured Phil Jones, rifled home the opening goal after 69 minutes and superbly laid on the second just two minutes later. Jobi McAnuff struck with ten minutes remaining to ensure a nervy finish for the home support, but United held on to secure a last-eight tie against Chelsea.

Sir Alex Ferguson had championed the depth of the talent pool at his disposal ahead of the game, and sought to demonstrate it with eight changes to the side which fought out a draw at Real Madrid five days earlier, with only Jones, David De Gea and Danny Welbeck retaining their places.

In a one-sided start to the game, Chicharito and Welbeck both came close within the first three minutes, while Ashley Young looked certain to side-foot home the opening goal until Sean Morrison flung himself in the way of the winger's effort. Reading looked overawed and disjointed, but gradually warmed to their task. Still, parity was preserved only by a fine double save from Adam Federici, who first pushed away Tom Cleverley's low effort, then brilliantly plunged to his right to somehow turn Young's follow-up around the post.

The most notable incident of the first period, unfortunately, was the withdrawal of Jones, who was left limping heavily after a crunching, 50-50 challenge with McAnuff. The defender was replaced by Nani, who quickly let fly with an outrageous first-time volley which thudded off Federici's right-hand post. Clearly keen to impact on the proceedings, the Portuguese then forced Reading's Australian stopper into action with a vicious, dipping left-footed effort which was only just pawed over the bar in the final act of the half.

After the restart, Nemanja Vidic's heavily deflected header needed to be cleared off the line by Noel Hunt, Federici comfortably parried away Anderson's right-footed effort and Nani scuffed a shot narrowly wide as United gradually cranked up the pressure.

The dam broke with 21 minutes remaining. Patient approach work between Cleverley and Antonio Valencia culminated in Nani controlling with his left and firing a 15-yard right-footed effort into Federici's far corner. Joy and relief mingled as Old Trafford roared its delight. That bellow had barely subsided when Adam Le Fondre hooked in a shot which required a fine reaction stop from De Gea. Decisively, United struck again just seconds later, as Nani sped down the right flank and curled in a magnificent cross, which Chicharito reached ahead of Federici to nod into the untended goal.

Game over? Not quite. Hunt's troublesome presence prompted the ball to bobble off Chris Smalling, and McAnuff pounced, holding off the attempted challenge of Alex Büttner and steering a finish past the exposed De Gea.

United could and should have put the tie to bed in the dying stages, as Federici twice made brilliant saves from Chicharito; Nani volleyed just wide of an empty net and then thundered a free-kick just over, but still there was one major fright to survive as Nicky Shorey curled in a fine free-kick which pinballed around the six-yard box before deflecting behind. Old Trafford breathed a sigh of relief as United held on to prolong their interest in all three major competitions.

The Teams

MANCHESTER UNITED: De Gea, Jones (Nani 42), Büttner, Smalling, Vidic, Valencia, Anderson (Carrick 83), Young (van Persie 64), Cleverley, Hernandez, Welbeck
SUBS NOT USED: Lindegaard, Ferdinand, Giggs, Kagawa

READING: Federici, Shorey, Mariappa, Morrison, Kelly, Karacan, Leigertwood (Guthrie 63), McAnuff, Le Fondre, Hunt, McCleary (Robson-Kanu 70)
SUBS NOT USED: Andersen, Gunter, Pearce, Daniel Carrico, Pogrebnyak
BOOKED: Hunt

The 2012-13 campaign had largely been a tale of frustration for Nani, but the Portuguese winger had taken the chance to showcase his unquestioned talents in a match-winning cameo to take United into the FA Cup quarter-finals – much to the delight of his manager, especially with rumours circulating about the winger's Old Trafford future.

'His contribution was terrific,' Sir Alex said. 'Just after coming on, he had two great strikes: one hit the post and the other one was saved. In the second half he got us the opening goal and I had the feeling he would win the match for us. I think he deserved it. He's a fantastic talent. You could see he was right on form when he came on. He's a good addition. If he keeps that form, it makes my job more difficult.

'We want to keep him, there's no doubt about that. He's capable of scoring incredible goals. The boy has an incredible talent for winning matches. He's one of the best match-winners in the game, and I include the whole of Europe in that. David Gill's been speaking to his agent for quite a few weeks. It's entirely up to the boy – he has a year and a half left. I think he wants guaranteed first-team football. He can guarantee himself that.'

'The manager has told us that he wants to win the FA Cup and we are very focused on this competition,' explained the 26-year-old winger. 'We prepared very hard for this game and we did well to win, which is the most important thing. I have been injured for a long time and it is always difficult when you come back, but I've worked very hard, and part of what I did on the pitch was because I've worked very hard. I will continue to work hard to do my best. It was nice to help the team, it was a beautiful evening and I have to keep working hard to try and help the team every time I get on the pitch.'

While Nani was contemplating forcing his way into Sir Alex Ferguson's plans on a regular basis, another prominent Old Trafford figure had decided to lessen his involvement. After a decade as Old Trafford's chief executive, David Gill announced that it would be his final season in office before stepping into a non-executive role on the board and handing over his duties to executive vice-chairman Ed Woodward.

Having enjoyed a close relationship with Gill, Sir Alex Ferguson admitted his sadness at the news: 'David has been a magnificent chief executive,' he said. 'Him stepping down is a big loss to me, but the fact that he is staying on the board encourages me that the reason for his departure is heartfelt, that he believes it is time for the club to move on. If I could have found a way of persuading him to stay, I would love to have done that. But he has made his decision and I respect him for it.'

Looking back on that choice, Gill sheds light on the whys and wherefores behind it. Scanning the Manchester skyline from his Old Trafford office, he admits: 'I decided just before Christmas. I'd put my name forward for the UEFA Executive position and I was looking at discussing that, and really I felt that the time was right to move on. It's the old adage: better for people to ask why you're stepping down than why you're not. I've loved the club. I spoke to Joel Glazer and discussed it, and for everyone it was agreed that it was appropriate.

'It's a difficult decision because it's been my life for sixteen years, ten as chief executive, so in that respect it's been a marvellous experience. I've always understood that I'm here as a custodian for a period and sometimes you need to move on, and I think it's the right time in my personal life and I do agree that the club will continue to grow and prosper and that continuity is there with Ed taking over from me.

'We'll see what happens. I might be sat down in a year's time thinking I've made a mistake, but you've got to look forward and I'm very much looking forward to playing a continued part within the club, albeit in a non-executive role with the football club. I've got the duties of the vice-chairman of the FA, hopefully this UEFA seat and we'll see what comes out of that. That's a good balance for me. I love the game, I love everything about Manchester United, so I can keep my involvement with the club but also play a wider role. I don't have to deal with agents anymore, so that's a plus! You never know in life, but the most important thing in life is to make a decision and move on, stand by it without any regrets.'

While Gill's successor, Ed Woodward, is a comparative unknown quantity to most United supporters, his predecessor speaks in glowing terms of the new man in charge. 'I've known Ed for a number of years,' says Gill. 'He's close to the owners who worked on the takeover with JP Morgan, and he joined as chief of staff and he's run the commercial operation very successfully. There's been a lot of investment in that area in the past few years and the quality partners we've got, the size of those partners is first class. He's a young man, a very bright individual. What he's got to get up to speed with – and this is where I'll work with him closely – is on the football side of the fence. It is different.

'It'd be silly to say it's the same as other commercial deals, but I know he's got the acumen, the intelligence and the desire to do well, and the key thing for me is to make sure the transition is effective and efficient, because when I'm sitting in that directors' box I want to be watching a team that's winning! We don't want a team that nobody enjoys! It might not be the team that Alex and I put on the pitch in terms of the transfers and contracts, but it's a team that I love watching, and if we're winning and getting to finals, then great. We've got to make that transition, so I'll be helping Ed in any way he wants to take over and develop that aspect.

'I've introduced him to key agents we have, people in the game that we know about, people in the Premier League and these are all things we have to do, but without doubt he's a very bright man and he's got the drive and enthusiasm to do an excellent job. We're very comfortable with it in the fact that he's come from within the club. I think it's positive and shows what Manchester United is about.'

The ideal way for Gill to depart his role would be having overseen a fifth Premier League title of his decade as CEO, and after two promising results in the Champions League and FA Cup, it was back to the nitty-gritty of league duties with a trip to bottom-of-the-table Queens Park Rangers. With Harry Redknapp's expensively assembled side showing signs of gelling after two successive hectic transfer windows, there was no room for underestimation in United's preparations.

'We have to treat these games as we would Real Madrid or anyone else,' said Sir Alex. 'It has to be won. We want to win. That's what our job is. There is an absolutely brilliant spirit in the place at the moment and a good determination about us. We have a problem picking teams at the moment, but that's where we want to be. QPR are fighting for survival and we know it is going to be a hard game. That is what we need anyway. We need to keep the awareness on making sure we do our job right.'

Phil Jones's 21st birthday fell the day before the trip to London, but the England international was unable to celebrate the milestone in style, with the ankle injury sustained against Reading quickly rendering him a major doubt to be ready for Real Madrid's visit to Manchester.

'We're working hard on it and I'd say Phil has an outside chance of facing Madrid – no more than that. He won't be fit for the weekend,' Sir Alex said, gravely. 'He was going in too brave. He tackled awkwardly. He tackled with the outside of his foot. He has dangled his foot in there, so that is why he has ended up with the injury he has got. But he has the courage and willingness to tackle. Bryan Robson was exactly the same. Bryan couldn't see danger and neither can Phil. That is a lot to do with the courage they have. The great thing Phil has got is that he doesn't care who he is playing against. There is no fear about playing against anyone. We will have to wait and see. The Madrid game is two weeks away. A lot can happen in that time.'

Sir Alex would also have to factor in the absence of Wayne Rooney with a sinus infection, while Paul Scholes had been sent to a specialist to assess the knee injury which had ruled him out of the Reds' previous five games. Nevertheless, with spirits high and form building, the leaders visited the division's bottom team in ruthless mood.

Barclays Premier League

Saturday 23 February | Loftus Road | Attendance: 18,337

QUEENS PARK RANGERS 0
MANCHESTER UNITED 2 Rafael (23), Giggs (80)

Rafael laid claim to United's goal-of-the-season award with a blockbusting effort, before Ryan Giggs wrapped up an impressive victory for United at Loftus Road.

The Reds' rampaging right-back arrowed a searing 20-yard drive past home goalkeeper Julio Cesar midway through the first half to give United the lead at Loftus Road, and Giggs strode through on goal and converted a low finish to wrap up another confident win for Sir Alex Ferguson's side. The only blight on the afternoon was a hip injury to Robin van Persie, who was forced off before the break in a physical encounter against Harry Redknapp's struggling side.

Rangers had previously taken home points off Manchester City, Chelsea and Tottenham, and made an energetic start against a strong United side. It took the Reds time to adjust to an uneven playing surface, but still the visitors created the game's first chance as Nani's tame header from an Ashley Young cross dribbled wide. Chicharito then twice went close in quick succession, firstly seeing his header well tipped over by Cesar before being inches away from connecting with Nani's low cross.

United increasingly had the answers to all QPR's questions, and it was no surprise when the league leaders forged ahead. The manner of the goal, however, did raise eyebrows. Van Persie battled his way to the byline and his drilled cross was palmed away by Cesar, but as the ball bobbled out of the penalty area, Rafael sprinted into view and walloped home an incredible strike which carried the resonance of a thunderclap.

Meanwhile, van Persie had picked up a hip injury after stumbling into a camera bunker just beyond the byline, and the Dutchman eventually made way for Danny Welbeck – though not before his fabulous first-time volley from a Rafael cross was brilliantly saved by Cesar.

At the opposite end, United could also thank a heroic effort from a Brazilian, as Rafael hacked Chris Samba's header off the line and away to safety. Nemanja Vidic came close to doubling United's lead with a glancing header from Giggs's free-kick, and the Reds' dominance continued into the second period.

Nani's header forced Cesar into action again, while Welbeck and fellow substitute Wayne Rooney both had powerful efforts blocked in the hosts' area. Another sub, QPR's Loic Remy, drew a fine reaction stop from David De Gea to remind the Reds that their narrow lead was precarious. Heeding that warning, a second goal arrived with ten minutes left, as Giggs ran onto Nani's slide-rule pass, steadied himself and fired home from an unforgiving angle.

Giggs almost doubled his tally when his looping shot bounced off the bar, and Welbeck was denied by a last-ditch tackle from Samba, but the Reds had already secured a cool, calculated victory which demonstrated invaluable resolve heading towards the nitty-gritty stage of the season.

The Teams

QUEENS PARK RANGERS: Julio Cesar, Traore, Bosingwa, Samba, Hill, Taarabt, Granero (Jenas 46), Townsend (Hoilett 72), M'bia, Mackie, Zamora (Remy 61)
SUBS NOT USED: Green, Onuoha, Park, Wright-Phillips

MANCHESTER UNITED: De Gea, Rafael, Evra, Ferdinand, Vidic, Giggs, Carrick, Nani, Young (Valencia 67), Hernandez (Rooney 61), van Persie (Welbeck 41)
SUBS NOT USED: Lindegaard, Evans, Anderson, Cleverley

'I can't remember scoring a better goal,' grinned Rafael, after his blockbusting opener teed up another vital win. 'The one at Liverpool was different because it was a curling shot, but I can't remember a better one than this. I think it's my best. I just saw the ball coming towards me and hit it as hard as I could. You can feel by the way you hit the ball that it's going in. I just hoped it wouldn't deflect off anyone. It was a good goal.'

Just as pleasing was United's growing defensive resolve, after a third successive Premier League shut-out. 'We're pleased to not be conceding and keeping clean sheets. We want to keep that going and continue picking up points,' added the Brazilian. 'The more clean sheets we keep, the more it improves our confidence. That consistency really helps us. We just have to keep winning.'

For Michael Carrick, a key midfield shield to the centre of defence, winning ugly posed no issue. 'It was just a case of battling it out at times,' he said. 'Sometimes you have to do that. Throughout the season it's not always going to be pretty. Sometimes you have to grind out results, work hard and make the most of your opportunities. We were able to cope with QPR and, at times, we played some good football. At other times we defended well and played on the break. All in all, I think we can be delighted with how the day's gone.'

Firmly in the winning groove and increasingly obstinate in defence, Carrick's delight could be widened to a successful month in February. Two-thirds of the way through the season and fast approaching the home straight, United were proving tough to keep pace with.

9

March

As winter meandered towards spring, United's man for all seasons again confirmed himself as a force of nature. Ensuring he would represent the Reds beyond his 40th birthday, Ryan Giggs signed a new one-year contract to extend his incredible run as a one-club man.

'What can I say about Ryan that hasn't already been said?' queried Sir Alex Ferguson. 'He is a marvellous player and an exceptional human being. Ryan is an example to us all, the way in which he has, and continues to, look after himself. His form this year shows his ability and his enjoyment of the game are as strong as ever.'

Within the dressing room, the news resounded just as positively. 'He is Mr Manchester United,' said Michael Carrick. 'He sets the tone around the dressing room. He doesn't say an awful lot, but when he does speak, everyone listens and everyone respects him. It leads onto the pitch. Not many people have lasted as long as Ryan. You have to take it year by year and see how your legs hold up. He is a one-off.'

While it appeared that there was no end in sight for a player who remained as important as ever to the United cause, even at 39, a fresh career path was beginning to loom large, according to his manager. When asked if a coaching role beckoned Giggs, Sir Alex told his pre-Norwich press conference: 'That will happen; that's the plan. We've done the same with Nicky Butt with the Reserves and when Paul Scholes finishes it will be exactly the same with him.

'We're good at that – we've got several former players installed in the club in different capacities. I think it's important we have people here who have the experience of being a player here. I think it's important that if anyone has ambitions to be a manager, then you should take on different roles before you get there, almost as a preparation. He [Giggs] has got to take his badges and he should go to the business school in Warwick, which I think is a very good one. He should spend time with the young players in the Academy and therefore prepare eventually to be a manager.'

Firstly, Giggs would have to pass yet another milestone. Incorporating his senior career appearances with United, Wales and Great Britain's Olympic squad, the Welshman's next outing would be his 1,000th. 'Phenomenal,' muttered Sir Alex. 'It's unique in the modern game, but I think it's more than that – I don't think it will ever be achieved again by anyone given the way that players' contracts are played out nowadays.'

The boss went on to confirm that his veteran would feature against either Norwich City or Real Madrid in two forthcoming Old Trafford encounters. Phil Jones, conversely, didn't have the luxury of such a choice, with the ankle injury he sustained against Reading ruling him out of both games.

'It was silly tackle,' he admitted. 'I probably should have looked after myself a bit more. I will learn from it as an experienced head would probably not have done that. But I will learn from that. It [enthusiasm] is in me; I like making tackles, I like defending. Injuries are going to occur in football, so I've probably just been unfortunate, especially at the start of the season. I tried everything to make the Madrid game. I was on the treatment table, having massages, in the pool and in the gym. But it was just too soon for me and I was gutted.'

But while Jones was battling in vain, with his sights set on the glamour tie against Jose Mourinho, Cristiano Ronaldo and company, Patrice Evra was wary of losing focus ahead of the visit of Norwich, who had inflicted the Reds' most recent league defeat back in November.

'Every game is important now,' said Evra. 'I hear a lot of people talking about the Treble and this is the wrong way – you have to think game after game. If we start to think about Madrid before Norwich, then you lose to Norwich. It's a big game and we have to win – if we go into Tuesday after losing against Norwich, it's going to be a nightmare.'

Fortunately for Evra, the Canaries' visit would provide a dream warm-up, for one man in particular.

Barclays Premier League

Saturday 2 March | Old Trafford | Attendance: 75,586

MANCHESTER UNITED 4 Kagawa (45, 76, 87), Rooney (90)
NORWICH CITY 0

Shinji Kagawa announced his goalscoring menace with a beautifully taken hat-trick in a comfortable victory over Chris Hughton's Canaries.

Wayne Rooney's late cracker rounded off the scoring, but it was the display of Japanese international Kagawa which stole the show, particularly after his late redeployment in a central attacking role yielded two impishly taken goals.

Sir Alex Ferguson fielded a strong side despite the impending visit of Real Madrid, yet the game still began at a sluggish pace. Quarter of an hour had elapsed before visiting goalkeeper Mark Bunn was called into meaningful action, diving at the feet of Robin van Persie to prevent the Dutchman from reaching Rooney's neat through-ball.

In the face of a steadfast defensive display from the visitors, United's approach was stifled for the vast majority of the first period. Rooney saw shots blocked by Michael Turner and Russell Martin, while van Persie ballooned a wayward effort into the Stretford End and frustration was just beginning to grip Old Trafford when the hosts finally found their feet in front of goal.

Antonio Valencia meandered down the right flank, cut onto his left foot and curled in a chest-high cross which van Persie did brilliantly to reach. Though the Dutchman's light touch appeared to be an attempt at control, the ball fell invitingly for Kagawa to nudge a first-time finish inside Bunn's near post with the outside of his right foot.

The deficit prompted Norwich to abandon their stifling game-plan, instead embarking on tentative forward forays at the start of the second half. Nemanja Vidic was forced to clear with Robert Snodgrass lurking, while Jonny Howson's drive deflected wide off Michael Carrick before Martin somehow skewed the ball over the bar from Grant Holt's knockdown, though the burly striker was penalised for fouling Patrice Evra.

Sir Alex rejigged his side, with the introduction of Danny Welbeck and Tom Cleverley for van Persie and Anderson, shunting Rooney forward to lead the line and moving Kagawa to a central role. The effects were immediate and sublime. Having latched onto Carrick's searching pass, Rooney held play up and squared for the onrushing Kagawa, who stroked the ball past the wrong-footed Bunn to have Old Trafford roaring its approval.

Another Rooney-inspired charge forward then led to Welbeck forcing a decent save out of Bunn, before the United substitute wound through the Norwich midfield and teed up Rooney to release Kagawa. The Japanese schemer strode into the Canaries' area and lifted a delightful finish over Bunn.

Three deftly taken strikes of subtlety had given Kagawa his first United hat-trick, and Rooney followed them all with a fourth goal of more conventional glamour. Moving infield into shooting distance, the England striker whipped a stunning drive over Bunn but under the bar to set the seal on a thumping victory.

The Teams

MANCHESTER UNITED: De Gea, Smalling, Evra, Evans, Vidic, Valencia, Anderson (Cleverley 74), Carrick, Kagawa, Rooney, van Persie (Welbeck 66)
SUBS NOT USED: Lindegaard, Rafael, Nani, Young, Hernandez

NORWICH CITY: Bunn, R.Martin, Bassong, Turner, Garrido, Johnson, Snodgrass (E.Bennett 73), Howson, Pilkington, Hoolahan (Kamara 72), Holt (Becchio 90)
SUBS NOT USED: Camp, Whittaker, R.Bennett, Fox
BOOKED: Turner, Garrido, Johnson, Snodgrass

'Shinji has shown some class since he came over,' says skipper Nemanja Vidic, 'but in that game especially it was a great performance. He had a good interaction with Wayne, exchanging a few passes and it seems like they worked very well together in that game – especially for that finish for the second goal, which was really cool. I was not sure if he wanted to shoot or have a touch!'

Having been imported by United himself when he joined from Red Star Belgrade in 2006, Vidic knows as well as anyone that it takes time to adapt to life at Old Trafford. 'It is obviously hard when you change the league, when you change the country and it is sometimes hard to show your quality straight away in the first games, but overall in his first season he has shown what class he has,' says the Serbian. 'I think that game lifted his belief and confidence. He is a great player.'

For Sir Alex Ferguson, redeploying Kagawa in a central role behind Wayne Rooney provided further compelling evidence that the Japanese playmaker could be cut out for the role. 'Midway through the second half, I didn't think it would end up four-nil, as I think we were a bit ragged for that period,' said the manager. 'But, when we brought Shinji into central midfield, it made a difference to us and he ended up with a hat-trick.

'It's brilliant for him. The lad is a good finisher and his second goal was so composed and an intelligent finish while his third was absolutely brilliantly taken. It's been a great day for him. He got that injury around October-November and was out quite a while. It knocked him back a bit, but he's gradually coming back and I think you'll see a really good player next year.'

Next week was the immediate focus for the manager, his players and the world's media, with all questions revolving around the visit of Real Madrid, who had warmed up for their trip to Manchester with two eye-catching wins over Barcelona. Robin van Persie had been removed after an hour against Norwich, as agreed with the player pre-match, while Ryan Giggs was spared involvement so that he could make his 1,000th appearance in a game befitting of the occasion.

Sir Alex admitted: 'I think both teams will score.' He went on to comment that his side's defensive shape 'probably will be the key to the game. As we know, Real Madrid are one of the best counter-attacking teams in Europe. That showed itself last Tuesday [against Barcelona] at the Nou Camp – they were absolutely stunning on the counter-attack, so we have to find a way of coping with that while also having our own threat in an attacking sense.

'If you're preparing for a game of football at our level, you have to respect the strengths of the other team, which we do. Every team we play against, we do work in terms of their shape, their tactics and who their best players are. You're only doing your job. That applies itself tomorrow. We obviously know the sense of our team anyway – we know our strengths and how to go about these games, and hopefully that helps us.'

While fervour continued to build around a game which Jose Mourinho claimed 'the world will stop to watch', Sir Alex insisted that his coaching staff's experience and tactical acumen would prove worthy of the occasion, while also stressing the need for trust in and among the players.

'We must trust the players,' he said. 'That's what we always do and they must trust each other. That's why we've had continued success for a long period. The continuity of management helps – myself and the coaching staff are very acquainted with all the things that are needed to relate to footballers, whether it be on the physical side, the nutritional side or the tactical side. We have the equipment to deal with all things. I've made up my mind for tomorrow what the theme of my motivation will be and my tactics talk. Certainly part of it will be about trusting themselves.'

There was, of course, the small matter of dealing with Cristiano Ronaldo. The Portuguese superstar had been well shackled in the first leg, yet had still managed to score Real's equaliser. Shorn of the defensive midfield diligence of Phil Jones, United would need to try an unorthodox means of shutting down their former number seven.

'My biggest concern is that he turns up!' joked Sir Alex. 'What do you expect when you play against a team with Ronaldo in it? You expect problems during the night. We have to try and curtail that as best we can. It won't be easy because he does it every week, it's not an accident about the lad. I don't think it's one we should fear. If we go in worrying about the damage Cristiano can do then we'll forget some of the things that we can do ourselves.'

The manager did, however, come up with a tactical masterplan to nullify Ronaldo by getting into the winger's head. After consulting stadium announcer Alan Keegan, the manager stressed that both team sheets must be read out in a different order from usual. As such, United's team was announced first, then Real's, but with Ronaldo left until last, ensuring a rapturous reception which thundered around the stadium and was still murmuring when the game kicked off. Sure enough, Ronaldo's head had been infiltrated and his influence was minimal. Unfortunately for United, there are some things in football for which you cannot plan.

UEFA Champions League

Tuesday 5 March | Old Trafford | Attendance: 74,959

MANCHESTER UNITED 1 Ramos (48 og)
REAL MADRID 2 Modric (66), Ronaldo (69)

United's bid to reach Wembley ended in painful, controversial circumstances as a perfectly executed gameplan was undone by a staggering refereeing decision which provided Real Madrid with the platform to pilfer progress into the Champions League quarter-finals.

The Reds took a deserved lead shortly after half time through a Sergio Ramos own goal and had controlled the contest for the best part of an hour until Nani was dismissed after challenging Alvaro Arbeloa for a high ball. Within 13 minutes, Luka Modric and, inevitably, Cristiano Ronaldo claimed an unlikely victory for the visitors.

The Portuguese again refused to celebrate after haunting his former employers, but he had seemed little more than an apparition for long periods as United's tactical approach totally stifled Ronaldo and his colleagues. Many post-match column inches were devoted to the decision to bench Wayne Rooney, but United's control of the early stages quickly validated Sir Alex's approach.

It appeared that the manager had everything right. Even his instructions to alter the reading of the team sheets before kick-off had the desired effect, with Ronaldo making a string of early mistakes and turning in a generally low-key display. Danny Welbeck, a scorer in the first leg, was again tasked with limiting the influence of Xabi Alonso and the lack of cohesion in the visitors' play spoke volumes for the striker's diligence. United's attacking play promised more, yet initially spawned only a spate of corners. From one, Nemanja Vidic thudded a header against Diego Lopez's post and Welbeck's rebound was blocked on the line.

Real twice reminded of their threat through Gonzalo Higuain, who forced an alert stop from David De Gea, then had a goal correctly ruled out for a prior Sergio Ramos foul on Robin van Persie. United's riposte was to go straight up the other end; van Persie chested down Patrice Evra's long ball and beat Raphael Varane on the turn before lashing a left-foot shot at Lopez. Real's shot-stopper then reacted quickly to divert Welbeck's rebound out for a corner and from Ryan Giggs's inswinging cross Vidic headed over.

An enthralling first period could boast talking points and tactical nuances galore, yet no goals to emboss it. It took just three minutes of the second half for the deadlock to be broken. Welbeck and then van Persie had shots blocked, but when Nani collected the loose ball and fizzed it into the box, Welbeck's slight touch of the ball deceived Ramos, who inadvertently turned it into the net to send Old Trafford wild.

Everything was going according to plan, until the 56th minute when Nani leapt to control a high ball and inadvertently caught Arbeloa. Indisputable contact, zero intent, yet referee Cuneyt Cakir

Former United star Cristiano Ronaldo is closely shadowed by Jonny Evans and Phil Jones during a gripping Champions League draw in Madrid.

Having entered the fray as a substitute, Nani turns in a match-winning display against Reading to take the Reds into the FA Cup quarter-finals.

Did you see that? Rio Ferdinand congratulates Rafael after the right-back's unbelievable strike at Loftus Road.

Shinji Kagawa strokes home a beautiful second goal against Norwich, en route to bagging his first United hat-trick.

Danny Welbeck stars against Real Madrid again, but his fine stifling of Xabi Alonso counts for little as the Reds controversially exit the Champions League.

Skipper Nemanja Vidic keeps calm under pressure from
Reading's Noel Hunt, as the Reds overcome the Royals
to move 15 points clear at the top of the table.

Anderson does his best to distract Sunderland keeper Simon
Mignolet ahead of a United free-kick at the Stadium of Light.

Tempers flare amid a hard-fought Manchester derby ultimately settled by Sergio Aguero's late solo goal.

Coach Rene Meulensteen congratulates Michael Carrick as the midfielder's first league goal of the season underpins a key win at Stoke.

Robin van Persie takes the acclaim for his stunning volley against Aston Villa, the second instalment of a title-clinching hat-trick.

Get the party started! Rio Ferdinand gets the champagne flowing in a jubilant home dressing room.

Bring on the champions: Arsenal's players form a guard of honour for the Reds ahead of a battling draw at the Emirates Stadium.

Signing off in style: Rio Ferdinand crashes home a late winner against Swansea and bags United's final goal at Old Trafford under Sir Alex.

The gaffer bids farewell to Manchester United with an impassioned speech befitting of 26½ glorious years at the club.

Rio Ferdinand plays compere as the champions embark on their Premier League trophy parade from Old Trafford to the centre of Manchester.

Superior support: among the thousands of Reds lining the streets, some brave fans take to scaffolding in order to catch a glimpse of their heroes.

Campeones! Skipper Nemanja Vidic leads the singing as the players revel in the spoils of their season's work.

Robin van Persie basks in the glory of individual recognition, picking up the Goal of the Season and Sir Matt Busby Player of the Year awards at the club's annual dinner.

Paul Scholes signs off in typical, no-nonsense style, picking up a booking in a pulsating 5-5 last-day thriller at West Bromwich Albion.

The final farewell: Sir Alex Ferguson salutes the travelling support at the Hawthorns after his 1,500th and last match in charge of United.

deemed the attempted control worthy of a red card and duly rerouted the tie. While the home support vented their fury in a frenzied din, Sir Alex and his players remonstrated in vain. The manager and Giggs both orchestrated the fans to try to haul the team over the line, but Jose Mourinho's response to events was to quickly introduce Modric. The little Croatian had been on the field for only seven minutes when he unleashed a fabulous long-range effort which flew in off De Gea's left post.

The balance of play had totally shifted and there was an air of inevitability about what would happen next. Three minutes after drawing level, Madrid established an insurmountable lead when Higuain's drilled cross found Ronaldo at the back post for a simple tap-in. Twenty minutes remaining, ten against eleven, two goals required. The numbers didn't stack up for United.

Not that sense has ever stopped Sir Alex's men from chasing in vain and, with Rooney and Ashley Young on in place of Tom Cleverley and Welbeck, United pressed forward valiantly. Michael Carrick and Vidic both forced excellent saves from Lopez with powerful headers, while Rooney blazed a volley over the bar, but there would be no late plot twists. The all-important one had already arrived, taking with it United's Champions League ambitions for another season.

The Teams

MANCHESTER UNITED: De Gea, Rafael (Valencia 87), Evra, Ferdinand, Vidic, Giggs, Carrick, Nani, Cleverley (Rooney 73), Welbeck (Young 80), van Persie
SUBS NOT USED: Lindegaard, Evans, Kagawa, Hernandez
BOOKED: Evra, Carrick
SENT OFF: Nani

REAL MADRID: Diego Lopez, Varane, Ramos, Coentrao, Arbeloa
(Modric 59), Khedira, Ronaldo, Ozil (Pepe 71), Alonso, Di Maria (Kaka 45),
Higuain
SUBS NOT USED: Adan, Albiol, Benzema, Callejon
BOOKED: Arbeloa, Pepe, Kaka

Devastated, shattered, distressed . . . the mood at Old Trafford after
United's European exit was embodied by Sir Alex Ferguson, who was
'too distraught' to face the media, according to assistant manager
Mike Phelan.

Asked whether Sir Alex had spoken to Turkish referee Cuneyt
Cakir, Phelan responded: 'I don't think he is in any fit state to talk
to the referee about the decision. I think it speaks volumes that I am
sat here and not the manager of this fantastic football club. We all
saw and witnessed a decision that seemed very harsh. We had a massive audience around the world with people watching in how many
countries I do not know, and everybody will be sitting there won-
dering what happened. A great performance was marred by one
decision.

'We felt we had the tactics right for such a big game. We felt as
though we were comfortable at times at nil-nil. We were where we
wanted to be. We scored the goal and that put us in a very commanding position. After that, we were in reasonable control and
created a few chances. We didn't convert as many as we should have
done, but in that one moment when you score the goal, you feel as
though the crowd is right behind you, they can see the finishing line.
The players sensed they were in control and then it drifted away. The
game totally changed. The decision was amazing. But we had to carry
on. In a game of this magnitude, with the whole world watching, we
feel very disappointed.'

An ITV interview with the typically enigmatic Jose Mourinho
yielded little more than the Portuguese insisting: 'Independent of the

decision, the best team lost. We didn't play well. We didn't deserve to win.' He then returned to the away dressing room.

Looking back on the heartbreak of the evening, Danny Welbeck and Nemanja Vidic feel United failed to respond properly to Nani's red card, such was their shock at the decision. 'It was actually going really well until the decision just after half time, which was a bit of a killer blow for us,' says Welbeck. 'It was just difficult from then on. They had some world-class players in their team and it showed through once we went down to ten men.'

'I think we played well again,' continues Vidic. 'They did not have any chances and David didn't have to make any saves until the red card. Then, the game changed and we were disappointed with the decision, which affected our game, I believe. I think we were not pre-pared for it and it was hard to take. That took some energy from us and we conceded the goals. After that, we stepped up and created a few good moments and chances, but in the end it was hard to leave the Champions League because I thought we could do more. We felt we could have done more in the competition because our form was getting better, but anyway, it has gone.'

The 2013-14 season will bring a fresh assault on the Champions League, but Vidic insists that United will not be fuelled by the per-ceived injustice of their exit against Madrid. 'No, that is not the way you think,' he says. 'You have to always start the pre-season and try to win every trophy, to prepare yourself to be ready for the teams that are coming. The priority for this club will always be the Premier League and Champions League. Next season will be no different. There are some good teams out there that are still looking to win the Champions League, the same as us. We have some quality that can bring us trophies. We have young players that will improve their abil-ities and qualities and that bodes well for the future.'

All round, sights had to be trained on the future. While Phelan admitted: 'The atmosphere in the dressing room was very, very solemn,' he preached perspective and urged the players to lift themselves for the real possibility of securing a domestic Double. 'This loss was not of our own making, so why should we be down and despondent when we've got everything to work hard for and everything to achieve? We've still got an FA Cup tie [against Chelsea] and we're still in a commanding position in the league. So we'll get over it, we'll bounce back.'

Before the Reds could take their first steps back on the road to recovery, an issue needed addressing. Wayne Rooney's exclusion prompted widespread media coverage, with several stories insisting the 'snub' from Sir Alex stemmed from a total breakdown in the pair's relationship. In true Ferguson fashion, the boss came out swinging at his next press conference.

'The Wayne Rooney issue first?' he asked at the start of the gathering. 'Or do you want to talk sense? The issue you're all going on about in the papers is absolute rubbish. There is absolutely no issue between Wayne Rooney and me. To suggest we don't talk to each other on the training ground is absolute nonsense.

'He understood the reasons for not playing him and that was completely tactical. And I think I was right. We don't always get it right, but I think we did get it right. Danny Welbeck is the best player we have in terms of operating in a double role. We had to choke Xabi Alonso's ability to control the game, which Danny did, and that took away Alonso's control of the game and his ability to go further forward and be an attacking player. We don't always get it right, but we definitely did on Tuesday. When you have the squad that we have ... goodness me, I left out Shinji Kagawa who scored a hat-trick, and nobody mentioned that. I thought I might get more criticism for that!

'My job now is to galvanise the troops and the fans, who were fantastic on Tuesday. We owe them a good performance on Sunday. There are a lot of things you can do when you lose a game. One thing we don't do is give in. We get up off our backsides and make sure we're ready for Sunday. Absolutely. A big game's probably best and we're at home, which is also good. It's a big game: the FA Cup. We have a hard game against good opponents. Chelsea have a terrific record in the FA Cup, probably the best of any team in the last decade. We haven't won it for almost ten years, so there are a lot of incentives for us.'

The FA Cup

Sunday 10 March | Old Trafford | Attendance: 75,196

MANCHESTER UNITED 2 Hernandez (5), Rooney (11)
CHELSEA 2 Hazard (59), Ramires (68)

A jaded United side squandered a two-goal lead and could consider themselves fortunate to be pencilling in a quarter-final replay after weathering a second-half siege from Chelsea at Old Trafford.

Goals from Javier Hernandez and Wayne Rooney put a dominant home side two ahead inside 11 minutes, but a second-half fightback from the visitors spawned goals from Eden Hazard and Ramires and earned the Blues a replay at Stamford Bridge. Sir Alex Ferguson's side looked to have buried the tie by the interval, but were punished for a lacklustre second-half display as Chelsea deservedly fought their way back into the tie. The visitors would have won, too, but for a stunning last-minute save from David De Gea to deny Juan Mata.

The manager made just four changes to the side that exited the Champions League against Real Madrid, with Wayne Rooney, Chicharito, Shinji Kagawa and Jonny Evans returning to the Reds' starting XI. While the pre-match atmosphere at Old Trafford failed to replicate the unyielding din that sound-tracked the previous

Tuesday's tie, it wasn't long before the home support had something to shout about.

There seemed little danger for the visitors when Michael Carrick meandered through central midfield, but without warning the Reds' chief string-puller dug out a magnificent diagonal pass that fell perfectly for Chicharito to loop a marvellous header over the stranded Petr Cech.

Less than five minutes had passed then, and the ten-minute marker bisected the award and conversion of a free-kick that doubled the Reds' lead. A lightning break from the hosts culminated in Victor Moses clumsily halting Nani's surge into the area. From the ensuing set-piece, Rooney's curling delivery narrowly missed Evans and David Luiz before nestling inside Cech's far post.

Chelsea briefly sprung into life as Frank Lampard fired straight at De Gea after neat approach work from Mata, but that was a mere blip in United's control, and Cech was called into a fine double save to block Rooney's shot with his legs, then tip the ball over the bar after Luiz miscued his clearing header.

With United seemingly in total control at the break, Chelsea began to claw their way back into the tie in the early stage of the second period. Hazard had been on the field little more than five minutes, but changed the course of the tie with a quite magnificent effort from the edge of the box which curled inside De Gea's far corner.

The visitors had wrested control of the tie – aided by sloppy possession play from the Reds – and Chelsea deservedly levelled with 22 minutes remaining when a breakneck counter-attack resulted in Mata releasing Ramires into the United area. The Brazilian cut inside on his left foot and steered a clinical finish inside De Gea's upright to send the travelling support wild.

Scenting blood, Chelsea dominated the closing exchanges as United appeared sapped of all energy reserves, and only last-ditch blocks from Carrick and Evans stopped Fernando Torres from nabbing a late winner. In the final minute of normal time, Mata looked set to have the final say after turning away from Evans, only for the Spaniard's close-range effort to be turned to safety by De Gea's staggering reflex stop with his right boot. When Howard Webb sounded the final whistle moments later, the Reds could be considered fortunate to still be in contention for a domestic Double.

The Teams

MANCHESTER UNITED: De Gea, Rafael, Evra, Ferdinand, Evans, Carrick, Nani (Valencia 45), Cleverley, Kagawa (Welbeck 76), Rooney, Hernandez (van Persie 62)
SUBS NOT USED: Amos, Vidic, Anderson, Young

CHELSEA: Cech, Azpilicueta, Cole, David Luiz, Cahill, Ramires, Lampard (Mikel 52), Mata, Oscar, Moses (Hazard 52), Ba (Torres 77)
SUBS NOT USED: Turnbull, Ivanovic, Terry, Bertrand
BOOKED: Luiz, Azpilicueta, Hazard

'Juan [Mata] came up after the game and congratulated me for the save, but he also took the mickey a bit, in a nice way,' laughed David De Gea, United's unlikely hero after a superb late save from his compatriot. 'It's difficult to attribute value to individual saves, because they're all important, but it's one of my best,' he declared.

'We're lucky to still be in the cup,' Sir Alex admitted. 'We just ran out of legs and Chelsea were far the better team in the second half. But I can't be critical of my side because the running they had to do on Tuesday night, against a really top side in Real Madrid, had its bearing on today's result, no doubt about that. The two full-backs are knackered and the two central midfielders tired badly. We kept giving the ball away and it made it a long day for us, going from one penalty box and back to our own. We could have been four-nil up in the first twenty-five minutes of the match. I think we needed that lead, because I could detect towards the end of the first half that the players' legs were starting to go.

'When you see teams giving the ball away, as we were doing, then you have to understand why. I think the emotions and the intensity of Tuesday took their toll on some of the players, understandably. I've no problems with that, but certainly they did feel it in the second half. The replay is not a problem for us. We've got plenty of time for it as we have no European games.'

To safeguard his players' fitness levels and allow the recharging of batteries, the manager gave his squad two days off, before a light session upon their return to Carrington. 'We came back in and got the legs going again, but it wasn't too hard out there on the training pitch,' revealed Jonny Evans.

'I think the mental side of it [the Madrid and Chelsea results] drains you. There were a lot of emotions during the week and we have to try to switch off from that and prepare for the next match. When you're at Manchester United, a lot of the time it's about preparing yourself mentally for every game. You know you have to be at the top of your performance and you can't let standards slip. I think what caught us out a bit against Chelsea at the weekend was we got off to a good start, but the mentally drained side really showed in the second half.'

Once the players were fully reintegrated to their regular preparations and the dust had settled, a clear picture remained: the team were streaking ahead in the title race and a replay away from an FA Cup semi-final against Manchester City at Wembley. Incentive aplenty to redouble efforts and go again with another push for the line and silverware, which, in the eyes of Wayne Rooney, would provide the platform for further glory in subsequent years.

'Being successful this season is really important because it would give us a great platform to kick on in the next few years,' said the striker. 'Once the young players get their first taste of silverware with the club, they'll realise how good it feels and they'll want to keep doing it again and again. Hopefully they'll get to taste it this season.'

United's hopes of doing so in the Premier League were further enhanced when Manchester City slipped to defeat at Everton, meaning that a win over rock-bottom Reading – who had just taken the surprising decision to sack Brian McDermott, January's manager of the month – would give the Reds a staggering 15-point advantage at the top of the table.

Barclays Premier League

Saturday 16 March | Old Trafford | Attendance: 75,605

MANCHESTER UNITED 1 Rooney (21)
READING 0

It was hardly eye-catching, but it needn't have been anything more than it was. One goal – a deflected Wayne Rooney strike midway through the first period – secured three hard-earned points against Reading to move the Reds a mammoth 15 points clear at the top of the Barclays Premier League table.

A game of few chances and even fewer talking points was fittingly settled by a scrappy goal, but Sir Alex Ferguson's side staved off any late jitters with a resolute defensive performance which negated any attacking shortcomings in a low-key display from the hosts.

The manager made eight changes to the team that drew with Chelsea six days earlier, but the much-rotated home side found the going heavy in the opening minutes. It took a quarter of an hour to fashion an opening, when Rio Ferdinand's stunning 50-yard diagonal pass found Ashley Young and the winger's shot fizzed across Stuart Taylor's goal.

The Reading goalkeeper soon had to race out of his area to prevent Young reaching Ryan Giggs's excellent through-ball, but he was helpless as United duly moved ahead. Ferdinand's ambitious run out of defence culminated in a neat pass to Rooney in space, and the striker's powerful effort deflected off Alex Pearce and looped over the stranded Taylor.

Later in the half, Rooney and Robin van Persie had long-range efforts that Taylor nervously saved, while Reading's sole testing shot came when Hal Robson-Kanu curled a 20-yard strike round David De Gea's right post. The Royals' only first-half effort of note acted as a springboard for a more ambitious second period, and United had to be alert in defending a flurry of corners in the opening ten minutes of the half.

The Reds, however, regained control and Danny Welbeck, Young and van Persie all had efforts on goal. The latter's was a vicious free-kick from 30 yards that Taylor punched clear, but for the most part the game drifted with neither side keen to force the issue. Reading were increasingly content to keep the deficit narrow in the hope of pinching a late leveller, while United were under no pressure to risk squandering a position of power.

Sir Alex introduced Michael Carrick for the dying stages of the game in order to ensure another layer of protection for his defence, but the midfielder actually sparked United into attacking life, quickly helping to conjure a chance for Giggs, whose shot from a narrow angle on the right was stopped by Taylor. As time ebbed away, Rooney laced a shot over the bar and van Persie acrobatically fired over in injury time, but three invaluable points had already been secured.

The Teams

MANCHESTER UNITED: De Gea, Smalling, Büttner, Ferdinand, Vidic, Anderson (Kagawa 85), Giggs, Young (Carrick 74), Rooney, Welbeck, van Persie
SUBS NOT USED: Lindegaard, Evans, Valencia, Powell, Hernandez

READING: Taylor, Shorey, Pearce, Mariappa, Kelly (Morrison 88), Karacan, Leigertwood, McAnuff, Robson-Kanu (Le Fondre 70), Hunt (Blackman 70), McCleary
SUBS NOT USED: McCarthy, Gunter, Harte, Akpan
BOOKED: Kelly, Hunt

'It wasn't a great performance but where we are now is not down to today, but the last six months,' said Sir Alex. 'The team has shown great consistency and played a lot of great football. Our goal difference is big over City now – thirteen goals. It's a great position to be in, but the only thing we can do is win our next game. You don't get points and medals for being complacent and we won't be.'

A fifth clean sheet in nine games laid the foundations for another three-point haul, with the Reds' defensive record markedly improved since the turn of the year. 'That's linked in with all our defenders coming back now,' explained Chris Smalling. 'It's just Phil [Jones] who is struggling, but I think he will be back soon and our strength is shown by the players that we have available.'

That raft of fit players was by no means guaranteed ahead of the Reds' next outing, at Sunderland, which would come a fortnight later after a two-game international break. The shock recall of Rio Ferdinand to Roy Hodgson's England set-up was the most noteworthy call-up, and after lengthy discussions between the defender and his club manager, then a London get-together with his international manager, it was decided that Ferdinand would withdraw from the squad as a result of his detailed pre-planned training and medical programme.

While that preserved one player's presence at Carrington, Sir Alex explained that special measures would be taken to ensure as many bodies as possible were available for United's trip to Sunderland; a jaunt quickly followed by the FA Cup quarter-final replay against Chelsea 48 hours later.

'They come back and then we've got a lunchtime game against Sunderland on Saturday and then it's lunchtime again against Chelsea on the Monday. Freshness is the name of the game now. It's not necessarily putting out your best team, it's picking the freshest. We're making arrangements for some players to fly home by privately hired jet after their matches, to make sure they get home as quickly and smoothly as possible.

'Tiredness is a great leveller, but we will do our utmost to make sure we field the freshest possible teams. Private planes are going to cost the club an awful lot of money, but it is something we feel we have to do. The players who have missed the international trips will be key players in the run-in.'

Among them was Nemanja Vidic, who relished the opportunity to work on his fitness during the lengthy lull at the usually vibrant Carrington hub. 'The international break is good for me,' admitted the skipper. 'I can work on my individual stuff, like fitness and other technical things. It is also always good to have a few days for yourself. When you have lots of games, like we have recently, you just manage yourself until the next one and you don't work on yourself that much. Sometimes it is nice to have these days to work on yourself.'

Vidic joined the likes of Ryan Giggs, Paul Scholes and Rio Ferdinand as the experienced heads who remained at Carrington, and Danish goalkeeper Anders Lindegaard insisted those senior figures were playing a vital role in setting an example for their younger peers, especially at a time when, in 2011-12, the campaign had started to fall apart, with disastrous consequences.

'I think you can feel it in the team now, especially with the more experienced players, that we're entering the late stage of the season when all the medals are going to be given out,' said the stopper. 'From Rio, Giggsy, Scholes and Vida, you can really feel it with the players who have done it before and see how determined they are and how important it is to them. The younger and less experienced players try to look to them leading us in the right direction, reminding us every day to stay sharp, not to relax and to keep going.'

Keeping going with another three points at the Stadium of Light would give the Reds a little piece of Premier League history: a record points total after 30 games. Returning to Wearside – with a squad mercifully bearing no new injuries from the internationals – for the first time since the final day of the previous campaign, Sir Alex insisted he bore no grudge to Sunderland's supporters for their joyous reaction to Sergio Aguero's last-gasp title winner.

'There's not any bitterness from my point of view,' he stated. 'It happens and we move on. We've dusted ourselves down and made a really good challenge in the league this year. The concentration has been fantastic and the team spirit is really good. So, in that respect, we've answered it as best we can.'

And, for good measure, the Reds would have one more final word on Wearside.

Barclays Premier League

Saturday 30 March | Stadium of Light | Attendance: 43,760

SUNDERLAND 0
MANCHESTER UNITED 1 (Bramble 27 og)

History was made as United ground out a gritty win over Sunderland to extend a record-breaking start to the Barclays Premier League season.

Robin van Persie's 27th-minute strike deflected off Phil Bardsley and Titus Bramble for the only goal of the game, making United the first team ever to win 25 of the first 30 games of a top-flight season in England. A mixed display from the Reds might have yielded more in a one-sided first period, but the relegation-threatened hosts improved markedly after the interval to keep United on the back foot for long periods.

From the first whistle, United were in charge of proceedings as Sunderland merely sat back and invited pressure without offering any attacking threat of note. Van Persie had the game's first attempt on goal as his long-range header from a Rafael cross drifted comfortably to Simon Mignolet, while Ashley Young overhit an inviting free-kick and Alex Büttner's solo run culminated in his toe-poked effort being deflected away by Mignolet.

The Belgian was helpless, however, as United moved into the lead shortly before the half-hour mark. Van Persie picked up possession on the left flank and bought time while he sized up his options. Having decided to shoot, the Dutchman's effort took an immediate nick off Bardsley, then a heavier touch off the thigh of Bramble and sped into the back of the net. Van Persie wheeled away in delight, his seven-game search for a club goal potentially at an end, pending the next sitting of the Premier League's Dubious Goals Panel. But to whom the glory belonged was a side issue; United were in front and a step closer to making history.

Moreover, the visitors continued to tighten their grip on the game. Though the injured Rafael made way for Jonny Evans, the Reds' dominance was uninterrupted. Mignolet spectacularly caught a Young free-kick and clutched van Persie's low, near-post effort, while only a heavy touch from Anderson spurned a delightful lay-off from Shinji Kagawa.

Van Persie twice came close to doubling United's tally in the closing moments of the half, first prompting Mignolet to tip over his fierce free-kick, then volleying over the bar after a sumptuous one-two with the superb Michael Carrick.

Inevitably, Martin O'Neill's players emerged for the second period clearly intent on committing to the cause; pushing greater numbers forward and charging into challenges. The home support cranked up their own contribution in keeping with events on the pitch, and it took a superb diving clearance from Evans to stop Stephane Sessegnon from giving the hosts even more to shout about.

Chris Smalling, who had switched to right-back after the introduction of Evans, made a fine headed clearance as Danny Graham steamed onto Adam Johnson's cross, before the ex-Manchester City winger drilled a long-range effort wide of De Gea's goal. Having absorbed the hosts' pressure, United set about searching for a killer second goal in the game's late stages.

Büttner's stinging right-footed effort was tipped wide and Nemanja Vidic planted a header off-target from the ensuing corner, and the final kick of the game might have yielded a goal for van Persie after a sweeping counter-attack, only for the Dutchman's close-range effort to be bravely fended away by Mignolet. There had been mightier displays from Sir Alex's side en route to making history, but the numbers drowned out the superlatives on this occasion: 30 matches, 25 wins and a 15-point lead over Manchester City, with eight games remaining.

The Teams

SUNDERLAND: Mignolet, Bardsley (Larsson 78), Rose (Colback 85), O'Shea, Bramble, N'Diaye, Gardner, Johnson (Wickham 76), McClean, Sessegnon, Graham
SUBS NOT USED: Westwood, Kilgallon, Mangane, Mandron
BOOKED: Bardsley, O'Shea, N'Diaye

MANCHESTER UNITED: De Gea, Rafael (Evans 32), Büttner, Smalling, Vidic, Valencia, Anderson (Cleverley 84), Carrick, Young, Kagawa (Welbeck 78), van Persie
SUBS NOT USED: Lindegaard, Evra, Nani, Powell
BOOKED: van Persie

After seven games without a goal, there was no doubt who Robin van Persie felt had scored United's winner. Asked if he was claiming it, the Dutchman responded: 'Of course, no question about that! It's been a while so it was good to score again, and it was an important goal. Today it was all about three points and we got them.

'We knew before that it was going to be tough; away at Sunderland is always going to be very hard. They work hard and play a game with lots of long balls, second balls and we had to dig in. We did that, everyone fought hard for a deserved win. This team, if you ask me, is just full of winners. I was never in doubt, even if it was still a small score at one-nil. Everyone knows what he has to do and we did it again.'

On this particular occasion, the victory demanded courage and sacrifice. The visitors lost Rafael to a groin injury in the first half and his replacement, Jonny Evans, played on after picking up a knock, while David De Gea was temporarily dazed by a clash of heads with Nemanja Vidic.

'I thought it was a battling performance by the players,' Sir Alex said. 'Courage got us through, particularly in the second half. They've shown a team spirit and focus in every game. It's also twenty-five wins in thirty league games, which is a record, and that's all down to the efforts of the players. It was an important win.'

Four more wins from eight remaining league games would sew up a 20th league title, but the looming FA Cup trip to Stamford Bridge would prove an enticing way to start April and prolong the Reds' hopes of a domestic Double.

10

April

'We took a big step in the league, but we want to go for both,' said Robin van Persie, eagerly anticipating United's FA Cup quarter-final replay at Stamford Bridge. 'It's going to be a big test, but I'm quite confident we can play well and get a good result. It's not ideal because it's only two days after the Sunderland game. It's a shame, but we can't do anything about it. We just have to deal with it. I think people have to realise not to expect a great game of football. That might not be possible. If it happens, great; but don't expect it – the games are too close to each other.'

Having seen his side narrowly avoid exiting the competition after Chelsea's second-half fightback at Old Trafford, Sir Alex Ferguson felt United had been feeling the after-effects of their Champions League heartbreak at the hands of Real Madrid. 'I thought we were lucky, to be honest with you,' he stated. 'I thought that tiredness had got into the team. That came, possibly, from the emotional intensity of the Real Madrid game and also the way we lost it. I think that affected two or three players. But we're fresher now and we've got a strong squad in terms of picking two teams.'

The FA Cup

Monday 1 April | Stamford Bridge | Attendance: 40,704

CHELSEA 1 Ba (49)
MANCHESTER UNITED 0

Hopes of a domestic Double were dashed as a superbly taken goal from Demba Ba sent Chelsea into the semi-finals of the FA Cup at the expense of United.

The quarter-final replay didn't match the excitement of any of the clubs' previous three meetings during the course of the season, as United never recovered from the double-whammy of Ba's brilliant volley and a world-class save from Petr Cech to deny Javier 'Chicharito' Hernandez a headed equaliser.

Sir Alex Ferguson made seven changes to the line-up which kicked off 48 hours previously at Sunderland, with only Chris Smalling, Michael Carrick, Antonio Valencia and goalkeeper David De Gea asked to start a second match in quick succession. The peculiar setting of the game – a replay, with an early kick-off, on a bank holiday – lent proceedings a surreal air, and both sets of players seemed unsettled in a disjointed opening 20 minutes. United managed to get within an incisive final pass of several promising situations, but every time were undone by a lack of concentration or sloppy play.

Chelsea had to recover from losing left-back Ashley Cole, who pulled up in a sprint duel with England team-mate Danny Welbeck, but still mustered the game's first shot on target when Ba forced De Gea to save with his legs from a powerful low effort. Longer-range efforts from Nani at one end and Eden Hazard at the other did not require action from the goalkeepers, but Cech made an unorthodox save with his right foot when De Gea found Chicharito with a kick from his hands, and the Mexican's resulting 20-yard shot took a wicked swerve.

After a moderately engaging first period, the second half began in sluggish fashion – though it didn't take long for Chelsea to serve up the game's one true moment of attacking quality. Juan Mata floated a fine ball over the top and Ba hooked a superb right-foot volley into the top left-hand corner, with De Gea rooted to the spot.

Tom Cleverley and Ryan Bertrand – on for Cole – both drew yellow cards for clattering fouls as the game suddenly developed an edge, and with United stung into action it appeared that a leveller was due to arrive, until Cech produced a breathtaking save. Welbeck's cross fell perfectly for Chicharito to meet and direct goalwards with a diving header, only for Cech to thrust out his left palm and push the ball to safety over his own crossbar – a save acknowledged with a rueful grin and congratulations from the Mexican.

Chelsea looked to hit United on the break as the visitors increasingly committed numbers forward, and De Gea did brilliantly to deflect Mata's powerful strike around the post and into the side netting, before Hazard wastefully dragged wide of the target from a promising position. Sir Alex sent on Robin van Persie and Ryan Giggs, and the former looked certain to level the scores when Patrice Evra burst into the Chelsea area and pulled the ball back, only for the Dutchman to blaze off target from eight yards out. With that, came and went United's final chance of Wembley glory, leaving the small matter of the Premier League title race to focus on.

The Teams

CHELSEA: Cech, Azpilicueta, Cole (Bertrand 21), Luiz, Ivanovic, Ramires, Mata, Oscar (Moses 90), Mikel, Hazard, Ba (Torres 90)
SUBS NOT USED: Turnbull, Terry, Benayoun, Lampard
BOOKED: Bertrand, Azpilicueta, Oscar, Mata

MANCHESTER UNITED: De Gea, Evra, Jones, Ferdinand, Smalling, Valencia, Carrick, Nani (Giggs 65), Cleverley (Van Persie 61), Hernandez, Welbeck (Young 80)
SUBS NOT USED: Lindegaard, Vermijl, Powell, Kagawa
BOOKED: Cleverley

'It's a massive disappointment for us,' lamented Patrice Evra. 'We didn't expect to lose and we really wanted to win the Double. A lot of players, including myself, haven't won the FA Cup and it was an important trophy for us. I think we lost the tie in the first match. We have to be realistic with ourselves – we gave the first game away. We were winning two-nil, they came back from two-nil down and we drew two-two. After that, we had another chance to win at Stamford Bridge, but Chelsea deserved to go through.

'We were really sad to lose in the Champions League; it hurt us a lot when we lost against Real Madrid, and this is another really sad day for the club, the players and the fans. Now we're going to focus on the league. It's nearly done but we have to win a few games.'

The Frenchman's evident air of disappointment was shared by every member of the away dressing room at Stamford Bridge but, with Manchester City's visit to Old Trafford looming large, the Reds would soon have the chance to make a statement and virtually end any uncertainty around the destination of the Barclays Premier League trophy.

'We must kick on,' insisted Sir Alex. 'We're disappointed and the players are down. They're disappointed because they know they can do better. To be honest with you, for the ninety minutes I thought only Antonio Valencia reached the standard that we expect of them. But we need to forget this result and look forward to the game with City. A positive result for us next Monday will just about seal the title for us.'

For Chris Smalling, the derby provided the ideal opportunity to bounce back from the disappointment of Stamford Bridge. 'It will take a couple of days to get over this, because a lot of us came into it with great confidence and we felt we were going to win this game,' he admitted. 'At least we have a good game next Monday, but we need to make sure that we rally together and win this title with aplomb. Our fans will be right behind us and we need to make sure that we give them a good performance.'

With a week to recharge and prepare for one of the season's biggest games, the players were given adequate time to ready themselves. In the lull between games, media reports suggested that Robin van Persie – who uncharacteristically missed an inviting late chance at Chelsea – was in need of a more substantial rest as his run of games without a goal moved to eight.

Sir Alex, however, disagreed. 'Robin doesn't need a rest, that's for sure,' insisted the manager. 'He's a strong lad with a great physique. The goals will come. All strikers have little dry spells – you always hope it ends quickly. It's just part of being a striker. I remember I had a spell at the start of one season when I had a little knee injury and didn't score until October and I still ended up with thirty-odd goals!

'You have to get through that period and not lose your faith and belief in yourself. My dad always used to say make sure you batter the ball when you're in there, don't tap it or try and side-foot the ball in the net, batter it! That's what I always tell strikers – when you get in the position, make sure you hit it. If the goalkeeper saves it, you can say "what a great save". But if you try to side-foot it in and the keeper just catches it easily, you'll get criticised for that.

'It's just being sensible and realistic. Robin's shot last week could have come off any defender because it was hit so well and that's the right thing to do. It's disappointing he wasn't awarded the goal at Sunderland – I can understand that because it took a wicked deflection. His shot was fantastic – it was hit with such venom that it's not surprising it took a deflection. But his ability to manoeuvre his position at that point was excellent.'

It appeared increasingly likely that van Persie could be joined in attack against City by the fit-again Wayne Rooney, while Rafael was also winning his personal race to return. With doubts over the availability of Nemanja Vidic and Jonny Evans, however, Phil Jones was earmarked to start in central defence.

Despite alternating positions between centre-back, right-back and defensive midfield, the England international could cope with his head-spinning rotation, according to his manager. 'Jones is going to be a fantastic player, his talent is unbelievable,' said Sir Alex. 'Yes [his best position is centre-back] but you could play him anywhere. I think you could play him centre-forward! He's just that type of player; he's an animal for football. He grasps the game, he understands it. Play him right-back? Brilliant. Play him centre-midfield? No problem. Play him centre-back? Terrific.

'He's just one of those unusual players you get now and again who can play anywhere. We've not had a player like him in terms of someone who can play at that performance level since, well, the closest you would get would be Brian McClair, who was a fantastic player.'

Much pre-match talk had centred on United's record return from the first 30 games of the season. Having dropped points in only five games, the Reds were on course to eclipse Chelsea's division record of 95 points, set in 2004-05. For Rio Ferdinand, however, setting such targets was a superfluous pursuit.

'It is just about winning,' said the defender. 'Anything that comes after that is great, but winning it is the most important part. If you win the league before the end of the season, then you can set other targets. For me, personally, we need to get the trophy first, and then you can think of all the other stuff that goes on around it.'

The old adage of taking each game as it comes may be a tired cliché, but winning 25 of 30 games had validated the mentality. Focusing on the next game would not prove problematic, however, with the stakes so high. Win and the title race would be virtually finished just over a week into April.

'It's a huge motivation, but that motivation has been there all season,' stressed Danny Welbeck. 'To be fifteen points ahead is a big margin, but we won't get complacent. Our mentality is always the same for every match – to win. That won't change. Of course, knowing victory would put us within a few points of the title is a massive incentive for us. Everyone has felt the excitement building in the city ahead of this match and it's one we're all looking forward to.'

Barclays Premier League

Monday 8 April | Old Trafford | Attendance: 75,498

MANCHESTER UNITED 1 Kompany (59 og)
MANCHESTER CITY 2 Milner (51), Aguero (78)

United missed the chance to all-but end the title race after Sergio Aguero's fine solo goal swung a fractious Manchester derby the way of Roberto Mancini's City.

Despite the considerable consolation of a 12-point advantage with just seven games remaining, the evening remained one of frustration for the Reds, who had harboured hopes of victory after Vincent Kompany's own-goal had cancelled out James Milner's deflected opener for the champions.

This was a match United desperately wanted to win as an assertion of dominance, while City wanted to land a telling blow in their increasingly despairing defence of the title. As such, both sides came out swinging in an unexpectedly open start to the game in which midfield was barely occupied.

Danny Welbeck had a glancing header saved easily by Joe Hart, while Milner's fiercely struck cross was palmed to safety by David De Gea, before Robin van Persie stroked an effort wide of the post, all inside the opening ten minutes. City took the initiative after that, however, and a spell of pressure led to a good opening after 20 minutes when David Silva's neat lay-off from Kompany's lofted pass was superbly anticipated by Phil Jones, who slid in to clear the ball from Carlos Tevez's toes.

Outright chances were few and far between as the game failed to deliver on its promising opening period, though referee Mike Dean allowed a healthily competitive game to unfold, with both sides flying into challenges throughout. The first half ended on a close call, however, as Rafael poked a shot against the bar from van Persie's lay-off inside the area.

The second half began in much the same fashion as the first: an open affair, with neither side dominating, but after a rare mistake from Ryan Giggs, whose attempted backheel released Gareth Barry, City struck the game's first blow on 51 minutes. Milner's powerful shot from just outside the area fizzed through a clutch of bodies, nicking Jones and narrowly evading De Gea's desperate dive.

To their credit, United responded by drawing level inside ten minutes. After Rafael had won a free-kick in an inviting, right-sided position, van Persie's thunderous, whipped cross beat Hart and was bundled over the line as Jones challenged Kompany. Old Trafford erupted and continued to buzz in expectation of a resounding victory, but instead the game lulled back into the balance before City took the spoils through a moment of individual excellence from substitute Aguero. The Argentine evaded four opponents and meandered towards De Gea's goal before thrashing an unstoppable finish high into the roof of the net.

The travelling Blues rejoiced in their hero's moment of inspiration, and the reigning champions held on through an ill-tempered end to the game to inflict United's first league defeat since November. Despite the galling manner of the setback, the Reds' excellence during that lengthy period ensured that the ramifications of City's win would go no further than wounded pride.

The Teams

MANCHESTER UNITED: De Gea, Rafael, Evra, Jones, Ferdinand, Giggs, Carrick, Young (Kagawa 90), Rooney (Hernandez 85), Welbeck (Valencia 80), van Persie
SUBS NOT USED: Lindegaard, Büttner, Nani, Cleverley
BOOKED: Rafael, Rooney, Valencia

MANCHESTER CITY: Hart, Zabaleta, Clichy, Kompany, Nastasic, Milner, Nasri (Aguero71), Barry, Silva (Lescott 89), Y.Toure, Tevez (Garcia 90)
SUBS NOT USED: Pantilimon, Kolarov, K.Toure, Dzeko
BOOKED: Kompany, Silva, Zabaleta, Barry, Tevez

No need for panic, just perspective. A game-by-game mentality had served the Reds well throughout the season and, after back-to-back setbacks, would be adopted once more. 'We've got seven games to go and it's a healthy lead,' said Sir Alex. 'But we're not taking anything for granted. We just have to kick on. The most important thing is to try and win our next game. We've got Stoke City on Sunday and it's a match we want to win and the performance tonight is a good indication.'

Certainly, Sir Alex's players were in agreement with their manager. 'We've got to bounce back,' urged Phil Jones. 'We'll get on the training pitch and do what we do best: recover, and we will.' Patrice Evra concurred: 'We must make sure we win at Stoke and show we are the best team in England.'

Any United defeat invariably meets a standard response within Carrington: the next game cannot come quickly enough. The Reds would have to wait six days until the short trip to Stoke, during which time Rio Ferdinand publicly decried the notion that United's season had not recovered from the shock of March's Champions League exit against Real Madrid.

'There has been no hangover at all,' said the defender. 'The Madrid game was a weird one – you're gutted obviously, but it didn't feel the same as when we lost to City because we didn't play well in that game. Against Madrid we did everything that was asked of us as players, but one decision took us off the rails and had a big impact on the way the game finished.

'We've had a couple of hard games against two teams [Chelsea and City] that are up there. We've got no divine right to beat those teams, but we should have beaten them given we were playing at home. That's the disappointing thing. But no, there is no hangover. Inevitably you have a bit of a down period for a day or so, but you've got to dust yourself down and move on, and that's what we're doing.

'We go into the Stoke game knowing we need to put a good performance and result together. What you aim for at the start of the season is to get some consistency within your team and that's what we've done. The results we've had have been churned out through hard work and applying ourselves in the right way and we've got to continue that. One defeat in nineteen is some going. We can't allow all that hard work to be undone by one or two bad results of late.'

Meanwhile, across Manchester, Roberto Mancini bemoaned the perceived fact that: 'No one plays well against United because they only play with fear. Every team that plays against United plays very soft because they think this game is difficult, that they can't beat them.'

Inevitably, the barb provoked a response from Sir Alex, who countered: 'I think that's absolute nonsense, I really do. There are a lot of games I've watched this season, teams like City, and I've said to myself: "Are they trying?" And of course they're trying. The English game is the most honest in the world, I think we all recognise that, and it has been for many, many years. And also you've got three thousand fans following you away. There's no way any team could come to Old Trafford and not do their best. That also applies itself to the Etihad, Stamford Bridge, the Emirates or Anfield. They all do their best because that's the nature of the English game. So it's absolute nonsense what he said. He was maybe looking for a bit of self-sympathy or something like that. But it's nonsense.'

The invariably hostile welcome in store at the Britannia Stadium could be counted on as a fixture which would validate Sir Alex's assertion. Fortunately, United were ready for the challenge.

Barclays Premier League

Sunday 14 April | Britannia Stadium | Attendance: 27,191

STOKE CITY 0
MANCHESTER UNITED 2 Carrick (4), van Persie (66 pen)

Back on track. United took another huge step towards the title with a solid, authoritative return to winning ways against a Stoke City side whose confidence was rocked early on and never resurfaced.

From the moment Michael Carrick prodded home the Reds'

early opener, the outcome never seemed in doubt, while Robin van Persie scored from the penalty spot to end his ten-game goalless run and tie up a vital victory.

Successive defeats to Chelsea and Manchester City made three points imperative for Sir Alex Ferguson's men, and with Stoke also in dire need of points to fend off the spectre of relegation, a strong start was exactly what the Reds required. Van Persie's cross led to right-back Phil Jones trying to hook the ball towards goal and, amid an untidy scramble, Carrick jabbed out a foot to direct the ball beyond Asmir Begovic and into the corner of the net for his first league goal of the season and United's 100th in all competitions.

With Wayne Rooney impressive in midfield, United took the game to the hosts early on. Patrice Evra lifted an attempt over the top after a van Persie corner, while Rooney forced a decent stop out of Begovic after unleashing a piledriver from long range. Stoke might have levelled out of nothing when Robert Huth headed wide from a Charlie Adam cross, but the hosts' response was otherwise muted.

Van Persie lobbed a cheeky effort well wide from 40 yards out after robbing Adam, before firing in a snap-shot that was fumbled behind for a corner by Begovic. Soon after, the Serbian breathed a sigh of relief when Rooney's free-kick from a promising position flew narrowly off-target.

Strangely, Stoke's famed passion and commitment rarely surfaced, despite their disadvantage, and United continued to boss matters in the second period. Superb passes by Rooney and Chicharito carved out an opportunity for van Persie, but the Dutchman lashed into the side-netting from a difficult angle. Then, just as the Potters began to show signs of life, with Adam trying his luck from distance and Kenwyne Jones blazing off target, United struck again. In a swift counter-attack, Phil Jones and Antonio Valencia worked the ball cleverly down the right and Rooney bided his time before releasing van

Persie. Andy Wilkinson made a reckless tackle as the Dutchman dummied back and conceded a clear penalty.

Calmly ignoring the strong winds – which initially blew the ball from the spot – van Persie stepped up to place his penalty wide of Begovic before sprinting off to the away dugout to indulge in warm celebrations with his manager, coaches and team-mates. The second goal prompted a minimal increase in pressure from the hosts, with De Gea forced to smother a strike by Ryan Shotton and Kenwyne Jones appealing for a penalty after tripping over a grounded Nemanja Vidic inside the area, but United saw out the game in almost total comfort. The only scare came when Adam's deep free-kick was well fended away by De Gea, preserving another clean sheet and an invaluable return to character for the runaway league leaders.

The Teams

STOKE CITY: Begovic, Cameron (Jerome 71), Shawcross, Huth, Wilkinson, Shotton, Whelan, Nzonzi, Adam, Jones (Crouch 84), Walters (Owen 77)
SUBS NOT USED: Sorensen, Palacios, Whitehead, Kightly
BOOKED: Jerome

MANCHESTER UNITED: De Gea, Jones, Evra, Ferdinand, Vidic, Valencia, Carrick, Kagawa, Rooney, Hernandez (Welbeck 77), van Persie
SUBS NOT USED: Lindegaard, Evans, Smalling, Büttner, Giggs, Cleverley
BOOKED: Valencia

'He nearly killed me!' joked Sir Alex, of Robin van Persie's enthusiastic goal celebration. 'He forgets I'm seventy-one! I always think you should celebrate goals – the boys celebrated right away and it was an emotional part of it. The supporters were encouraged by that. It was an absolutely tremendous penalty under pressure, with the wind blowing the ball off the spot two or three times. He arrowed it right in the corner, a perfect penalty. He and the rest of them will think they've done a great job today, very well justified in terms of the performance and having to dig in deep to get that result.'

With a first goal in ten games safely tucked away, it's little surprise van Persie was so elated – though he conceded that the pressure was on as he faced Asmir Begovic. 'I had to score that one and thankfully it went in, and after that the relief of a couple of weeks came out, I would say,' laughed the Dutchman. 'I wanted to celebrate with everyone; with the players, the staff, with all the players involved even on the bench, because they've been great to me from day one. Even when sometimes it is a little bit harder, they still believe in me and they still support me and help me wherever they can. That's why I wanted to join everyone.'

Wayne Rooney paid tribute to van Persie's bravery in deciding to take the penalty, with the weight of expectation bearing down after so long without a goal. 'I'm sure he would have thought about it [the drought] before he took the penalty, but he showed a lot of courage to step up and put it away,' said Rooney. 'Credit to him for that. Every player in the world has had a few games on the run without scoring. Robin's kept his head down, kept working and thankfully today he's got his goal and hopefully that'll kick him on because he'll be a massive player in the next few games for us.'

Next up, with barely time to return to Carrington, would be West Ham at Upton Park, a venue equally as inhospitable as the Britannia Stadium. A similar direct, physical approach would undoubtedly be in store for the Reds in East London, and Nemanja Vidic – never one to shirk any manner of challenge – was eager for a repeat performance against the Hammers.

'Stoke is always a difficult place to go to, but we fought for every ball, played some good football and, in the end, I think we deserved to win. It was physical. You know Stoke are going to get the ball to the forwards, they're good at set-pieces, they're going to challenge defenders. Now it's West Ham and we have to play well again. They play in a similar style to Stoke – we're going to have long balls and set-pieces to deal with. You think you're almost there [in the title race], but you have to win the games.'

Between games, Vidic and his colleagues passed a good deal of their time indulging in light-hearted ribbing of their leading goalscorer, whose celebration at the Britannia Stadium continued to be the topic of debate among the squad. 'It has been difficult for Robin,' confided Patrice Evra. 'He has had a lot of stick from us. For two or three days we have been getting at him!

'To be fair, Robin told us he was really emotional. He had not scored for ten games. He just showed the passion and the way he wanted to win. He said to us: "Hands up, guys, it was an emotional game. I did it, it is okay, we can move on now." It was nice. I can see a lot of love and emotion. It is the first time we saw that [from Robin]. It is good to see love like that on the pitch sometimes. I always say the atmosphere at this club is great. That is a big strength for Manchester United.'

Barclays Premier League

Wednesday 17 April | Upton Park | Attendance: 34,692

WEST HAM UNITED 2 Vaz Te (16), Diame (55)
MANCHESTER UNITED 2 Valencia (31), van Persie (77)

Robin van Persie struck a late equaliser as United twice came from behind to register a battling draw with West Ham at Upton Park. While the Reds missed out on a valuable three-point haul, the spirit on show in Sir Alex Ferguson's side demonstrated the resolve of champions.

Ricardo Vaz Te's opener was cancelled out by Antonio Valencia's first goal of the season, only for Mohamed Diame's fine strike to nudge the Hammers back in front. Shinji Kagawa, who also set up Valencia's effort, hit the woodwork in the 77th minute and Robin van Persie converted the rebound to salvage a point.

A long, draining evening looked to be on the cards from the first few minutes, as West Ham flew out of the traps, hassling and harrying United throughout the opening exchanges, albeit with little creative reward for their bluster, until Matt Jarvis beat Rio Ferdinand and crossed for Andy Carroll, who headed down for Vaz Te to dive and nod past Rafael and Nemanja Vidic on the line.

United's response was a gradual one, with Jussi Jaaskelainen almost totally untroubled. Then, shortly after the half-hour, an equaliser arrived following a fine move down the left flank. Van Persie threaded a pass through James Collins's legs to work the ball back to Kagawa and the Japan international sauntered his way into the area and to the byline before teeing up Valencia for a simple tap-in.

Diame got the better of Michael Carrick to lash a drive into the side-netting and Vaz Te thumped well wide as Sam Allardyce's side produced a positive reaction, while Kevin Nolan tumbled under the merest touch from Vidic in a desperate bid to win a penalty. Referee Lee Probert was unimpressed, but then was mysteriously similarly unmoved by Carroll's bizarre charge on David De Gea from a corner.

The start of the second half saw an immediate improvement from the visitors, with van Persie heading Wayne Rooney's precise cross frustratingly behind Phil Jones, who was unable to make a proper connection when a goal would have been certain. Yet United's upsurge in tempo merely galvanised the hosts. Carroll, unconcerned by collecting a booking for another flare-up with De Gea, smashed a long-range effort just off-target, before another spectacular attempt put the Hammers back in front. After peeling away from Rooney on the edge of the box, Diame thrashed a superb, curling effort through a crowd of players and into the far corner. Upton Park erupted.

Jussi Jaaskelainen suddenly needed to earn his match fee. A superb stop from van Persie was ultimately a moot incident, with the Dutchman called offside, but the Finn was then fortunate when a scuffed Rooney shot skipped past him, only for Gary O'Neil to hack away off the line. A wonderful one-handed save by Jaaskelainen kept out van Persie's header from a Valencia centre, and Sir Alex introduced Ryan Giggs for Rooney in a bid to build on United's growing momentum.

That meant that Kagawa moved into a central position, with Giggs stationed on the left, and the former Borussia Dortmund schemer was heavily involved in the second equaliser. Collecting a Carrick pass, he blasted in a splendid shot that hit both posts and van Persie was on hand to emphatically lift the rebound into the roof of the net. The Dutchman had been lurking just offside, an infringement missed by officials. Substitute Chicharito looked set to pinch the spoils when Giggs curled in a magnificent cross, only for Carroll – of all people – to make a heroic sliding clearance to secure a deserved share of the points for both sides.

The Teams

WEST HAM UNITED: Jaaskelainen, Reid, O'Brien, Collins, Demel, Nolan (Taylor 82), Jarvis, Diame (Collison 82), O'Neil (Noble 67), Carroll, Vaz Te
SUBS NOT USED: Henderson, Pogatetz, C.Cole, Maiga
BOOKED: Carroll

MANCHESTER UNITED: De Gea, Rafael, Evra, Ferdinand, Vidic, Valencia, Jones, Carrick, Kagawa (Hernandez 79), Rooney (Giggs 71), van Persie
SUBS NOT USED: Amos, Evans, Nani, Cleverley, Welbeck .

While a point represented another shuffle in the right direction, the display of David De Gea – more for his withstanding of the

Hammers' rugged approach than any shot-stopping – demonstrated the great strides taken by the young Spanish goalkeeper in his time at Old Trafford.

'We know how they play,' shrugged Sir Alex. 'The ball is in the air most of the time and you have to defend those things. They were very aggressive as you've seen. There's no doubt it's a red card [for the challenge on De Gea]. It's obvious. The referee saw it differently. We're looking for players to be protected and didn't get that.

'David has been improving all the time and is developing into a fantastic keeper. It's just a matter of experience in the English game – he's got stronger. His training performances are really good and he's shown that again tonight. As we've been saying for quite a while, he's developing into a first-class goalkeeper. Steeley [goalkeeping coach Eric Steele] kept reminding David he would be top. The improvement is the physical part as he's put on nearly a stone now in terms of muscle. He's much stronger and dealing with the physical part much, much better. He's quick, he's got good composure and his use of the ball is good. He's got no problems now. He took a real buffeting at West Ham and it didn't affect him at all.'

De Gea wasn't the only one bearing the battle scars of the midweek draw at Upton Park when the boss came to assess his resources for the visit of Aston Villa to Old Trafford. 'We've got a few bumps and bruises,' reported the manager. 'Vidic has got a beautiful bruise on his cheekbone and after coming out of that war zone, we're quite happy no one was seriously injured.'

Ashley Young, however, would not be involved again in 2012-13. The winger had attended Upton Park on crutches after visiting a specialist in London for further insight on the ankle injury sustained against Manchester City, and had not been given good news.

'It's unfortunate and it's a bad blow,' said Sir Alex. 'We thought it'd be maybe two or three weeks but now he's been down to the specialist and that's why you saw him at the game on Wednesday. The prognosis was not very good at all. We're going to lose him for the rest of the season.'

Better news abounded for three other United players, with Robin van Persie and Michael Carrick nominated for the PFA Player of the Year award and Danny Welbeck in contention for the junior equivalent. For Carrick in particular, individual recognition had been slow in arriving from outside the club. Within its confines, however, there was no doubt over his value to the squad. 'Michael has been fantastic for United this season,' opined Tom Cleverley. 'Growing up here, I've been really lucky all the way through, as I've always had fantastic midfielders to learn from. He's one of those. With his forward passing and calmness on the ball, he just knows how to control and win games, so I can always be learning from him.'

Carrick's form had been key to United's title charge, but suddenly the Reds were handed an unexpected leg-up by Manchester City's late defeat at Tottenham. Just as the Blues' form had suggested that the title race still had legs, they had charged into the final hurdle, leaving United only one win from a 20th domestic crown.

Barclays Premier League

Monday 22 April | Old Trafford | Attendance: 75,591

MANCHESTER UNITED 3 Van Persie (2, 13, 33)
ASTON VILLA 0

A first-half hat-trick from Robin van Persie confirmed the return of the Barclays Premier League title to Old Trafford on an unforgettable evening of champagne football from Sir Alex Ferguson's champions.

The Dutchman's 31-minute treble – including a staggering volley – had the outcome beyond doubt by the interval, and a relatively low-key second period passed without major incident as United ascended the throne in comfortable fashion. After Manchester City's defeat at Tottenham, the Reds knew that victory would wrench the Premier League trophy back with four games to spare, and Sir Alex sent out a side so eager to do so that it took them just 81 seconds to forge ahead.

After Wayne Rooney's sublime crossfield ball had released Antonio Valencia, the Ecuadorian teed up Rafael, whose deep, first-time cross was beautifully cushioned across goal by Ryan Giggs for van Persie to gleefully sidefoot home. Old Trafford shook with joy, and the first renditions of 'campeones' were ringing around the brimming stadium when van Persie passed up the chance to double his tally, volleying just over from Valencia's deflected cross in the third minute.

As a rampant United start continued to promise goals, the Dutchman unselfishly headed down for Shinji Kagawa after more sterling work from Giggs, only for the Japanese schemer's close-range effort to be blocked by Ron Vlaar. Villa were quickly indebted to the woodwork as Rafael's swerving shot thudded away off Brad Guzan's right-hand post, but Christian Benteke fired wastefully off-target almost immediately to remind the hosts of their defensive duties.

If that was a sobering moment for the Reds, Rooney and van Persie quickly combined to intoxicate Old Trafford once again with a goal of undiluted brilliance. Already looking sharp in a deep, roving role, Rooney clipped a magnificent 40-yard pass into the path of van Persie, whose audacious, first-time volley hurtled across Guzan and into the bottom corner. A roar of amazement filled the air, before again making way for chants commemorating United's increasingly inevitable feat. Though Villa, to their credit, continued to probe for an unlikely route back into the game, the attacking incision of Rooney, van Persie, Giggs and Kagawa gave them no respite in defence.

The latter trio combined shortly after the half hour to seal the Dutchman's double-quick treble. Kagawa's fine through ball sent Giggs scampering into the area, and the veteran astutely squared for van Persie to take a touch, plot a path past Guzan and belt a finish in off the upright. Having all-but sealed United's 20th title, the Reds' number 20 was also homing in on personal glory, moving to the top of the Premier League's scoring charts with his 24th strike of the season.

Van Persie's first contribution after the interval came at the other end of the field, clearing Andreas Weimann's header off the line as the visitors made a bright start to the second period. David De Gea was forced into a low save by Benteke, then a wonderful, full-length tip over the bar to keep out substitute Karim El Ahmadi's fine long-range effort.

Guzan's involvement was comparatively muted, facing only sporadic attempts from the hosts. Rooney twice came close in a matter of seconds before making way for substitute Danny Welbeck, while Kagawa undid a beautiful feint by blasting high into the Stretford End after fine wingplay from Valencia. There would be no fourth goal, leaving van Persie as the man in the spotlight. It was a fitting state of affairs on the evening that Sir Alex and his indefatigable players rescaled the pinnacle of the Premier League, surveying all below them as worthy champions.

The Teams

MANCHESTER UNITED: De Gea, Rafael, Evra, Jones, Evans, Valencia, Giggs, Carrick, Kagawa, Rooney (Welbeck 72), van Persie
SUBS NOT USED: Lindegaard, Ferdinand, Büttner, Nani, Cleverley, Hernandez
BOOKED: Evra

ASTON VILLA: Guzan, Vlaar, Bennett (Clark 80), Baker, Lowton, N'Zogbia (El Ahmadi 46), Westwood, Delph, Agbonlahor, Benteke, Weimann
SUBS NOT USED: Given, Holman, Sylla, Bent, Bowery

'It's a great feeling,' beamed Robin van Persie, with no small hint of understatement after scoring a hat-trick to clinch the first championship of his long career. 'I had to wait a long time and I've been thinking and speaking about it with Rio, for example, in the car and he's been telling me: "Listen, whatever happens, that's the standard." He's right. From now on, our new standard is we want to be champions every year and we want to win more.

'We are even more hungry than we were last season because you could just tell, from day one, everyone wanted this. I want to win it again. I want to win more stuff. I want to win the FA Cup, the Champions League, the Capital One Cup. I want to win it all. This is a trophy for all of us – the management, staff, all the players, and the fans have been brilliant, too. They've been absolutely amazing, cheering us on every single game, home and away, so credit to them as well.'

A packed Old Trafford swayed and bellowed in unison to salute the new champions, and while van Persie was a relative greenhorn in the situation, Michael Carrick – just a year the Dutchman's senior – was digesting his fifth title. 'I said before I came here that if I won a league that would have meant everything to me,' explained the midfielder. 'Strange as it is though, as soon as I won that first league it left me hungry for more.

'Whether that is from being here, or just the feeling that came with the opportunity for getting more here, I don't know. Before I came here, one trophy would have been a big success from where I came from. But the satisfaction of winning it is such a good feeling you want it again and again, and you get hungrier to win it again.

'I definitely want more. The season is not over yet – we haven't even got the trophy – but we will come back next year and give it everything again. We will be as hungry as ever. That is how we bounce back from this so well. Regardless of whether we have been successful the year before or not, we are trying to achieve again. What is gone is gone. We lost against City and we bounced back. It is something we pride ourselves on. There are not many teams who could have come back from that.'

To have come back at all was commendable, but to have done so in record-breaking fashion spoke volumes for the steely determination pulsing through the club, in the eyes of Sir Alex Ferguson. 'The players' focus was fantastic this season,' he said. 'They didn't get themselves annoyed by what happened last season. A lot of teams – most teams in the country – would have melted. But not this bunch.

'They went on and did what Manchester United expects of them and raised the bar. You could go on and on and on about losing a title, and we've had to do that in my time. I think our consistency for the last twenty years has been unbelievable. It's been a marvellous performance. We've got eighty-four points with four games left – fantastic.'

That four-stop victory parade would begin at Arsenal's Emirates Stadium. Though United's aim had been achieved with time to spare, the Gunners' need to garner points in the chase for Champions League qualification underlined that plenty of teams still had important targets to play for, and that the champions could not switch off. Even though the win over Villa had sounded the starter's pistol on an evening of unconfined celebration in Manchester for the players, there was insistence from within the squad that there would be no easing up thereafter.

'We'll approach it the same as always, because our pride dictates that we want to win the game,' said Carrick. 'We've won the league but we won't go there and relax; we want to put on a good performance and try to play as if the title depended on it – that's how we'll approach it. Of course we're in a position where we can play with a bit of freedom, but we still want to get a result, so we won't be taking anything lightly. We don't want to take our foot off the gas; we want to carry on until the end of the season. It's only fair to us and the other teams that we do as much as we can.'

For one man in particular, the trip to the Emirates carried special significance. Robin van Persie, who had left Arsenal in search of major honours, would return to his former club less than a year on, having already achieved his ultimate aim. What's more, the Dutchman would return with a bang.

Barclays Premier League

Sunday 28 April | Emirates Stadium | Attendance: 60,112

ARSENAL 1 Walcott (2)
MANCHESTER UNITED 1 Van Persie (44 pen)

Robin van Persie scored on his return to the Emirates Stadium to dent his former side's chance of Champions League qualification, but United's hopes of a record Premier League points total were dashed by a 1-1 draw with the Gunners.

Just two minutes after welcoming the champions onto the field with a guard of honour, Arsenal forged ahead through Theo Walcott's finish, only for van Persie to win and convert a penalty shortly before half time. United could have pilfered victory in the dying stages, with substitute Ryan Giggs coming closest, but it would be missed chances which prevented the Reds from executing an ideal counter-attacking strategy.

Arsène Wenger's players commendably formed a guard of honour for United and, despite a smattering of boos for van Persie, who emerged last out of the tunnel, the home fans were soon cheering.

Tomas Rosicky's threaded pass set Walcott racing towards goal and, though the winger had been offside when the ball was played to him, he was allowed to continue, slot past David De Gea and send the Arsenal fans wild.

Buoyed by their start, Arsenal adopted an aggressive approach to proceedings. After a few strong early challenges from the home side, it was surprising that, on 18 minutes, Phil Jones was the first of four first-half bookings for United after a committed challenge on Mikel Arteta. Undeterred, he went on a rampaging run from midfield, linking first with Wayne Rooney and then van Persie, whose lofted cross was a glorious invitation to level matters, but Jones's header was misdirected from eight yards.

Lukas Podolski forced a save from De Gea with a powerful shot from a tight angle after 32 minutes, but United grew in stature throughout the half and should have levelled when van Persie headed Nani's cross into Wojciech Szczesny's face, and again two minutes later when Jones headed wide again from an Antonio Valencia cross.

When the equaliser did arrive, it was wholly avoidable from Arsenal's perspective. Van Persie capitalised on Bacari Sagna's mistake and raced into the box. Sagna, attempting to recover, slid in and chopped down his former team-mate for a clear penalty award. The Dutchman shrugged off the wall of hostility behind Szczesny and smashed his spot-kick high into the net to level the scores and complete an entertaining half.

United continued to look the more dangerous in front of goal after the break as Rafael fired a 54th-minute shot over the bar and Rooney latched onto a Patrice Evra cross but headed the ball straight at Szczesny. The tackles continued to fly in, too, and Sagna could consider himself lucky to stay on the field for a wild, late challenge on Evra. As the open game gradually descended into a jaded slugfest, United almost landed a knockout blow when substitute Ryan Giggs was released by Rooney's wonderful pass, but the veteran winger's bottom corner-bound shot was deflected wide to ensure that an entertaining game ended all square.

The Teams

ARSENAL: Szczesny, Sagna, Gibbs, Mertesacker, Koscielny, Rosicky (Wilshere 61), Arteta, Walcott, Ramsey (Oxlade-Chamberlain 78), Cazorla, Podolski (Gervinho 71)
SUBS NOT USED: Mannone, Vermaelen, Monreal, Jenkinson
BOOKED: Sagna, Walcott, Oxlade-Chamberlain.

MANCHESTER UNITED: De Gea, Rafael (Anderson 73), Evra, Ferdinand, Evans, Jones, Valencia, Carrick, Nani (Giggs 82), Rooney (Hernandez 88), van Persie.
SUBS NOT USED: Lindegaard, Büttner, Cleverley, Kagawa
BOOKED: Rafael, Jones, Evans, Valencia, van Persie

'We expected a tough game and we got a tough game,' smiled Sir Alex. 'It swung back and forth. In the first twenty minutes, we were surprised by Arsenal's aggression and some of their tackles. That put us on the back foot. We probably had the best chances – we had four fantastic chances from headers. We went through time and time again in the last third of the field and perhaps with a bit more composure we would have won the game.'

That the Reds even had a solitary point to take back to Manchester owed entirely to the coolness of Robin van Persie. 'He kept his nerve, that was important,' the boss said. 'It was a difficult time for him. The chanting from the fans doesn't help, but he kept his cool.'

'People forget what he achieved for [Arsenal],' added Patrice Evra. 'But he showed them that he hasn't made the wrong choice. It was a long time that he didn't win the league [at Arsenal]. He has come to Manchester United and won the league. He did a good job for

Arsenal and I was really disappointed for him. I think he felt it as well. To take that penalty he showed what a world-class, top player he is. He kept his nerves down to score that penalty and I am happy for him.'

If it was a game of mixed emotions for United's number 20, that theme continued into the evening, when he attended the PFA Player of the Year awards dinner. While beaten to the main individual award by Tottenham's Gareth Bale – who also beat Danny Welbeck to the junior equivalent – van Persie could find solace in being one of four Reds in the PFA Team of the Year, alongside David De Gea, Rio Ferdinand and Michael Carrick. But as the Reds returned to Manchester, few in the squad could have envisaged that a month of such historical significance, of a record-extending 20th league title, would be followed by an even more seismic chapter in the club's history in May.

11

May

With the Premier League title already wrapped up, United sailed into the final month of the season faced with three games which, on first view, carried no real meaning. For Chelsea, however, their visit to Old Trafford provided a key test of their ability to secure one of two remaining Champions League qualification berths, and Sir Alex Ferguson was wary of a side who had hit their stride under interim manager Rafael Benitez.

'Chelsea are chasing a Champions League place as well and we'll be playing the strongest team we can,' he confirmed. 'We did pretty well at Arsenal last weekend and should've won it with the chances we had. Chelsea have done fantastically well over the last few weeks and they are in the final of the Europa League. It should be a good game. We need to play with good enthusiasm and enjoy it. We should express ourselves and try to finish off a good season.'

'The most important thing is to win the games and keep that winning mentality,' echoed Nemanja Vidic. 'Sometimes when you play without the pressure you can have a good game and enjoy it more. There is enough of a motivation for us. We are motivated every time we step out at Old Trafford. When we go into the games we have a mentality to win which is not going to change against Chelsea or anyone else. The only difference is we are relaxed. We are not chasing points for the trophy. We have won that so we can enjoy the game. We will try to win. We don't want to lose the last three games. We want to finish in a good style.'

Unfortunately for United, it would be Chelsea's greater need which would shine through.

Barclays Premier League

Sunday 5 May | Old Trafford | Attendance: 75,500

MANCHESTER UNITED 0
CHELSEA 1 Jones (87 og)

United failed to score in a Premier League game at Old Trafford for the first time since December 2009, as Chelsea edged a dour affair to boost their hopes of qualifying for the Champions League.

Juan Mata's 87th-minute shot nicked Phil Jones's leg and spun inside Anders Lindegaard's post in a rare moment of excitement within a game which rarely showcased either side's finer play. United also finished the game with ten men – a first in the league all season – as Howard Webb dismissed Rafael for aiming a kick at Blues defender David Luiz after Chelsea had moved ahead.

That frantic final few minutes was out of keeping with a game which began in muted fashion and rarely rose above mediocrity. Demba Ba headed a Mata cross off target under no pressure and Rafael made an important block from the striker as Chelsea enjoyed the better of the opening exchanges, and it took a fine save from

261

Lindegaard to paw Oscar's shot onto an upright after a surging run forward.

United, conversely, seldom tested Petr Cech beyond his most basic duties. The Blues goalkeeper fielded a low effort from Ryan Giggs and a dangerous cross from Rafael, while Tom Cleverley's arrowed, left-footed effort thudded against Anderson when it appeared to be goal-bound. Giggs was again involved when his sublime curling pass released Robin van Persie but, from a tight angle, the Dutchman's first-time shot bounced a foot wide. In a strong finish to the first period, Giggs stabbed a volley off target from an Antonio Valencia centre and van Persie had a header saved by Cech.

The early stages of the second period again had Chelsea probing with greater intent, but one flowing counter-raid from United should have yielded more than Jones's errant cross ahead of van Persie. Sir Alex introduced Wayne Rooney and Alexander Büttner in place of Anderson and Cleverley, with the Dutch defender operating on the left side of midfield, while the England striker quickly headed off target from another Valencia cross.

Chelsea's greater need shone through in the late stages, however, and after Mata had inexplicably failed to nod home Frank Lampard's inviting cross, the tricky Spaniard finished off a clinical counter-attack with a low shot which crucially struck Jones and bobbled into the goal off Lindegaard's upright.

United's frustration was compounded – and, indeed, embodied – in the game's final event of note. As Rafael jostled with Luiz for possession, United's Brazilian took exception to his compatriot's unabashed use of his elbows and caught the Blues defender with a wild kick. While Luiz flashed a hidden grin to the home support as he lay prostrate, Rafael was given his marching orders by referee Webb to set a fitting seal on an afternoon of exasperation for the champions.

The Teams

MANCHESTER UNITED: Lindegaard, Rafael, Evra, Vidic, Evans, Anderson (Rooney 69), Jones, Cleverley (Büttner 68), Valencia (Hernandez 90), Giggs, van Persie
SUBS NOT USED: De Gea, Ferdinand, Scholes, Kagawa
BOOKED: Jones, Vidic
SENT OFF: Rafael

CHELSEA: Cech, Azpilicueta, Cole, Ivanovic, Luiz, Ramires, Lampard, Mata (Ake 90), Oscar, Moses (Torres 76), Ba
SUBS NOT USED: Turnbull, Ferreira, Cahill, Terry, Benayoun
BOOKED: Luiz

'It's hard to put my finger on why we weren't up to our normal standards,' said Jonny Evans. 'We've had a hectic couple of weeks, but Chelsea have been our rivals and we're disappointed not to get three points against them. Maybe they had more intensity in their play because they are pushing for a Champions League spot, but it is hard to say. I think they deserved their victory in the end.'

For the Northern Irishman, failing to win either of the Reds' two games since clinching the title was not good enough. A historic season needed a fitting sign-off. 'We will lift the trophy next week against Swansea, which will be a big day for us and we want to win that game,' he said. 'It's then the last game of the season against West Brom and we want to win that as well. We want to win every game and, going into these last two games, I'm sure the lads will be up for it and we want to make sure we put on a good performance for the fans.'

Soon enough, it would transpire that there was further motivation to end the season on a high. The visit of Chelsea had coincided with growing rumours in the media that Sir Alex Ferguson was considering retiring at the end of the campaign, with David Moyes put forward as the likeliest replacement. As the rumours gathered pace, so they infiltrated the following day's Manchester United Foundation charity golf day. The players gave little more than cursory attention to the talk, but arrived at Carrington the following morning and quickly became aware that something seismic was unfolding.

'We came in and there was a notice on the board to say there was a meeting,' says Rio Ferdinand. 'There were rumours in the papers about maybe the manager was going to leave and stuff like that, and we were a little bit like: "Nah, there's no chance he's going to leave; he's just got too many good things going on at the club and things that could happen in the next couple of years with the squad that he's building."'

Once the squad had assembled, however, all doubt was removed when the manager confirmed that he would be retiring. Ferdinand recalls: 'I think the thing I'll probably remember from it is that there was just dead quiet in the room. Even when he left there was just a real, mad silence and I think it was just a combination of disappointment and respect as well for the manager's decision, and for what he's done for the club and for each of us as individuals and as a team.'

'What I had to do, and I think I did it well, I didn't show my emotion too much,' reflected Sir Alex. 'When I announced it to the staff, I got a bit blubby, you know, but it wasn't easy.' The manager went on to confirm that he had known the end of his reign was nigh as far back as Christmas, when his sister-in-law passed away.

'Things changed when Cathy's sister died,' he revealed. 'She's isolated a lot now and I think I owe her a lot of my own time. For forty-seven years she's been the leader of the family, looked after three sons and sacrificed for me. I think she's lost her best friend, her sister Bridget, so I think I owe her time, that was important.

'I wanted to go out a winner, that's really important. That was an issue when Cathy and I chatted about this at Christmas. In March I let the club know. Sometimes, when we were with the family, you'd forget you were talking about next year and were afraid you might blurt something out. We didn't tell the family, my sons, until the end of March. My son Jason knew earlier, because he works a lot with me. I only told my brother the night before it was announced. He wasn't too pleased; I got a bit of invective off him!'

Within an hour of telling his staff and players, the news had been confirmed to the world via a statement containing the most pertinent line: 'It is the right time.' In spite of the inevitability that the day would eventually come, and even considering the media rumours which had preceded the announcement, there was no escaping the shock caused by the decision. While the world digested the news, United's players travelled to Chester race course for a pre-arranged day of team bonding which, naturally, took on a more subdued air than anticipated. Conversations speculating on the manager's successor would prove moot, with an announcement made the following day that David Moyes would indeed be coming to Old Trafford on a six-year contract.

'We are all delighted,' said Rio Ferdinand. 'I think it was important that the club made a decision quickly and it all got sorted out. I think the club have acted impeccably in that sense. The manager, I'm sure, thought long and hard about his own decision, he made it and then the club acted swiftly and it's great to see the new manager coming in.

'Another reason I think it's a good appointment is that David Moyes will be very, very open and sympathetic to the traditions of the club and he'll try to continue that and not come in and make changes in terms of the whole characteristics of the club. That's important for a club of this size and important from what's gone on before. The manager that we've got now has implemented a fantastic system, a working system, and we've been successful this year and hopefully we can continue that and I'm sure he is the right man to do that and take us forward.'

Doing so after such a stunning announcement would not be easy. The long-term future could wait, however. In the short term, two games remained in the champions' season, with Old Trafford geared up to pay an almighty farewell to one of its greatest servants, as the Reds hosted Swansea in the final home game of Sir Alex's reign. An unforgettable occasion was already assured, but the confirmation on the eve of the game that Paul Scholes would also be retiring merely heightened the emotion.

While Sir Alex opted against conducting his usual pre-match press conference, there was no avoiding the sense of occasion building around the manager's final game at Old Trafford. But rather than allow maudlin sentiment to pervade, Ryan Giggs set the perfect tone when insisting simply: 'It should be a celebratory occasion.'

Nobody would be disappointed.

Barclays Premier League

Sunday 12 May | Old Trafford | Attendance: 75,572

MANCHESTER UNITED 2 Hernandez (39), Ferdinand (87)
SWANSEA CITY 1 Michu (49)

On an unforgettable afternoon at Old Trafford, Manchester United supporters heralded their champions and bade emotional farewells to Sir Alex Ferguson and Paul Scholes before, during and after a 2-1 victory over Swansea.

Chicharito slid home the opening goal of the game shortly before half time of a game in which United bossed possession, only for Michu to draw the visitors level early in the second period. Swansea

266

improved markedly after the break, and either side could have secured victory in an open second half, but it was left to unlikely hero Rio Ferdinand to blast home a Stretford End winner with just three minutes remaining.

It was a thrilling finish to a game which flickered without igniting for large periods, but however exciting the spectacle had been, it would never have matched the occasion. Old Trafford swayed and resounded for long portions of the afternoon in appreciation of two of United's greatest servants and the return of the Barclays Premier League trophy.

Both teams and their staff formed a guard of honour ahead of kick-off, allowing Sir Alex to enter the arena to a rapturous, spine-tingling reception in which over quarter of a century of residual gratitude poured in the direction of one man. The manager's team selection had hinted at an open, attacking approach, with Chicharito, Robin van Persie, Danny Welbeck and Shinji Kagawa all included in a fluid forward line, and the quartet duly served up some delicious interplay in the opening stages.

In the fifth minute, van Persie sent Chicharito through on goal, on the left side of the area. Unfazed by his tight angle, the Mexican lifted a left-footed effort against the underside of Gerhard Tremmel's crossbar. As the ball rebounded to safety, Phil Jones seized upon it and drove into the area after two sublime one-two exchanges with van Persie and Chicharito, only to lose control of the ball at the vital moment.

Demonstrating their willingness to partake in an open encounter, Swansea instantly counter-attacked at speed and should have opened the scoring, only for Pablo Hernandez to send his effort comfortably wide of David De Gea's far post. As both sets of supporters continued to set a booming soundtrack, the party continued irrespective of events on the field. When United struck with half time looming, however, the volume was ratcheted up to new levels.

Van Persie's curling free-kick from the right flank was poorly defended by the visitors, ricocheting off Ashley Williams and falling perfectly for Chicharito to slide home a simple finish.

Van Persie almost doubled United's advantage before the break, unleashing a piledriver which Tremmel did well to smuggle wide, but a positive start to the second period from the visitors quickly had the scores levelled. A sustained spell of pressure culminated in Nathan Dyer crossing from the right, and Michu reached the ball ahead of the diving Jones and flicked an unstoppable finish past De Gea.

Swansea quickly pressed for the lead and Wayne Routledge almost provided it, stabbing just wide after a neat one-two with Michu. Although United steadied and began chasing the lead once more, another quick counter from the visitors led to Pablo Hernandez bringing a sharp stop from De Gea. When Scholes left the fray to a rapturous reception after 65 minutes, the outcome was very much in the balance.

The midfielder was joined by Welbeck in making way for Anderson and Antonio Valencia, and the Brazilian was quickly in the thick of the action, crossing for Chicharito to head wide, via a deflection, then drilling a low volley just off-target with Tremmel beaten. It took brave, last-ditch defending from Jones and Nemanja Vidic to prevent Chico Flores from turning home on two occasions in quick succession as Swansea continued to play in free-spirited fashion, but Vidic almost pinched the points with a back-post header which sneaked wide of Tremmel's goal.

It was, rather, the Serbian's central defensive partner Ferdinand who had the game's final say, taking advantage of poor defending by lashing home after van Persie's corner had been allowed to bounce through to him. The goal – making Ferdinand the 20th United player to score a league goal in the 20th title-winning season (a record) – provided the momentum for another wave of sound which would carry through, beyond the final whistle, until the day's main events: United's coronation and fond farewells to two of the club's most-loved servants.

The Teams

MANCHESTER UNITED: De Gea, Jones, Ferdinand, Vidic, Evra, Welbeck (Valencia 66), Carrick, Scholes (Anderson 66), Kagawa, van Persie, Hernandez (Giggs 76)
SUBS NOT USED: Lindegaard, Evans, Büttner, Cleverley

SWANSEA CITY: Tremmel, Tiendalli, Williams, Chico, Taylor (Davies 66), Dyer, Hernandez (Agustien 87), Britton, de Guzman, Routledge, Michu (Rangel 74)
SUBS NOT USED: Cornell, Monk, Lamah, Shechter

All eyes were on one man. Sir Alex took the microphone from stadium announcer Alan Keegan and admitted: 'I've got absolutely no script in my mind; I'm just going to ramble on and hope I get to the core of what this football club's meant to be. First of all, it's a thank you to Manchester United. Not just the directors, not just the medical staff, not just the coaching staff, the players or the supporters, it's all of you. You have been the most fantastic experience of my life.

'I have been very fortunate to manage some of the greatest players in the country, let alone Manchester United. All these players here today have represented your club the proper way – they've won the championship in a fantastic fashion. Well done to the players.

'My retirement doesn't mean the end of my relationship with the club; I'm able to now enjoy watching them rather than suffering with them. If you think about it, those last-minute goals, the comebacks, even the defeats, are all part of this great football club of ours. It's been unbelievable, thank you for that.

'I'd also like to remind you that when we had bad times here, the club stood by me, all my staff stood by me, the players stood by me and your job now is to stand by our new manager. Before I start blubbering, I just want to pay tribute to Paul Scholes . . . he's unbelievable; one of the greatest players this club has ever had and will ever have. Paul, we wish you a good retirement and I know you'll be around to annoy me! Also I'd just like you to join me in wishing Darren Fletcher a speedy recovery.

'The players . . . I wish the players every success in the future. You know how good you are, you know the jersey you're wearing, you know what it means to everyone here and don't ever let yourself down. The expectation is always there. I'm going home, well, I'm going inside for a while, and I want to say thank you again from all the Ferguson family. Thank you.'

Old Trafford erupted, glowing in gratitude and adulation for the man who had hauled United back to its feet, dusted it down and marched it to unparalleled success. There could only be one man to lift the Premier League trophy – the Reds' 20th league title and Sir Alex's 13th – and another primal roar burst forth as the 71-year-old held aloft the most coveted piece of silverware in the land.

'It was nice for the boss to enjoy a final Old Trafford victory,' reflects Rio Ferdinand, the Reds' unlikely match-winner. 'The first thing I thought was: "We're going to win the game." The second thing that filled my head was that it was a late goal, and that's typical of the boss's era, so it was great to be a part of that. Then I thought about my kids: it was the first time they've been in the stadium and I've scored when they've actually known about it. Five years! So for them to be there and witness it was great, and it just brought it all together nicely.

'This is the way the manager, in his dreams, would have liked to leave the club: in a fit state for someone else to come in and take the reins and not be looking up at any other teams. He wanted to be at the top of the league, looking down at everyone and saying: "Come and catch us." I think the new manager's in a fantastic position. Obviously they're massive, massive shoes to fill, but he couldn't be walking into a healthier situation. There are young players here who are hungry, who want to win stuff, and there are senior players here who've won a lot of things but have still got the desire and the work ethic that the manager has instilled in us. I think that's vital for the future of the football club.'

There would be ample opportunity, however, to revel in the present for just a little longer. The retirement of Paul Scholes had been intentionally announced at a time when Sir Alex's departure had hogged the limelight, but there was no way the veteran midfielder would depart without praise from within the squad ringing in his ears.

'Scholesy still doesn't get enough credit as he should for me,' said Michael Carrick. 'He is not regarded as highly in the game as he should be. If you ask anyone who has played against him or played with him, he is right at the top of their tree of players. It has been such a privilege to play with him. Even against Swansea, knowing it was his last Old Trafford game, it really meant a lot to me and I really enjoyed it. I made the most of it. It is sad to see him go, but he has earned his retirement, he has done more than enough in the game and everyone has learned more than enough from him. I'm sure he'll enjoy himself.'

Scholes and Carrick would be reunited again on board the following evening's trophy parade through Trafford and Manchester. Starting at Old Trafford and snaking through the city centre, the scenes on Deansgate invoked memories of the staggering turnout which welcomed the Treble-winning Reds home from Barcelona in 1999.

'It is just brilliant,' gasped Ryan Giggs, still imbued with the memories of 14 years earlier. 'Obviously, it gives us a chance to share this great achievement with the fans and they have turned out in their thousands – it's an amazing atmosphere. In 1999, that was probably my greatest memory. I remember turning down Deansgate and not being able to see Deansgate for all of the fans. Tonight is similar to that.'

An incredible occasion, either for a veteran of all 13 titles under Sir Alex or for a player enjoying his first, as Robin van Persie grinned: 'Everyone is so happy, it's just incredible. The medal hasn't left my neck since yesterday; it's been here all night! This trophy is for the fans, the players, the staff . . . the one thing I really like is it's made so many people so happy. You see kids, babies, women, men, all sorts of people are so happy and I'm very pleased to see that.'

'There have been mixed emotions with the news that the manager is leaving,' continued Giggs. 'It has been hard, it has been tough, especially for the players who have known him for a long time, but I am happy and delighted that we could end on a high by winning the league in his last season.'

As well as gathering to salute a season of achievement, the thronging crowds perched on anything remotely flat or load-bearing to again pay tribute to their departing manager, capping an emotional period for all concerned, but most of all Sir Alex – and the events took their toll.

'The whole last few days have been hard,' he conceded. 'After the parade, I slept for ten hours, I think for the first time in my life! I was absolutely gone, knackered. I didn't go in [to work the next morning]. As it got to. . . I don't know what time it was, I kept feeling the presence of Cathy coming into the bedroom. I think she was just checking to see if I was still alive!'

But still the prior engagements loomed large. The club's annual awards dinner took place ahead of the final-day visit to face West Brom, and from within the collective effort which had brought back the title, two players were elevated: Michael Carrick and Robin van Persie, named players' player of the year and supporters' player of the year respectively, while the Dutchman also bagged the goal of the season award for his sublime volley against Aston Villa.

'It was instinct,' he says, looking back on the moment he thundered home Wayne Rooney's fabulous crossfield pass. 'I looked up and thought: "This ball is so nice, it's too beautiful to take a touch." Had it been half a metre to the left or right I couldn't have hit it. Wayne and I had been talking about playing balls in behind the right centre-back all week. We'd talked about it in training almost every day, then before the game Wayne said: "Robin, don't forget that ball, I'll give you that ball today." And it was the perfect pass, it was phenomenal. All I had to do was time my run correctly. In the last second I decided to hit it and I was lucky everything fitted together.'

That had been the story of the Dutchman's entire debut campaign at Old Trafford. 'This whole year has been incredible,' he says. 'I have to be fair – it's beyond expectations. I have to thank all the boys, the staff and the fans, who since day one, have been unbelievable. It's been an honour. It's made such a big impact on me and I'm still thrilled about what's happened in the last ten months or so. I have to say that winning a trophy is fantastic. It's great, but the road to the whole trophy is maybe even nicer. Being together every day and working on details, getting better step-by-step, beating opponents and then the best feeling of all that is the result and the trophy. Hopefully, we can do even better, crack on and win even more trophies.'

Before sights could be set too far forward, however, there was still one more game to play in 2012-13, against West Bromwich Albion at the Hawthorns. For all the warm farewells already afforded him, Sir Alex was presented with a slightly different tribute at his final press conference, as the assembled media unveiled a cake shaped like a hairdryer in a nod to the manager's famed method of animatedly expressing his views.

'It's been an amazing last week,' he conceded. 'I have been overwhelmed. Sunday was unbelievable and, as for the parade on Monday, I thought nineteen ninety-nine could not be beaten. But, this time, seeing all the people on the scaffolding was incredible. I think it was better than ninety-nine. The memories are all there in twenty-six years at United – the whole thing. The day I came here was a privilege. The day I leave, I feel honoured.'

There was still housekeeping to do. The manager had revealed after victory over Swansea that Wayne Rooney had expressed a desire to leave the club in April, but conceded that the situation may unfold differently under the future management of David Moyes. 'I'm no longer interested in that,' he said. 'Quite rightly, David is going to deal with it. I am happy with that.'

Rooney would be absent from the trip to face West Brom, but missed out with the club's blessing after his wife went into labour. Regardless, Sir Alex was looking forward to rotating his squad for the final instalment of a 1,500-game tome.

'Fifteen-hundred games… it's incredible,' he admitted. 'West Brom have done fantastically, every team wants to win their last home game and obviously I want to win this one more than last week's even. I don't have many injury problems. I'll make a few changes – maybe a few younger players will play. I'm looking forward to it. It's going to be great.'

Barclays Premier League

Sunday 19 May | The Hawthorns | Attendance: 26,438

WEST BROMWICH ALBION 5 Morrison (40), Lukaku (50, 80, 86), Mulumbu (81)
MANCHESTER UNITED 5 Kagawa (6), Olsson (9 og), Büttner (30), van Persie (53), Hernandez (63)

Sir Alex Ferguson's final match at the Manchester United helm provided a staggering spectacle as the Reds and West Brom contrived to serve up a ten-goal thriller at the Hawthorns.

On a sun-soaked afternoon in the Midlands, United turned in a scintillating attacking display which had yielded five goals by just after the hour mark, only for a late defensive collapse to allow the hosts to roar back and snatch an unlikely point on a breathless afternoon.

The champions came out to a guard of honour before both sides applauded the departing United manager onto the pitch, and the visitors' early play looked set to provide Sir Alex with a fitting farewell. As the ball was neatly worked out of defence, Alex Büttner's pass into the right-hand channel released Chicharito to supply a pinpoint cross for Shinji Kagawa to head down and past former United keeper Ben Foster.

Just three minutes later, Kagawa fed Antonio Valencia on the right flank, the Ecuadorian – operating as full-back for the afternoon – smashed the ball across goal and Jonas Olsson poked it past Foster to double the lead. The Reds were rampant. Olsson almost put through his own goal again, Foster clutched Phil Jones's shot and Chicharito missed a free header, but a third goal was soon forthcoming. Michael Carrick's pass found Tom Cleverley, whose neat tee-up invited Büttner to bury a low drive into the far corner of the net.

West Brom were stung into life by the Dutchman's strike and began to feel their way back into the game. After Chicharito had skewed Valencia's pass off-target, James Morrison beat Jones to tuck Graham Dorrans's low cross past Anders Lindegaard and provide the home support with faint hope of a revival. Both sides threatened to score again in the five minutes before the break. Foster made a stunning save to fend away Gareth McAuley's inadvertent attempt at his own goal, while Jonny Evans made a fine challenge to deny Shane Long.

A thrilling first period was merely a prelude, however, to a maddening second half. Substitute Romelu Lukaku beat Lindegaard with a tame shot, but United looked to have extinguished the hosts' revival when Robin van Persie steered a shot high into Foster's net and

Chicharito tapped home substitute Ryan Giggs's cross. Rather than close out a comfortable victory, United somehow failed to round off the season with three points. Lukaku skimmed the side-netting from another promising position, then ran onto a Markus Rosenberg through ball to notch his second goal.

From their next attack, West Brom struck again. Youssouf Mulumbu strode through unchallenged to touch in a Jones pass and the comeback was very much on, before Lukaku bundled the ball home from virtually on the goal-line to tie the scores with time almost up.

While a far from ideal climax to his 1,500th and final game at the United helm, Sir Alex nevertheless enjoyed one last goodbye at full time, at the behest of his players. 'Go,' urged Giggs, pointing towards the travelling supporters. With just a little reluctance, the lone figure stepped forward, towards the overspill of gratitude and admiration, threw up his arms and merely said 'thank you', before taking a bow, blowing a kiss and departing to resounding applause – a fitting finale to the most magnificent managerial reign in the history of British football.

The Teams

WEST BROMWICH ALBION: Foster, Jones, McAuley, Olsson, Ridgewell (Lukaku 46), Yacob, Morrison (Fortune 79), Mulumbu, Dorrans, Brunt, Long (Rosenberg 79)
SUBS NOT USED: Myhill, Popov, Dawson, Tamas

MANCHESTER UNITED: Lindegaard, Valencia, Büttner, Jones, Evans (Ferdinand 83), Anderson, Carrick, Cleverley (Giggs 60), Kagawa (Scholes 69), van Persie, Hernandez
SUBS NOT USED: De Gea, Evra, Vidic, Januzaj
BOOKED: Scholes

'Emotional. Very emotional.' And with that, Sir Alex was gone. There would be no final farewell conducted through the media, as the departing manager opted to let others do the talking for him.

'The impact Sir Alex has had on me is massive,' said Chicharito, scorer of the final United goal of the manager's reign. 'He gave me this big chance to play at the biggest club in the world. He has taught me a lot and I only have thankful words for him. It [Sir Alex's retirement] is not only a loss for the British fans, but he has changed football across the world. He has been here for twenty-six years and made the impossible dream come true.

'It's the first time in my career that I've been involved in a game with ten goals! It was a crazy match and also a bit frustrating because we wanted to win it. I think we thought we had it won, which was a mistake because we relaxed a little bit and West Brom made very good substitutions which helped their team. It's frustrating, but the most important thing is we have won the league.

'All the players and fans are expecting things for next season, but we need to take this break, look forward and enjoy the fact we have the trophy back.'

Michael Carrick, who skippered the Reds at the Hawthorns, admitted that, although difficult, the time had come to look to the future. David Moyes would be in charge when the squad reported back for their first day of training ahead of the 2013-14 season, and the England midfielder admitted: 'I think you have to be excited.

'We have to take on the challenge and it is obviously a new challenge. It is going to be a slightly different feeling coming back to pre-season and not really knowing what is going to happen. We know we have got the tour and where we are going, but in terms of day-to-day things, it is going to change. How much change we'll have to wait and see because there is not too much wrong, but we have a new manager with new opinions. David Moyes is his own man and

I am really looking forward to working with him and moving forward both as a team and as individuals.'

'We've got to prove ourselves under the new manager,' adds Rio Ferdinand. 'He's going to come in, he's going to have new ideas, there are going to be new rules and a new regime. It doesn't matter how long you've been here – the likes of Giggsy and myself have been here many years, but we're going to be in the same boat as people like Danny Welbeck, Phil Jones, Tom Cleverley. We'll all be looking to prove ourselves to make sure he thinks we're the right people to start each game.'

Thanks to the sterling work of Sir Alex Ferguson and his staff, the new manager would be working with a squad brimming with talent and character, imbued with positive and negative experiences and galvanised by both. David Moyes would inherit a squad full of champions.

Acknowledgements

MUTV
ManUtd.com
United Review
Inside United
Photographs: John and Matt Peters

Sincerest thanks to everybody at Manchester United for their co-operation and support in the writing of this book, particularly Sir Alex Ferguson, his staff and players for their time and insight.

While many people around the club have been helpful throughout the course of the season, special gratitude must be extended to Ian Marshall, Mark Froggatt, Karen Shotbolt, John Allen, Paul Thomas, James White and Daniel James for their help at various points in the production of this book.